Virginia Woolf

Virginia Woolf

and the
Politics of Style

PAMELA J. TRANSUE

State University of New York Press

The author gratefully acknowledges permission from the following sources to quote from Virginia and Leonard Woolf's published and unpublished materials: Mr. Quentin Bell, the University of Sussex Library, Mrs. M. Parsons, the British Library, the British Broadcasting Corporation, and the Henry W. and Albert A. Berg Collection of the New York Public Library (Astor, Lenox and Tilden Foundations). Excerpts from *Between the Acts, Jacob's Room, Mrs. Dalloway, Night and Day, Orlando, The Pargiters, A Room of One's Own, To the Lighthouse, The Voyage Out, The Years*, and *The Waves* are reprinted by permission of Harcourt Brace Jovanovich, Inc. Copyright 1920 by George H. Doran, renewed 1948 by Leonard Woolf; copyright 1923, 1925, 1929, 1931, 1937, 1941 by Harcourt Brace Jovanovich, Inc., copyright 1928 by Virginia Woolf, renewed 1951, 1953, 1956, 1957, 1959, 1965, 1969 by Leonard Woolf; copyright 1977 by Quentin Bell and Angelica Garnett.

Published by
State University of New York Press, Albany

© 1986 State University of New York

Printed in the United States of America

For information, address State University of New York
Press, State University Plaza, Albany, N.Y., 12246

Library of Congress Cataloging-in-Publication Data

Transue, Pamela J.
  Virginia Woolf and the politics of style.

  Bibliography: p.
  Includes index.
    1. Woolf, Virginia, 1882–1941—Political and
social views.   2. Woolf, Virginia, 1882–1941—Style.
3. Politics in literature.   4. Feminism in literature.
5. Humanism in literature.   I. Title.
  PR6045.072Z883   1986   823'.912   85-27952
  ISBN 0-88706-286-5
  ISBN 0-88706-287-3 (pbk.)

59,244

Contents

Acknowledgments

For help, both personal and professional, in bringing this process to fruition, I wish to thank Stuart Grover, Elizabeth Inglis, Bob Jones, Marlene Longenecker, John Muste, Elizabeth Perry, Barbara Rigney and Roseanne Rini. I am grateful as well to The Ohio State University for providing the financial support which made possible my research at The New York Public Library, the British Library, and the University of Sussex Library.

Introduction

In her essay on "The New Biography," first published in the *New York Herald Tribune* (October 30, 1927), Virginia Woolf repeated a conviction which influenced her aesthetic choices throughout her writing career: the truth of fact and the truth of fiction are separate and must remain so. "For though both truths are genuine, they are antagonistic; let them meet and they destroy each other. . . . Let it be fact, one feels, or let it be fiction; the imagination will not serve under two masters simultaneously."[1] Woolf's tone here is one of confident conviction, and yet in all her novels and essays we sense an uneasy truce between these two opposing modes. And she is, after all, the same artist who wrote, in her introductory essay to *The Pargiters*, "This novel, 'The Pargiters,' moreover is not a novel of vision, but a novel of fact. It is based upon some scores—I might boldly say thousands—of old memoirs. . . . My intention, that is to say, is to represent English life at its most normal, most typical, and most representative."[2]

The obvious contradiction which emerges here does not represent merely a momentary aberration in Woolf's aesthetic code. Woolf was persistently skeptical of organized political movements in any form and shied away from feminist groups, yet she was intensely critical of the patriarchal social and political system of values in the western world, particularly as it related to women, and her fiction became a vehicle for her criticisms. One of the most fascinating possibilities for a critical investigation of her work, then, focuses on the ways in which Woolf, who pointedly opposed didacticism in fiction, transformed this polemical material into art. The importance of this question goes far beyond its implications for Woolf scholarship. Often, in literature courses, students object that a given novel is too political, or not political enough. Sometimes students feel a novel has a design on them and resent being manipulated. A novel, they believe, should tell a story, should involve them in an experience which allows them to make their own evaluations.

If one were asked to name the differences between a novel and an essay, this tendency of the novel to withhold, or at the very most only to imply judgment, or a system of values, is one of its most salient characteristics and requires an entirely different method from the essay. Values must be evoked via a convincing situation and credible characters. In the novel, readers enter into a "willing suspension of disbelief," as Coleridge described it, only when they feel that they will be permitted to form their own conclusions. Authors who never relent in their determination to teach us a lesson have chary readers. While this may be a relatively recent phenomenon, didactic literature having been generally accepted up through the eighteenth century, most modern readers view fiction which is openly didactic with disapprobation. Although this poses a dilemma for the feminist artist, it is not an altogether unique dilemma since it must be confronted by the Marxist artist, the Christian artist, indeed any artist with a strong value system. How can art serve as a vehicle for political ideology and yet remain successful art? What can be done to prevent it from degenerating into mere propaganda?

This issue has been addressed by Marxist philosophers and aestheticians ever since *Das Kapital*, though without ever culminating in any kind of consensus. Engels, for example, was eager to protect the aesthetic purity of art and maintained that theses "must spring from the situation and action itself, without being explicitly displayed."[3] As he maintained in a letter to Ferdinand Lassalle, "The more the author's views are concealed, the better for the work of art."[4]

Mao, on the other hand, was optimistic that art could maintain its integrity and still function as effective propaganda: "Works of art which lack artistic quality have no force, however progressive they are politically. Therefore, we oppose both the tendency to produce works of art with a wrong political viewpoint and the tendency towards the "poster and slogan style" which is correct in political viewpoint but lacking in artistic power."[5]

As a person with strong, though rather eccentric, feminist convictions Virginia Woolf struggled with the issue of how, when and whether to express her views throughout her writing career. Like Engels, she felt that fiction should further a given value system only implicitly. Her most consistent objective as a writer was a mind which would "consume all impediments" and create a work of art whole: aesthetically unified and unfettered by the private grievances of its author. For this reason, she has severe words for two of her predecessors in the art of fiction, George Eliot and Charlotte Brontë:

> In *Middlemarch* and in *Jane Eyre* we are conscious not merely of the writer's character, as we are conscious of the character of Charles Dickens, but we are conscious of a woman's presence—of someone resenting the treatment of her sex and pleading for its rights. This brings into women's writing an element which is entirely absent from a man's, unless, indeed, he happens to be a working-man, a negro, or one who for some other reason is conscious of disability. It introduces a distortion and is frequently the cause of weakness. The desire to plead some personal cause or to make a character the mouthpiece of some personal discontent or grievance always has a distressing effect, as if the spot at which the reader's attention is directed were suddenly twofold instead of single.
>
> The genius of Jane Austen and Emily Brontë is never more convincing than in their power to ignore such claims and solicitations and to hold on their way unperturbed by scorn or censure. But it needed a very serene or a very powerful mind to resist the temptation to anger. The ridicule, the censure, the assurance of inferiority in one form or another which were lavished upon women who practised an art, provoked such reactions naturally

enough. One sees the effect in Charlotte Bronte's indignation, in George Eliot's resignation. Again and again one finds it in the work of the lesser women writers—in their choice of a subject, in their unnatural self-assertiveness, in their unnatural docility. Moreover, insincerity leaks in almost unconsciously. They adopt a view in deference to authority. The vision becomes too masculine or it becomes too feminine; it loses its perfect integrity and, with that, its most essential quality as a work of art.[6]

Woolf, then, is intensely aware of the manifold temptations to anger that a woman writer must face. She sympathizes, yet steadfastly maintains that this anger, however justified, is potentially disastrous when it enters a work of art. Charlotte Bronte's dissatisfaction with the restrictions placed on her own life is revealed in Jane Eyre's persistent yearning for experience in the world, and in Woolf's view, this bitterness ruins the artistic integrity of the novel. Brontë's anger shatters her ability to "get her genius expressed whole and entire."[7] Throughout history, Woolf suggests, women who wished to write have had to grapple with this problem, and those who have been unable to transcend anger are now lost in oblivion. To prove her point, in *A Room of One's Own* Woolf resurrects for us Lady Winchelsea, a poet of the late seventeenth century who wrote some singularly beautiful lines but whose work as a whole is "harassed and distracted with hates and grievances." It was perhaps just this inability to overcome her anger, Woolf suggests, that made it possible for Pope or Gay to dismiss her as "a blue-stocking with an itch for scribbling." What if, Woolf asks, this same woman had been free, encouraged, unharassed?[8] She and others like her might have made a worthy contribution to our literature.

When the woman novelist is angry, Woolf maintains, she is thinking of "something other than the thing itself"[9] and her art suffers. Her characters lose their integrity because the reader becomes aware of a "double focus," of an unwillingness to free a given character from the author's predilections. Woolf's objection to this is not merely aesthetic. It is political as well. For the writer who motivates characters through her own anger is not performing an act of creative vision but reacting to patriarchal dominance. And this is true whether the character views her plight with indignation or whether she simply resigns herself to masculine domination; thus Woolf's criticism of George Eliot. It is interesting to note, as

Miyeko Kamiya points out, that Woolf often states in her diary that she is writing her novels "furiously," "ferociously," or "fiercely."[10] While these adverbs all denote anger, they become transformed in the "act" of writing into pure energy. Since this anger rarely surfaces on the semantic level, the novels themselves would seem to represent in part successful sublimations of that anger.

The need to approach the art of fiction with an unfettered mind was not, in Woolf's view, a problem limited to women writers. Meredith and Hardy were not true novelists because they "had things to say that they could not say suitably and with freedom in a novel. In the first place they want to give us a philosophy, and are not content to let us infer it for ourselves from listening and watching."[11] Woolf seems to be advocating a kind of "negative capability": as Keats described it, "capable of being in uncertainties, Mysteries, doubts, without any irritable reaching after fact and reason. . ."[12] The successful writer must, like Shakespeare, be able to create from a higher state of mind unfettered by the torments of injustice, and must, as Coleridge suggested, cultivate the androgynous mind. In Woolf's words:

> . . . it is fatal for anyone who writes to think of their sex. It is fatal to be a man or woman pure and simple; one must be woman-manly or man-womanly. It is fatal for a woman to lay the least stress on any grievance; to plead even with justice any cause; in any way to speak consciously as a woman.[13]

And yet, as Herbert Marder reminds us, Woolf was proud of being called "the most brilliant pamphleteer in England."[14]

Again, a seeming contradiction. But although Woolf had strong and persistent convictions about the destructiveness of patriarchy in all its manifestations, she never relaxed in her judgment that polemic should be confined to the essay. The novel, as an aesthetic creation, could not tolerate didacticism. As Marder puts it, "Works of art, she believed, should say what cannot be said by other means."[15] In *Three Guineas*, Woolf herself expresses it this way: "If we use art to propagate political opinions, we must force the artist to clip and cabin his gift to do us a cheap and passing service. Literature will suffer the same mutilation that the mule has suffered; and there will be no more horses."[16]

Although feminist in the sense that she advocated greater responsibility and influence for women, Woolf was wary of, and at times even hostile toward, organized feminist political organizations. She saw in them the same destructive pigeonholing of people into hierarchical slots that she judged to be the pattern of patriarchy. Feminists, in allying themselves with the masculine tendency to convert and to impose definite solutions upon indefinite situations, were merely perpetuating the patriarchal system of power. In *Mrs. Dalloway*, Woolf brandished this point of view in her identification of Miss Kilman with Sir William Bradshaw. As Clarissa realizes, religious ecstasy and causes make people callous.[17] For this reason, feminism, although essential to Woolf's conception of reality, is latent in her novels, processed through a series of filters. And because "the 'reality' of society is always seen through the observations, words or reflections of individual human beings," as Berenice Carroll points out, Woolf appears to be a writer of sensibility rather than a feminist.[18] Herbert Marder notes that although the novels are not "didactic in the narrow sense of pleading for specific reforms . . . they illustrate the dangers of one-sidedness and celebrate the androgynous mind. Woolf's main emphasis, in the novels and in the essays, is on self-reform, and on art as a means to that end."[19]

Even when Woolf's feminism is fairly obvious, it is usually tempered by a tentative quality which is often achieved through incorporating it into a process of discovery on the part of one of her characters. In the manuscript version of a story related to Mrs. Dalloway's party, a young woman begins to understand both the fear and the ecstasy aroused by her approaching adulthood:

> But what was the whirlpool? Oh it was made up of a million things—Westminster Abbey, the sense of enormously high solemn buildings surrounding them; being grown up; [illegible]; being a woman. Perhaps that was the thing, when all the rest was melted down, remained, and the dress accentuated it, and all the little chivalries and respects of the drawing room; all made her feel that she had come out of the chrysalis and was being proclaimed what in the [illegible] comfortable darkness of childhood she had never known—this frail and beautiful creature, this limited and circumscribed creature, this butterfly with a thousand facets to its eyes, delicate fine plumage, and difficulties, weaknesses innumerable: a woman.[20]

This evocation of the male mystique and one young woman's response to it succeeds far better than straightforward invective in posing the female dilemma. When, later on in the same manuscript, Woolf's young woman experiences a moment of shock as she suddenly understands the element of humiliation which her new role imposes, the insight has been carefully prepared for by the tentative process of discovery which has preceded it:

> And to worship, to adorn, and to embellish was her part, and her wings were for that. But he talked about his [illegible] with gluttonous passion. And as he talked he killed a fly. He pulled the wings off its back, with his clever strong hands. But it was necessary, she said, thinking of the churches, the parliaments and the blocks of flats, and so tried to cower and crouch and fold her wings [illegible] flat over her back.[21]

Because Woolf's character is so totally receptive to impressions, so naive and malleable, a strongly feminist perception can be offered without its seeming dogmatic.

This emphasis on the personal and emotional as opposed to the public and political is characteristic of all of Woolf's writing. The reader who assumes the personal and the political are unconnected, however, has missed Woolf's point entirely. As Barbara Rigney points out, "Woolf maintains throughout *Three Guineas* that the public world is but a reflection of the private world, that the system which approves tyranny of women in the home will also condone the tyranny of humanity in general. Thus, Woolf sees no distinction between feminism and humanism."[22] It is perhaps for this reason that Woolf feared the co-optation of women who assumed power in the existing social structure and advocated instead a society of "Outsiders," a concept she develops fully in *Three Guineas*. As Berenice Carroll suggests, Woolf felt that society could only be changed if women refused to participate in either the policies or the practices of patriarchy, including patriarchal honors, such as honorary awards and degrees, which she herself refused.[23] The male political model has to be avoided at all costs. Solutions to oppression were of necessity private and individual, though they might be shared among an informal network of "Outsiders."

To a certain extent, the force of Woolf's feminism is softened by her concern with more cosmic issues. Woolf's fiction emerges from a world plagued by war and poverty on a global scale. Although she ultimately blames many of these problems on patriarchal institutions, she sees men and women equally as victims of the destructive effects. As David Daiches remarks, the dominant theme of all her fiction is "time, death, and personality and the relations of these three to each other and to some ultimate which includes them all."[24] In all her novels, as Lucio Ruotolo perceives, at least one of the characters experiences a moment of absolute doubt—of the sense of the unreality of life and the world.[25] This ontological vertigo is intensified by the absence of a consistent and shared system of belief.

Although Woolf never allows us to forget that the relationship of one's personality to time and death is a human problem in the broadest sense, she also perceives that men and women, as writers and as human beings, may approach these and other issues differently:

> It is probable, however, that both in life and in art the values of a woman are not the values of a man. Thus, when a woman comes to write a novel, she will find that she is perpetually wishing to alter the established values—to make serious what appears insignificant to a man, and trivial what to him is important. And for that, of course, she will be criticized; for the critic of the opposite sex will be genuinely puzzled and surprised by an attempt to alter the current scale of values, and will see in it not merely a difference of view, but a view that is weak, or trivial, or sentimental, because it differs from his own.[26]

At first, this statement seems to contradict Woolf's insistence elsewhere on the importance of androgynous vision in the writer. But the differences in emphasis that are a product of the female vision are not, in Woolf's view, indicative of limitation determined by sex. Masculine values, Woolf suggests, have dominated fiction for so long that they have become the norm. It will be the gift of the woman artist to rejuvenate the novel through correcting this one-sidedness and providing us with a more harmonious vision. The task is difficult because writers emerge from a tradition, in this case a largely masculine tradition, which is unsuitable as a vehicle for expressing the unique observations of women.

The extent to which Woolf herself had to struggle with this problem is indicated by such manuscripts as her unpublished story entitled, "Scenes from the Life of a British Naval Officer." In this effort, which is undated and probably early, Woolf offers a very tedious, plodding, stereotyped protrait of a classic military man: square, rough-hewn features, erect bearing, decisive movements, manly silence, and so on.[27] It is a singularly undistinguished piece, largely because it is entirely conventional. Because the female artist's vision of reality is different, new forms must be metamorphosed from the old:

> To begin with, there is the technical difficulty—so simple, apparently; in reality, so baffling—that the very form of the sentence does not fit her. It is a sentence made by men; it is too loose, too heavy, too pompous for a woman's use. Yet in a novel, which covers so wide a stretch of ground, an ordinary and usual type of sentence has to be found to carry the reader on easily and naturally from one end of the book to the other. And this a woman must make for herself, altering and adapting the current sentence until she writes one that takes the natural shape of her thought without crushing or distorting it.[28]

Throughout Woolf's work, we see her doing just that; adapting, shaping and molding the sentence to fit the form of her thoughts and perceptions. As Sydney Kaplan perceives, "The kind of movement from self to the object of perception, to self again, to past and immediate past and present, the movement from perception to reflection and back again is characteristic of these sentences which illustrate the movement of the mind."[29]

For Woolf, the conception, the idea of what she wanted to do, always preceded the means of doing it, so that Geoffrey Hartman's description of Woolf's novels as "mirrors held up to the imagination" is perceptive and accurate.[30] Thus, when she came to write perhaps her greatest novel, *Mrs. Dalloway*, she did not, as some critics have suggested, begin with a method and find a content to fit it, but quite the reverse. As she puts it, " . . . the idea started as the oyster starts or the snail to secrete a house for itself."[31] The idea gave rise to the form. And the extent to which this form departs from previous modes of rendering a fictive reality is perhaps the measure of Woolf's success. In David Daiches' words, Woolf is able to establish through her technique a "texture of revery"—the setting and maintenance of mood which allows the kinds of reflections simply not possible in

Victorian novels which revolve around "public symbols, gain or loss of money, sudden fortune or sudden disgrace, or obvious emotional changes concerned with love or hate or hope or disappointment."[32]

Through Woolf's technique, for which "stream-of-consciousness" is not a very good name, we are aware of Clarissa as a whole being—of who she is and what she was and what she might have been—almost simultaneously, so that her presence evokes for us, at any given moment, a multitude of associations. Outer events become important only insofar as they function as catalysts to the mind's imaginings.

Not every moment, of course, is capable of inspiring a rich outpouring of associations. Most of life, as Woolf saw it, consisted of "non-being," of the unmemorable banalities which she also referred to as the "cotton wool" of daily existence. Woolf's awareness of these "dead periods" which comprise so much of our lives is evident even in her earliest diary, kept when she was fifteen in 1897. When nothing happened in the course of a day to stimulate her imagination, she saw no value in recording the events.[33] Sometimes these days of "non-being" would melt into weeks, even under conditions which might be expected to inspire her. In the journal recording her trip through Italy in 1906, for example, she explicitly states that there has been nothing worth recording.[34] And yet sometimes, a seemingly unimportant occurrence triggered an outpouring of creative energy. The issue here is the importance Woolf assigned throughout her life to the workings of imagination. Time Woolf viewed as a discontinuous flow, consisting of periods of "non-being" in which time is irrelevant, punctuated by moments of perception in which a given instant is expanded in an onrush of vision. Memory consists in the recollection of these moments of expanded and ultimately frozen time.

Woolf's resistance to the perception of time as a dogged cataloguing of events detached from the element of vision is amusingly revealed in an unpublished sketch entitled "Monday, Tuesday—The Diary." When a male friend suggests to the narrator that she keep a diary and presents her with one which has each day marked out, she settles on Friday the thirteenth and proceeds to completely undermine the diary's arbitrary divisions with a series of fascinating reflections which have nothing to do with the actual events of that particular day.[35] This refusal to concede to divisions, categories, and "rules" which she considered arbitrary is perhaps one of Woolf's greatest strengths. Her insistence on being true to herself and her vision of the world led ultimately to her ability to transform the novel into a suitable instrument for that vision.

Although it is tempting at times to take Woolf's stylistic innovations for granted, to see them as resulting naturally and without effort from her own unique view of the world, the difficulty she encountered in finding an appropriate style and form should not be overlooked. Like Flaubert, Woolf agonized over her writing, subjecting her work to innumerable revisions so that each of her novels took years to produce. An interesting insight into this process is provided by a series of manuscripts of a short story initially entitled "What the Telescope Discovered" and begun in 1929. This story was subjected to eight radical revisions and yet, even at that, was apparently never completed to Woolf's satisfaction. This series of revisions does, however, offer an excellent opportunity for studying Woolf's method of composition.

In the first version, which is very conventional and straightforward in terms of plot and development, a mother, father, and son live in a very solitary, learned atmosphere in a ruined castle. One night, the son turns his telescope from the moon to the earth, more precisely to the farm two miles away. When the telescope reveals to him a boy kissing a girl, he undergoes a moment of shock and races out into the night. While the idea may be interesting, the story is in fact tedious, largely because of the rigid conventionality of the style in which it is told. In the next version, Woolf begins by having her narrator discuss the limitations of mere fact and the importance of creative transformation, then moves on to an illustration from a forgotten biography which forms the germ of the ensuing story of the boy in the tower with the telescope. In this version, when the boy is startled by the sight of the boy and girl kissing, he runs off and becomes, she thinks, a colonial officer. Although this version is an improvement, since the events now exist in a context of what it means to write fiction, the story is still not handled with her usual skill.

In the seven subsequent revisions, the story opens with a description of an English town, Freshwater, in the 1860's. Woolf's whimsical humor is increasingly more in evidence, as is apparent when she has the rooks cry "Maud, Maud, Maud." Once the reader has become comfortably situated in the town, the narrator moves to an observation of a boy and girl, obviously in love, who are taking a stroll. The boy, it turns out, is none other than Henry, the boy with the telescope who becomes the colonial officer.[36] The primary interest in studying these revisions lies in observing the increasing sophistication of the ways in which the story is told. While Henry remains the focus of the story throughout the revisions, in the later versions he emerges from a context of ideas and description which do much to enhance the reader's interest. The narrative focus, in passing through a series of displacements, gains depth and texture. Although other writers have certainly employed similar strategies, one might argue that such indirection suggests a feminine revision of traditional plot progression.

The extent to which the elements of Woolf's style were influenced by the periods of mental breakdown which plagued her is difficult to judge but provides fascinating material for speculation. Miyeko Kamiya, a psychiatrist who greatly admires Woolf's work, points out that the analogies between certain aspects of her style and syntax and the processes of psychic disintegration which occurred during her periods of breakdown are very strong. In particular, her preoccupation with "inner states of mind . . . metaphysical themes of life and death, time and eternity, fragmentation of personality, the blotting out of the self, the rush of images and absence of logical structure" all correspond very closely to her description of what she experienced during these periods of instability.[37]

Whatever their sources, Woolf's stylistic innovations function as subtle vehicles of a feminist consciousness. Realizing the impossibility of using the traditional novel to express what was, after all, a new way of seeing reality, Woolf developed a new form, one which would clothe her vision without distorting it. As Roger Poole points out, Woolf's methods and modes of perception were diametrically opposed to "rational" Bloomsbury.[38] Eschewing the logical processes of thought espoused by her Cambridge-educated peers, she dove beneath the surface of life to the unconscious where she could, in Ellen Rogat's phrase, "discover language unfettered by masculine values." As Rogat goes on to point out, Woolf's style brings this sensual, enigmatic, unconscious material to the surface in vivid concrete images which are suggestive rather than programmatic, thus functioning in much the same manner as dreams do.[39] The cathexis Woolf achieves by concentrating emotional intensity in physical images is also characteristic of dreams.

Woolf's feminism can be viewed as latent, then, insofar as it has become merged with the subnarrative elements of structure, style, point of view, and so on. These are not, however, the only techniques employed by

Woolf to embody a feminist vision. At times, Woolf's political convictions appear in their raw state in her novels, untempered by artistic manipulation. At other times, her convictions are processed through a series of filters which have analogues in the psychological processes of sublimation, transference, displacement and condensation. There is, obviously, a certain irony in using psychoanalytic concepts in discussing Woolf's work, given the skepticism and distrust with which she viewed these techniques, especially in the hands of mass manipulators like Sir William Bradshaw. Nevertheless, Woolf's positive response to certain psychoanalysts in her own life suggests some inconsistency on that point, and the Hogarth Press did print the first collected edition of Freud.

In defining sublimation, Freud points out that the sexual instincts in human beings are both more strongly developed and more constant than in the higher mammals. For this reason, sexuality "places extraordinarily large amounts of force at the disposal of civilized activity, and it does this in virtue of its especially marked characteristic of being able to displace its aim without materially diminishing in intensity. This capacity to exchange its originally sexual aim for another one, which is no longer sexual but which is psychically related to the first aim, is called the capacity for 'sublimation.'"[40] The musical prowess of Rachel Vinrace in *The Voyage Out* and the extraordinary vitality and "civilizing influence" of Clarissa Dalloway and Mrs. Ramsay can be seen as providing fairly clear examples of the process of sublimation. It is noteworthy as well that the libidinal instincts are often associated with death. The metaphorical connection of orgasm with death throughout literature is well-known. Mrs. Ramsay's identification with the elemental forces of nature and the recurring motif of the death-wish which seems so central to Clarissa's psyche can be viewed, I think, as sublimations of repressed libidinal energy. To the extent that this preoccupation with death results from the scarcity of responsible or creative activities in which this sublimated energy could be employed, it is a feminist issue. And Woolf manages to convey through her sensitivity to these processes a powerful impression of the disjunction between the public and private lives of these women.

Although Freud's concept of transference cannot be directly applied to these novels since it has reference, in the strict sense, only to the therapeutic relationship between doctor and client, the idea on which it is based provides a useful analytical tool. The phenomenon of transference, as Freud defines it, involves the substitution of the analyst for various persons in the client's past, usually the father or mother, and a working out of earlier conflicts with these persons as if they were occurring at the present moment. The patient, then, "replaces some earlier person by the person of the physician . . . [and] a whole series of psychological experiences are revived, not as belonging to the past, but as applying to the person of the physician at the present moment."[41]

In *The Voyage Out*, Helen Ambrose and Richard Dalloway can be seen as substitutions by Rachel for a dead mother and an absent father inasmuch as she gains maturity in defining herself against them through a series of psychologically crucial encounters. In much the same way, Katharine Hilbery in *Night and Day* is ultimately able to develop a set of values more congenial to her personality than those with which she has grown up through defining herself anew against the paternalistic figure of William Rodney.

Another useful concept in analyzing Woolf's fiction is that of "displacement." As Freud points out, in analyzing our dreams it becomes clear that "the elements which stand out as the principal components of the manifest content of the dream are far from playing the same part in the dream-thoughts."[42] Very often, the most important figures or episodes in dreams remain in the background and become recognized as central only when the dream is analyzed:

> . . . things that lie on the periphery of the dream-thoughts and are of minor importance occupy a central position and appear with great sensory intensity in the manifest dream, and *vice versa*. This gives the dream the appearance of being displaced in relation to the dream-thoughts, and this displacement is precisely what brings it about that the dream confronts waking mental life as something alien and incomprehensible.[43]

Also, since dreams are completely egoistic, one's own ego is represented not only directly but is displaced onto various other figures in the dream.[44] In the novels of Virginia Woolf, the concept of displacement is useful in understanding such things as the evolution of Septimus as Clarissa's alter ego in *Mrs. Dalloway* and the deflection of Clarissa's sexual and emotional energies from Sally Seton to Peter Walsh. And if we view Septimus, Sally, and Peter as aspects of Clarissa's personality, a much fuller understanding of her character is possible.

It is in Woolf's skillful handling of "condensation," however, that one of her greatest strengths as a writer emerges. Certain key images in Woolf's work, such as the lighthouse and the recurring image of a "blot fringed with flame" have a haunting resonance. Part of the magic of these images is that they can never be fully explained. Although one can hardly avoid viewing them as symbolic, critics can never agree on just what it is that they symbolize. This is due in part to the seemingly endless complex of associations which they generate. In this sense, the key images in Woolf's novels bear a striking correspondence to the function of images in dreams. Freud describes the work of condensation as follows:

> Dreams are brief, meagre and laconic in comparison with the wealth and range of dream-thoughts. If a dream is written out, it may perhaps fill half a page. The analysis setting out the dream-thoughts underlying it may occupy six, eight or a dozen times as much space . . . . it is in fact never possible to be sure that a dream has been completely interpreted . . . . [45] Each element in the content of a dream is 'overdetermined' by material in the dream-thoughts; it is not derived from a *single* element in the dream-thoughts, but may be traced back to a whole number. These elements need not necessarily be closely related to each other in the dream-thoughts themselves; they may belong to the most widely separated regions of the fabric of those thoughts. A dream-element is, in the strictest sense of the word, the 'representative' of all this disparate material in the content of the dream. [46]

Similarly, images such as the lighthouse seem to encompass, in their stark simplicity, everything of any importance in the lives and minds of Woolf's characters. Just as in dreams, these images constitute "nodal points"[47] upon which a great number of associations converge.

The following chapters will explore Woolf's strategies for transforming her feminist vision into an art unfettered by the tone of grievance. Because she so clearly recognized the problems inherent in using fiction as a vehicle of feminist convictions, Woolf offers a rare opportunity for the study of the processes by which ideology can be transformed into successful art. As James Naremore maintains, "To perceive life differently was to place oneself in opposition to the social status quo; to change the form of the novel, or to write fictions which in many ways do not seem like novels at all, was to challenge the prevailing European social order and its methods of defining humanity. Hence, contrary to the way most people have described it, Virginia Woolf's program for modern fiction was an aestheticism which was also deeply political."[48] Woolf's committed feminism combined with her integrity as an artist and her outstanding capacity to metamorphose ideology into art make her work particularly suitable for a study of the complex relationship of polemic to aesthetics. There is hardly a more crucial issue for the feminist artist today, who must seek to reconcile creatively her program with her art. For the student of this art, a recognition of these processes and a means of evaluating their success or failure is essential.

I   *The Voyage Out*

> "Our views about men and women are doubt-
> less quite different, and the difference doesn't
> matter much; but to draw such sharp and
> marked contrasts between the subtle, sensitive,
> tactful, gracious, delicately perceptive, and
> perspicacious women, and the obtuse, vulgar,
> blind, florid, rude, tactless, emphatic, indeli-
> cate, vain, tyrannical, stupid men, is not only
> rather absurd, but rather bad art, I think."
> Clive Bell on *The Voyage Out*

> "I never meant to preach, and agree that like
> God, one shouldn't. Possibly, for psychologi-
> cal reasons which seem to me very interesting,
> a man, in the present state of the world, is not
> a very good judge of his sex; and a 'creation'
> may seem to him 'didactic.'"
> Virginia Woolf's response to Clive Bell
> (Quoted by Phyllis Rose in *Woman of Letters*)

In this first novel, Virginia Woolf is hindered by her attempt to work within traditional novelistic conventions. One senses a disjunction between what she wants to do in the novel and the tools she has for doing it. Her plot is too weak to carry the weight of her impressions and instead simply interferes with the open-ended exploration of consciousness which is her strength. Despite its weaknesses, however, this novel is engaging and it provides a good starting point for understanding the development of Woolf's aesthetic in that her feminism is relatively undisguised. In some cases, feminist ideas are openly discussed, and in other cases, Woolf merely lends credence to the feminine point of view when it comes into contact with masculine values.

In establishing the character of Mr. Pepper, for example, a representative if somewhat unflattering portrait of the male academic, Woolf describes his intellectual accomplishments in considerable detail. Yet all this is thoroughly undermined by Helen's query, "Has he ever been in love?"[1] Throughout the novel, Woolf's feminism is perhaps most obvious in her protrayal of the social interaction between men and women. While the men are forever holding forth, the women, half-listening, are forever supporting their disquisitions. Nor can we overlook the fact that the men in general are hypochondriacal, complaining, and helpless, constantly in need of female care and reassurance.

Throughout this novel, Woolf is also engaged in a subtle but persistent undermining of patriarchal institutions, a function which is accomplished primarily through the point of view of Helen Ambrose. Helen, who has instructed her children to think of God as a kind of walrus, openly expresses her contempt for a number of the more sacred male institutions, including religion and the army. She despises war, and "it seemed to her as wrong to keep sailors as to keep a zoo" (p. 69). As for making a fortune in trade, Helen considers that twice as bad as pursuing the role of a prostitute (p. 308). One can, surely, view Helen's passion on these subjects as in part a displacement of her contempt for the men around her. Since these feelings cannot be expressed, partly because she only half understands them herself, her contempt shifts to a condemnation of male institutions in general. As is often the case for women, Helen's anger baffles and confuses her insofar as it is generated by her personal life and consequently is displaced onto impersonal institutions, in this case onto institutions which do, in fact, oppress her as a woman. Helen is, for this reason, an interesting role model for the ingenue heroine, Rachel.

Like most other young women of her time, Rachel has been kept deliberately naive. Her reading has been carefully censored, she is without experience in the world, and she has virtually no friends of her own age. Her one refuge is in her music. Though her aunt is afraid she will ruin her arms by using them too much, Rachel is a superb pianist. Having discovered that people in general are appalled by honest emotion, Rachel turns to her music as the only outlet for her considerable passion. People strike Rachel as being overly conventional, insincere, symbols rather than realities. For this reason, Richard Dalloway's kiss assumes tremendous importance since it represents the first genuine, unprogrammatic human interaction that Rachel has ever experienced.

While Woolf's feminism is obvious in her use of characterization, it is equally apparent in the overall theme of the novel. The issue, broadly speaking, is whether a woman's emotional and intellectual needs can be fulfilled within the framework of traditional marriage. In exploring this question, Woolf offers us a variety of different perspectives in the numerous courtships, engagements, and marriages around which this novel revolves. The Ambroses, for example, appear to be a stable couple, relatively comfortable in their marriage of many years and secure in their feelings for one another. Yet, even this marriage, which is a good one, is ambiguous in its overall effect: "When two people have been married for years they seem to become unconscious of each other's bodily presence so that they move as if alone, speak aloud things which they do not expect to be answered, and in general seem to experience all the comfort of solitude without its loneliness" (p. 195). Though this comfort is appealing, there is something rather chilling about it as well.

Although Helen Ambrose has clearly managed to maintain her vitality and independence of mind despite the silences of her marriage, there is also an aura of loneliness about her. And so the quarrelsome Hirst becomes for her like a breath of fresh air: " . . . he took her outside this little world of love and emotion. He had a grasp of facts" (p. 304). Helen, although she loves her husband, is stifled by marriage and the limitations it imposes on her intellectual growth. And as Terence Hewet so tellingly perceives, Helen's efforts at keeping her husband happy place her in a false position: "She gave way to him; she spoilt him; she arranged things for him; she who was all truth to others was not true to her husband, was not true to her friends if they came in conflict with her husband. It was a strange and piteous flaw in her nature" (p. 242).

Clarissa and Richard Dalloway, who are very different from the Dalloways we meet in Woolf's later novel, have even more rigid and polarized roles in their marriage. Clarissa quite literally worships Richard and parrots his opinions unquestioningly, as if it has never occurred to her that she might have an independent thought:

> "I often wonder," Clarissa mused in bed, over the little white volume of Pascal which went with her everywhere, "whether it is really good for a woman to live with a man who is morally her superior, as Richard is mine. It makes one so dependent. I suppose I feel for him what my mother and women of her generation felt for Christ. It just shows that one can't do without *something*" (p. 52).

The reader should not miss Woolf's irony here. The absence of a shared system of belief, while freeing women from the patriarchal dominance of the church, may have increased their dependence on their husbands and on masculine judgment in general.

The Dalloway marriage is based on complete submission of woman to man. For Clarissa there is no privacy: "He kissed her passionately, so that her half-written letter slid to the floor. Picking it up, he read it without asking leave" (p. 51). Richard, on the other hand, is so secure in his privacy and in his masculine privilege that after lecturing the virginal Rachel on the nobility and superiority of men he shows no compunction in inflicting himself on her physically.

Richard is a pompous man who sees himself as the guardian of civilization, the defender of all that is worthy and proper. Clarissa's role is to pamper this image and dedicate herself to providing Richard with every comfort:

> "I never allow my wife to talk politics," he said seriously. "For this reason. It is impossible for human beings, constituted as they are, both to fight and to have ideals. If I have preserved mine, as I am thankful to say that in great measure I have, it is due to the fact that I have been able to come home to my wife in the evening and find that she has spent her day in calling, music, play with the children, domestic duties—what you will; her illusions have not been destroyed. She gives me courage to go on. The strain of public life is very great," he added (p. 65).

One wonders whether it might not be Richard's illusions rather than Clarissa's which have not been destroyed, although he assures Rachel that he has none. Rachel, indeed, is particularly appealing to Richard simply because she is so naive, because whatever he says is received with a kind of awed acceptance. While Helen, as an older woman, can merely dismiss Richard's pomposity, Rachel hangs on his every word.

In part, of course, Woolf's object in describing the Dalloways is to present a satirical portrait of the aristocracy. Richard is a temporarily displaced member of Parliament who views himself as the guardian of civilization. His opinions are considered irrefutable by the other characters on board, based as they are on careful observation: "In Spain he and Mrs. Dalloway had mounted mules, for they wished to understand how the peasants live" (p. 39). Although one can hardly imagine a more caustic remark on the part of our narrator, Woolf carefully softens the satiric impact of this statement by burying it in a descriptive paragraph, so that the reader can easily pass over it unheedingly.

At other times, however, Woolf's satire becomes painfully apparent, perhaps too much so. Clarissa's persistent insincerity and dilettantism are agonizing, though perhaps still believable. There is perpetually a disjunction between what she says and what she feels. At one point, she quotes passionately from Shelley while expounding on the great admiration she has for stockbrokers, who are really much better than poets. This may, of course, be in part due to Richard's influence, since he is forever bringing up the poets in order to catalog their lack of importance when compared to the political man. Clarissa, in her reverence for Richard, parrots his opinions without even seeming to realize that they contradict her own. Although this is often amusing, the resulting insincerity gives Clarissa a vacuous quality. Among other things, she maintains that she would give ten years of her life to learn Greek, yet when she is given the opportunity to do so, she fails to take advantage of the lessons which are offered her. She distrusts music, because it is too emotional. She also maintains an unflaggingly optimistic attitude: "'I've never met a bore yet!' said Clarissa" (p. 55). Given what we've seen and heard of her husband, this is a remarkable statement. Woolf rescues Clarissa from pure satire only by managing to convey the winsomeness of Clarissa's absurdity, her high spirits, geniality, and charm. While she can hardly been seen as a model to which women should aspire, she does befriend Rachel and treat her with consistent respect.

The Dalloway marriage is never openly condemned either by Woolf's narrator or by the other characters. Woolf presents the relationship and in some sense governs our response through the material she chooses to convey, but judgment is left to the reader. We are never simply told how we are supposed to feel.

There are other established marriages in the novel, each with its own problems, but primarily they serve as a backdrop against which the entry into matrimony by the younger characters can be measured. The two first to fall are Susan Warrington and Arthur Venning. Dazzled by each other, they accept the roles that each will play without question. Rachel and Terence, who come upon the lovers accidentally, have a somewhat different perspective:

"Love's an odd thing, isn't it, making one's heart beat."

"It's so enormously important, you see," Hewet replied. "Their lives are now changed for ever."

"And it makes one sorry for them too," Rachel continued, as
though she were tracing the course of her feelings. "I don't know
either of them, but I could almost burst into tears. That's silly,
isn't it?"

"Just because they're in love," said Hewet. "Yes," he added after
a moment's consideration, "there's something horribly pathetic
about it, I agree" (pp. 140–141).

As time goes on, Susan's increasingly obsessive concern for domestic
trivialities becomes more and more oppressive. Rachel, after listening to a
long and boring monologue on Susan's domestic duties and how busy they
keep her, is inspired with a violent dislike. The force of Rachel's response,
of course, is only exacerbated by her own fear of being swallowed in
marriage.

In Terence Hewet, however, Rachel finds a man who is more in tune
with her own turn of mind. Like Rachel, although more sophisticated
than she, he is a reflective person who views marriage critically:

All the most individual and humane of his friends were bachelors
and spinsters; indeed he was surprised to find that the women he
most admired and knew best were unmarried women. Marriage
seemed to be worse for them than it was for men (p. 241).

Unlike most of the other men in the novel, Terence sees a value in women
which is wholly unrelated to their potential desirability as wives. Indeed,
he is dismayed at the cost to personal development in women that marriage appears to exact. Rachel, too, is intensely ambivalent about the
prospect of marriage, so much so that at one point she proclaims that the
sexes "should live separate; we cannot understand each other; we only
bring out what's worst" (p. 156). This extreme point of view is not,
however, the point of the novel, but just one of a surprising number of
perspectives on marriage that the reader is asked to consider.

Yet another point of view is offered by Evelyn Murgatroyd, the novel's
token feminist. She shares with Rachel and Terence a skepticism about the
value of marriage, but her ideas are undermined because of her lack of a
firm character. Evelyn is a chameleon, lacking identity because she lacks a
strong family base, and in her we find a sometimes caustic portrait of a
feminist do-gooder which reflects Woolf's persistent mistrust of organized

political activity. Perhaps even more to the point, Woolf appears to be suggesting that people who cling blindly to ideologies, including feminism, do so because they lack security in their own identities. Although Woolf is ambivalent about Evelyn, and seems to waver between distaste and a kind of amused fondness, Evelyn clearly strikes her as somewhat absurd and becomes the target of some of Woolf's keenest wit. Unfortunately, this tends to weaken the novel. To the extent that Evelyn is denied complexity and humanity, she emerges as a caricature and becomes detached from the rich texture of the fictional world. We begin to sense the author's presence and to become aware of a point of view which instead of growing naturally from the context of the novel has been imposed upon it from the outside.

Fortunately, Woolf is skilled enough to soften the destructive effects of her barbs by allowing Evelyn a few genuinely perceptive moments, unclouded by fanatic enthusiasm:

> Love was all very well, and those snug domestic houses, with the kitchen below and the nursery above, which were so secluded and self-contained, like little islands in the torrents of the world; but the real things were surely the things that happened, the causes, the wars, the ideals, which happened in the great world outside, and went on independently of these women, turning so quietly and beautifully towards the men. She looked at them sharply. Of course they were happy and content, but there must be better things than that. Surely one could get nearer to life, one could get more out of life, one could enjoy more and feel more than they would ever do. Rachel in particular looked so young— what could she know of life? (p. 320).

These musings at least lend a poignancy to Evelyn's character, although Woolf herself viewed the causes, wars, and ideals which Evelyn longs to be part of with great suspicion. Evelyn's yearning for heroism is not, however, treated as a simple absurdity, and we are likely to feel sympathy as well as amusement when the men around her consistently undermine her desire for friendship by proposing marriage.

That Woolf should poke fun at Evelyn's feminism may strike some readers as inconsistent given the vehemence of Woolf's own arguments for female independence. For that reason, the point needs to be made that Woolf's objection to Evelyn's brand of feminism, here and elsewhere, is that it is a closed system. As such, it tends toward platitudes of the sort that Woolf despised. True feminism, in her view, should foster creativity and expand the human spirit. She therefore opposed those feminists whose only goal appeared to be greater power within a social structure which she considered destructive. She supported greater involvement by women in the affairs of the world but feared the possibility that women would simply be absorbed into patriarchal patterns of behavior. This ambivalence led her to value the civilizing influence of the domestic virtues at the same time that she resented the confinement of women to the domestic sphere. As Herbert Marder perceives, marriage in her novels is both a destructive "patriarchal institution" and "the ultimate relation." It is "associated with oppression" but it is also "a profound symbol of community."[2]

Woolf's opinion of organized religion was far less uncertain. In the church service which takes place about midway through the novel, once again we are confronted with relatively undisguised polemic in which religion is presented as mindless, mewling, and fatuous. Susan Warrington sits through the service in a kind of bovine placidity, following the remarks "with the same kind of mechanical respect with which she heard many of Lear's speeches read aloud. Her mind was still serene and really occupied with praise of her own nature and praise of God—that is of the solemn and satisfactory order of the world" (p. 227). Rachel, on the other hand, is appalled by the enervating tone and content of the service and by the bland docility of the congregation: "One after another, vast and hard and cold, appeared to her the churches all over the world where this blundering effort and misunderstanding were perpetually going on, great buildings, filled with innumerable men and women, not seeing clearly, who finally gave up the effort to see, and relapsed tamely into praise and acquiescence, half-shutting their eyes and pursing up their lips." Even before the end of the service, Rachel has "rejected all that she had before implicitly believed" (pp. 228–229).

Woolf's criticism of organized religion is pointed and thorough. There are, however, three factors which prevent this incursion into more or less pure polemic from seriously weakening the novel. First, the repudiation of organized religion is not the point of the novel but a relatively minor side issue. In addition, Woolf does not go so far as to posit, through her characters, any kind of solution to the problem, such as shutting down the churches. She criticizes, but she does not plead for action. Finally, and perhaps most importantly, Rachel's passionate indignation to a large extent springs from her frustration with Terence Hewet. At this point in the novel, she is very uncertain of his feelings and terribly frustrated by this lack of resolution. She cannot, however, express these feelings openly, partly because she only half understands them, so that it is not surprising that they should be displaced onto anger and contempt for religious complacency in general.

Several other political and social issues, most of them concerning women, are raised in the novel, and for the most part Woolf presents her material dialectically. We learn about Rachel very early on, for example, that her education has been eclectic and shallow: "Her mind was in the state of an intelligent man's in the beginning of the reign of Queen Elizabeth" (pp. 33–34). Although she possesses an extraordinary talent for the piano, she is discouraged even in this by her aunt's anxiety that too much practicing will spoil her arms. The crux of the issue develops when Hirst ponders Rachel's naivety and tries to assign it a source: "'You see, the problem is, can one really talk to you? Have you got a mind, or are you like the rest of your sex? You seem absurdly young compared to men of your age . . . It's awfully difficult to tell about women' he continued, 'how much, I mean, is due to lack of training, and how much is native incapacity'" (p. 154). Even Terence, a far more sympathetic character, is sometimes nonplussed by Rachel's vagueness: "You've no respect for facts, Rachel; you're essentially feminine" (p. 295).

Nevertheless, it is Terence who most adroitly voices a sense of indignation at the plight of women. Testing his ideas on Rachel, he posits that women have an inordinate respect for men and are easily bullied, so much so that winning the vote will make very little difference. It will be generations before women are sufficiently thick-skinned to enter the professions, he suggests, and even then they will be hindered by a long-standing tradition which educates sons at the expense of daughters.* At this point, Terence asks Rachel to describe a typical day in her life at home and the rigidity and vacuity of the scene Rachel describes are appalling (p. 214). This leads Terence to ponder the situation of women on a broader scale:

> "I've often walked along the streets where people live all in a row,
> and one house is exactly like another house, and wondered what

---

*The reader may recall, at this point, the persistent emblem of this oppression in *Three Guineas*: "Arthur's Education Fund."

on earth the women were doing inside," he mused. "Doesn't it make your blood boil?" he asked suddenly turning upon her. "I'm sure if I were a woman I'd blow someone's brains out" (p. 215).

Woolf shows considerable shrewdness in assigning these sentiments to Terence. Were Rachel to utter them, Woolf would have created the same sort of distracting "double focus" for which she later criticized Charlotte Brontë. Intriguingly, Elizabeth Heine's study of the extant earlier manuscripts of *The Voyage Out*, which took Virginia Woolf eight years to finish to her satisfaction, "indicates that Woolf rewrote the novel almost completely after her marriage, changing the heroine, Rachel Vinrace, from an intelligent, outspoken, critical young feminist to the vague and innocently naive dreamer of the published text." Whereas Rachel is very much at ease with adults and particularly with women in the earlier versions, "in the published novel she approaches all other adults rather tentatively."[3]

It was perhaps Woolf's uneasiness with the air of grievance which hangs over some of Jane Eyre's speeches and her opinion that this betrays an authorial bitterness which disrupts the fiction that prompted her to use a male character as a spokesperson against the oppression of women. It is also true, of course, that Rachel is too inexperienced and unformed to have many strong opinions while Susan Warrington is incapable of these feelings and the reader would discount them coming from Evelyn Murgatroyd. Nevertheless, by ascribing these sentiments to Terence, Woolf avoids the appearance of using her fiction as a platform for her own political convictions.

Terence's ideas are counter-balanced in the novel by Hirst's impatience with feminine vagueness and Richard Dalloway's patronizing condescension. Hirst, who is abrasive and openly misogynistic, somehow emerges as a largely appealing character, partly because of his candor and his willingness to entertain whatever opinions are offered. Richard, on the other hand, has an opinion on every subject which he dispenses with an air of unquestioned authority. Jane Austen is "the greatest female writer we possess," for the simple reason that, unlike every other woman, ". . . she does not attempt to write like a man" (p. 124). On the subject of suffragists, Richard waxes sentimentally paternalistic in one breath and outraged in the next:

"No, I pity them, I confess. The discomfort of sitting on those steps must be awful" . . . "Nobody can condemn the utter folly and futility of such behaviour more than I do; and as for the whole agitation, well! may I be in my grave before a woman has the right to vote in England! That's all I say" (p. 43).

Richard is delighted to have found such a seemingly willing audience for all these sagacious pronouncements as Rachel Vinrace. As he correctly perceives, Rachel is still in the process of forming her ideas and therefore has no rejoinders to Richard's assertions, however specious they may be. He particularly enjoys needling Rachel by investing her with feminist leanings and then chiding her for them:

"Well, then; no woman has what I may call the political instinct. You have very great virtues; I am the first, I hope, to admit that; but I have never met a woman who even saw what is meant by statesmanship. I am going to make you still more angry. I hope that I never shall meet such a woman. Now, Miss Vinrace, are we enemies for life?" (p. 67).

Richard is clearly confident here that the threat of losing his approval is more than sufficient to dissuade Rachel from adopting a feminist course in life. Indeed, he is so confident in his attractiveness that he does not hesitate to impose himself upon Rachel sexually.

Although their encounter is in fact limited to a passionate kiss, the totally inexperienced Rachel is traumatized by the event. That night she is tortured by a nightmare in which she finds herself in an increasingly narrow tunnel which opens into a damp vault from which there is no escape. Once inside the vault, she is confronted by a gibbering, deformed, animal-like little man by whom she feels horribly threatened (p. 77). The vaginal and uterine images of the tunnel and vault and the threatening dwarf-like figure are fairly common themes in the dream imagery of women writers, and seem to suggest an association of sex with intimidation, torture, and entrapment. In this case, however, during the course of the following day, Rachel's terror is transformed into anger:

"So that's why I can't walk alone!"
By this new light she saw her life for the first time a creeping

hedged-in thing, driven cautiously between high walls, here turned aside, there plunged in darkness; made dull and crippled for ever—her life that was the only chance she had—the short season between two silences.

"Because men are brutes! I hate men!" she exclaimed (p. 82).

Rachel's experience with Richard and her reaction to it are crucial, since they provide a springboard for Rachel in her search for identity and security. Although she is still uncertain about what she wants in life, she is increasingly clear about what she doesn't want. All that is represented by Richard Dalloway—pomposity, masculine privilege, contempt for assertive women—becomes symbolic of an orientation which she will henceforth resist. It is not surprising, then, that she should react so strongly to Susan Warrington's unbounded feminine submissiveness and that she should be drawn to the reflective, unpatronizing Terence Hewet. With Terence, Rachel discovers that there are, in fact, alternatives to the walled-in life of conformity which she had visualized.

Woolf's evocation through Rachel of the process of falling in love is nothing short of brilliant. Rachel's emotion, which she only half understands, elevates her and set her apart. When, confronting Gibbon's *Decline and Fall of the Roman Empire*, she finds herself exultant at the prospect of learning, she realizes vaguely that her excitement has something to do with love, but she is unable to see the connection clearly. The notion of sublimation is unfamiliar to her. Gradually, the people at the hotel become objects of wonder to Rachel, even though the reader is more struck by the great triviality of their lives which Rachel's curiosity brings into focus. Her naivety is poignant:

> Everyone who stayed in the hotel had a peculiar romance and interest about them. They were not ordinary people. She would attribute wisdom to Mrs. Elliot, beauty to Susan Warrington, a splendid vitality to Evelyn M., because Terence spoke to them (p. 223).

She is also subject, not surprisingly, to periods of melancholy, restlessness, and depression. She suffers the sensation that she is in fact asleep and dreaming. At one dramatic juncture, her dissatisfaction with Hewet, who is frustrating her through inattention, is displaced onto Helen in the form of genuine, though groundless, rage. Just those feelings which Rachel finds it necessary to repress about Hewet are showered on Helen. Helen, fortunately, is wise enough in the ways of love not to take Rachel's attack personally (pp. 262–263).

Ultimately, of course, Hewet proposes and Rachel accepts, although they are both overwhelmed by the sense of unreality which surrounds such a momentous decision. The unfamiliarity of the surroundings, in this case the Amazon jungle, serves to reinforce that feeling. The symbolic connection of the mysterious, exciting, but vaguely ominous Amazon jungle with the feeling of Rachel and Terence as they contemplate marriage is dramatically effective, and is a fine example as well of how Woolf uses symbols. The connection between the symbol and the thing symbolized is less than obvious and tends to be a matter of association rather than logic. Often, in consequence, Woolf's symbols have a kind of echoing quality which is reminiscent of the way symbols function in dreams.

This associational use of symbols is one of the most salient characteristics of Woolf's style in all her fictional works. In one of her last compositions, a short sketch entitled "The Symbol" and dated March 1, 1941, the narrator compares the mountain outside her window with her earlier anticipation of her mother's death. The mountain, in its unrelenting presence, is associated with the narrator's ambivalence in that it suggests, simultaneously, the force of the maternal presence and the personal freedom and release that the narrator anticipates will be hers when her mother dies.[4] Both the Amazon jungle of *The Voyage Out*, then, and the mountain of this very late story, function on a variety of levels to suggest the confusion of emotion accompanying a major change in one's personal life. The awesomeness and strangeness of the settings engender a sense of unreality, of a disorientation which is both exciting and terrifying. In both cases as well, the combination of terror and excitement which is reinforced by these exotic images suggests the sense of "loss of foothold" women often feel when confronted by a major change in their lives. While the death of a mother or impending marriage may be momentous events in a man's life as well, he very often has other occupations or responsibilities which reduce the potential trauma or disorientation of such events.

As Rachel and Terence begin to plan their life together, this initial sense of unreality fades and is replaced by a creative vision of how men and women might better relate to one another in marriage. Together, Rachel and Terence envision a new kind of marriage which will not stifle them as individuals. Their children, too, will be encouraged to develop independent minds: ". . . their daughter should be required from infancy to gaze at a large square of cardboard, painted blue, to suggest thoughts of infinity, for women were grown too practical; and their son—he should be taught to laugh at great men, that is, at distinguished successful men, at men who wore ribands and rose to the tops of their trees" (pp. 294–295).

All these plans and hopes are shattered, of course, by Rachel's untimely illness. As the novel draws to its close, Rachel's movement toward consummation becomes a movement toward death, and the link between Eros and Thanatos which informs so much of Woolf's work is established. The eroticism which Terence has awakened in Rachel is, like the jungle, both enticing and terrifying. On the one hand, it suggests to Rachel the ultimate human experience, but on the other, it threatens her with the loss of a selfhood which she is only just beginning to establish. As in all of Woolf's novels, sexuality, though mysterious and alluring, brings in its wake fear, anxiety, and death.

The subtlety with which Woolf communicates this ambivalence is notable. From beginning to end, the images of *The Voyage Out* reinforce this central conflict, but they operate so unobtrusively that few readers are likely to be consciously aware of them. Even in her most casual descriptions, however, Woolf is carefully reinforcing her themes. James Naremore points out Woolf's description of the old lady gardeners at the hotel as one such example: ". . . millions of dark-red flowers were blooming, until the old ladies who had tended them so carefully came down the paths with their scissors, snipped through their juicy stalks, and laid them upon cold stone ledges in the village church." As Naremore correctly perceives, the apparent tranquillity of this scene is jarred by the image of the scissors cutting the "juicy stalks" of the "dark-red flowers."[5] Sex and death are the real subjects here, not charming old ladies tending their flowers.

On a more or less subliminal level, then, the reader has been carefully prepared for Rachel's entry into fever and death. In a sense, given the anxiety with which intimacy has been associated throughout the novel, her death seems inevitable. Mitchell Leaska's notion that "Rachel's ability to become detached from a threatening closeness is, in effect, her only means of self-protection, even survival" is probably accurate. And as Leaska goes on to say, "By the end of the novel, we know that no sacrifice was too great to safeguard that tragically helpless independence, with all its watery solitude."[6]

Significantly, Terence is reading the address to Sabrina from *Comus* to Rachel when she falls ill, and images and verbal echoes from *Comus* permeate the description of Rachel's fever. Like Sabrina, or like Lycidas for that matter, Rachel's virginal self does indeed reside in a watery solitude, which, though tragic, allows her to retain an integrity of self and a sense of personal power which is vital. In a sense, then, as Mitchell Leaska perceives, ". . . hers is a death consciously unresisted, unconsciously sought—it is a *self-willed* death."[7] While there is something horrifying in this notion that one must choose between loss of integrity or death, it is in fact a recurring theme in Woolf's work. In *Jacob's Room*, the hero's early death allows him to escape the "world's slow stain"; in *Mrs. Dalloway*, the suicide of Septimus "clutching his treasure," his integrity, to his bosom, allows Clarissa, in her identification with him, to go on living; and in *To the Lighthouse*, Mrs. Ramsay's death imbues her with a "mythic integrity" which would not have been hers had she lived. Virginia Woolf herself offers some justification for this disquieting paradox in her essay "On Being Ill":

> Human beings do not go hand in hand the whole stretch of the way. There is a virgin forest in each; a snowfield where even the print of bird's feet is unknown. Here we go alone, and like it better so. Always to have sympathy, always to be accompanied, always to be understood would be intolerable. But in health the genial pretence must be kept up and the effort renewed—to communicate, to civilize, to share, to cultivate the desert, educate the native, to work together by day and by night to sport. In illness this make-believe ceases.[8]

It is, nonetheless, disturbing that Woolf should have Rachel die, since so many of the possibilities the novel has been exploring die with her. Too often in novels of the past, one feels, heroines have been punished with death for choosing untraditional paths. It may be, however, that Woolf was forced to recognize that not even Rachel and Terence could conquer the obstacles posed by the institution of marriage:

> It seemed to her now that what he was saying was perfectly true, and that she wanted many more things than the love of one

human being—the sea, the sky. She turned again and looked at the distant blue, which was so smooth and serene where the sky met the sea; she could not possibly want only one human being (p. 302).

Given this perception of the insufficiency of love, Woolf may have elected to kill her heroine rather than sentence her to a life of disillusionment. Or it may be that Woolf was troubled by the more or less polemical nature of the novel and its focus on the pros and cons of the institution of marriage. By having Rachel die, she can attenuate her message about traditional marriage and its limitations by placing it in the larger context of pondering the meaning of individual life against the background of time and death. It is, after all, just this question which engages Rachel fairly early in the novel: "And life, what was that? It was only a light passing over the surface and vanishing, as in time she would vanish, though the furniture in the room would remain" (p. 125). As James Naremore points out in his discussion of Woolf's novels, "On the one hand is the world of the self, the timebound, landlocked, everyday world of the masculine ego, of intellect and routine, where people live in the fear of death, and where separations imposed by time and space result in agony. On the other hand is the world without a self—watery, emotional, erotic, generally associated with the feminine sensibility—where all of life seems blended together in a kind of 'halo,' where the individual personality is continually being dissolved by intimations of eternity, and where death reminds us of sexual union."[9]

It is this second state of being, "the world without a self," which becomes available in moments of "vision." But because these visionary moments involve the temporary suspension of individual identity, they are associated with death. And as Alice van Buren Kelley points out, because love is often the catalyst to vision, it too becomes associated with death. While death offers an extraordinary solace, it demands, like love, the surrender of the self which it has been the function of life painstakingly to create. Since the "loss of self" is both attractive and terrifying, love and death are viewed with an edgy ambivalence.[10]

When Rachel dies, Terence momentarily experiences perfect happiness. Death, like the marriage proposal, marks such a momentous transition as to become unreal. At the moment of death, Terence is overwhelmed by the sense that it makes no difference, that death is only "to cease to breathe" (p. 353). His peace, though momentary, is real.

The inconsequence of individual life and the absurdity of death is reinforced when Woolf moves back to the other characters for their reactions. Mrs. Paley, because she is virtually deaf, must ask repeatedly "Eh? What's that?" when she is told that Rachel has died. And then, when she finally understands the message, she is unable to remember just exactly which young woman Rachel was (pp. 361–362). Ultimately, however, the apparent callousness of the other characters has its reassuring side as well. Hirst, who has remained at Terence's side throughout Rachel's illness, is a wreck physically and emotionally and is much reassured by the sight of life going on at the hotel. Gratefully, he is absorbed into this company as the novel ends (pp. 374–375).

In the treatment of Rachel's death, Woolf manages to convey with considerable subtlety a major feminist dilemma. Marriage, even with so enlightened a partner as Terence, is too bound by tradition to accommodate the kind of change that Rachel's feminist vision demands. Feminism has expanded Rachel's horizon; marriage necessarily contracts it.

Most of the feminist issues addressed in *The Voyage Out*, however, are handled with considerably less subtlety than Rachel's death. In this first novel, Woolf is only beginning to develop the techniques for which she is famous. Events unfold in simple chronological order and are never melded by those powerful, ambiguous, recurring images which become so central in her later work. We have, as well, a standard omniscient narrator and a point of view which is largely confined to Rachel and the narrator, although we occasionally see things from the perspectives of Clarissa, Helen, and Hewet. The structure of the novel is simple, and in some ways even crude. Events are used, not very imaginatively, to throw characters together, so that we move from the initial voyage to the picnic to the dance to the expedition to Rachel's final illness rather mechanically. The picnic, interestingly, has much in common with the one which occurs in *Emma*. Woolf's inexperience becomes particularly obvious when she has Rachel move from person to person, room to room in the hotel in order to suggest Rachel's changing consciousness. As readers, we are too aware of this structural manipulation. And in no other novel does she come nearer to preaching than she does here.

If Woolf avoids an aesthetic disaster in *The Voyage Out*, it is because even in this first novel she recognized the dangers of undisguised polemic. Never does the reader sense, except perhaps in the church episode, that the author herself is angry or full of grievances. To be sure, she uses characters like Richard Dalloway, Mr. Ambrose, and St. John Hirst to expose the outrages of patriarchy, but the narrator never steps in to evaluate and judge these characters. Instead, the reader is offered a variety of points of view and is left to make his or her own judgment. And although Woolf may at times seem almost merciless in exposing the faults of her characters, these faults are sufficiently balanced by favorable qualities to preclude a flat, one-sided characterization. Richard Dalloway, Hirst, and Evelyn are not altogether unattractive. They have appealing qualities as well.

If Virginia Woolf does not manage "to get her genius expressed whole and entire" in this novel, it is because she is stifled by the traditional form. The shape of the sentence, plot, structure, characterization—all work against the delicate and adroit exploration of consciousness which was to become Woolf's greatest strength. Nevertheless, in Rachel's fever and death and at certain other points in the novel, we can see a new form taking shape. Virginia Woolf's "voyage out" as a writer is full of promise.

II *Night and Day*

> "When philosophy is not consumed in a novel,
> when we can underline this phrase with a
> pencil, and cut out that exhortation with a pair
> of scissors and paste the whole into a system,
> it is safe to say that there is something wrong
> with the philosophy or with the novel or with
> both."
>
> (Virginia Woolf,
> *The Second Common Reader*)

Virginia Woolf's second novel, *Night and Day*, was written during the first World War, although the story can be dated about 1912, before the war. According to Winifred Holtby, Woolf was ill when she wrote it and could only work about an hour a day.[1] As in *The Voyage Out*, the principal themes of this novel are marriage, and the ambiguity of its advantages, feminism, and the ambiguity of its claims, and domesticity, and the ambiguity of its value. Jane Marcus maintains that *Night and Day* depends "structurally on Mozart, stylistically on Jane Austen, and thematically on Ibsen."[2] Mary Datchet is the committed feminist of *Night and Day*, and the suffrage society to which she belongs is in many ways an object of satire. As Herbert Marder points out, "The total effect is interesting; women's problems are taken seriously, but the feminist societies are not. Both too much and too little is made of feminism as a theme—too much for it to remain mere background; too little for it to become a significant part of the fictional pattern."[3]

Perhaps because she lives alone and takes an active role in current social and political issues, Mary appears very clever and free to other women, particularly Katharine Hilbery, who views Mary's life wistfully. Unlike Evelyn Murgatroyd in *The Voyage Out*, Mary is far more than a mere enthusiast. She is an open-minded, committed, intelligent worker, and has a mature sense of personal identity. Woolf's decision to make Mary

Datchet an appealing character was fortunate. Otherwise the novel would almost certainly have degenerated into mere satire.

As it is, the disdain which might have been lavished on Mary is deflected onto Mrs. Seal and Mr. Clacton, Mary's co-workers. Even Mary views her office mates as lacking "some essential part."[4] Mrs. Seal, in particular, is a ludicrous figure, a perpetual enthusiast who loves a cause, any cause, although she is especially passionate on the subject of women. Mrs. Seal is an ax-grinder and, as Woolf makes clear, given her way, she would happily force people to share her vision of the way things ought to be. She is worthy of Dickens.

Unfortunately, such unmitigated caricature does not fit easily into the kind of novel Woolf was trying to write, and it constitutes a weak spot in the narrative. Because Woolf was ambivalent about feminist organizations, disliking their methods on the one hand and yet, as Holtby notes,[5] she chose to treat the suffrage office comically. One senses an uneasiness in Woolf's writing about the suffragists, however, as if she is in part questioning her own motives in dismissing them so lightly. The author's presence is intrusive in these passages and creates a tension which interferes with the fictional integrity of the novel.

Part of the reason for Woolf's critical attitude toward the suffrage organization, according to Margaret Comstock, is that it "is headed by a man who recapitulates the patriarchal and oppressive orderliness associated with men like Mr. Hilbery."[6] Nevertheless, it is through the musings of the urbane Mr. Hilbery that we gain some insight into Woolf's uneasiness with political organizations:

> "It's curious," Mr. Hilbery continued, agreeing with his daughter, "how the sight of one's fellow-enthusiasts always chokes one off. They show up the faults of one's cause so much more plainly than one's antagonists. One can be enthusiastic in one's study, but directly one comes into touch with the people who agree with one, all the glamor [sic] goes" (p. 100).

Given what we know about Woolf's persistent aversion to organized political activity, Mr. Hilbery's statement is fascinating. Suffrage societies, it would seem, are distasteful because one's point of view becomes tarnished and vulgarized when it is shared with others. Woolf reveals a basic mistrust here, an inability to join with others in a common cause which may spring from a fear of losing identity, of having one's uniqueness swallowed in a sea of mediocrity.

This fear of mediocrity was surely a product, at least in part, of the intellectually competitive atmosphere in which Virginia Woolf was reared. Around Sir Leslie Stephen and his colleagues or later on her brother Thoby's Cambridge friends, she was intent on being clever. As such, she was a successful product of her class. She was keenly aware, however, that the advantages of class exact a cost as well by creating chasms between people that can be difficult if not impossible to bridge.

Much of Ralph Denham's adverse initial reaction to Katharine, and to the Hilberys in general, springs from an envy for the tradition, luxury, taste, culture, and ease which they represent. Because Ralph has been denied these perquisites by an accident of birth, he resents Katharine for having them. Because Ralph is unable to admit to feeling such a base emotion as envy, his animus takes the form of contempt. When Katharine tells him that nothing interesting ever happens to her, for example, Ralph's response is little short of vicious:

> "I think you make a system of saying disagreeable things, Miss Hilbery," he broke out, again going further than he meant to. " I suppose it's one of the characteristics of your class. They never talk seriously to their inferiors" (p. 62).

Significantly, as the novel progresses, it becomes increasingly clear that the distinctions between classes are, in fact, real. The Hilberys are paragons of taste and deportment whose social behavior displays an ease and grace which is never ruffled. The Denhams, on the other hand, live in a house which is overcrowded, worn by constant use, in need of repair, noisy, and cluttered with objects of questionable taste. The industry of the Denham household forms a striking contrast with the relaxed urbanity of the Hilbery quarters.

Woolf was a singularly adept observer of these differences, and the issue of class tension has begun to develop as an interesting theme in *Night and Day* when it is substantially abandoned. After the first few chapters, Woolf focuses almost entirely on personal tensions which she has carefully detached from their origin in class differences. In doing so, Woolf avoids committing herself politically, but she also loses the opportunity to ground an otherwise conventional love story in a complicated and believable social context. Thus, although we are aware that Katharine does not quite fit when Ralph finally gets around to introducing her to his family, Woolf does little to exploit this scene for its obvious implications about the ways in which class determines character.

Katharine Hilbery, whose activities are in fact very limited by her class, suffers from an overdose of domesticity. As Marder describes her, "She is starved for abstract ideas, for facts, and shrinks from her emotions."[7] Like most house-bound women, she has little privacy, and consequently can devote little time to her secret vice—the study of mathematics. Although Katharine's life may strike us as stifling and wearisome, however, at one point the narrator offers a surprisingly different evaluation: "Katharine . . . was a member of a very great profession which has, as yet, no title and very little recognition, although the labor of mill and factory is, perhaps, no more severe and the results of less benefit to the world. She lived at home. She did it very well, too" (p. 44).

Woolf's obvious and persistent admiration for domestic skill should not be construed as anti-feminism. In admiring Katharine's skill, the narrator insists that such labor is of equal if not greater value than that which men perform in the workplace and should be respected as such. The domestic wisdom which has been cultivated and perfected by women through the centuries should have a broader spectrum in which to operate, but it is far too valuable to be rejected. Indeed, for Woolf this wisdom constitutes a female culture which is the necessary corrective to patriarchal values and modes of behavior.

Both Katharine and her mother, Mrs. Hilbery, are hindered by the notion that as women their intellectual pursuits should be confined to composing the biography of their famous *pater-familias*, the poet Richard Alardyce. This is acceptable because its intent is to enhance the reputation of the family's famous man. Unfortunately, it is a task to which Katharine and her mother are very ill-suited. Katharine's true interest and talent lie in mathematics, although "she would rather have confessed her wildest dreams of hurricane and prairie than the fact that, upstairs, alone in her room, she rose early in the morning or sat up late at night to . . . work at mathematics. No force on earth would have made her confess that" (p. 45). Katharine sees math as the antithesis of literature, a supposedly congenial interest, and consequently her passion for math makes her feel like a traitor. Unfortunately, Katharine's aptitude for literature is not great and she does not enjoy phrase-making. Since she is the well-born grand daughter of a famous poet, however, most other options are closed.

Similarly, Katharine's mother, who is always reciting or jotting down snatches of poetry, is clearly more suited to pursue the poetic vocation of her father than to compile his biography: ". . . in the spring her desire for expression invariably increased. She was haunted by the ghosts of phrases. She gave herself up to a sensual delight in the combinations of words" (p. 304). For Mrs. Hilbery, however, the idea of being a poet is inconceivable. Her duty is the biography, for which she is hopelessly ill-equipped.

Katharine and her mother are not the only women in this novel who are crippled by false limitations imposed by convention. Ralph Denham has the burden of supporting a family of capable females who are prevented by societal expectations and restrictions from supporting themselves. And Katharine's bright, energetic cousin, Cassandra, has been educated in such a haphazard manner that "she could never possibly earn her living" (p. 431). It is only when we see Katharine and Cassandra together, in fact, that Katharine's unconventionality in the seriousness with which she approaches her work becomes obvious.

As in *The Voyage Out*, one of the predominant themes of this novel is marriage and its questionable capacity to gratify the needs of those who enter it. For Katharine, the choice between William Rodney and Ralph Denham is crucial, since they represent very different attitudes toward the mutual responsibilities of husband and wife. In this attempt to explore the institution of marriage and how it might best be shaped to suit the needs of the characters, three issues seem to predominate: love, and the question of whether it is advisable to love one's potential spouse; happiness, and the lengths to which one should go to achieve it; and passion, and the decision as to whether or not it should be indulged. The cultural assumption, of course, is that marriage is necessary for wholeness in women, that they are only half-alive, half-real, without it. But for the characters, the choice of an appropriate partner inspires all sorts of questions. How much importance, for example, should be assigned to passion, and is it a destructive or positive force in marriage?

In the privacy of her own thoughts, Katharine indulges in fantasies of total passion and surrender, but consciously, and in terms of actual behavior, she is fully able to contemplate a totally loveless marriage (p. 107).

When, indeed, we learn from Mrs. Hilbery's letter that Katharine is to be married, we are likely to be shocked by the total absence of emotion in Katharine's announcement. She has made, it appears, a simple, practical decision, rather like deciding to order a new chair (p. 143). Ralph Denham, who is shocked by the news that the woman who haunts his dreams is about to marry another, sublimates his thwarted passion into a vision of himself leaving London, settling into an isolated country cottage, and writing a great book (pp. 225–226). By contrast, Katharine's fiance, William Rodney, is made distinctly uneasy by the passionate aspect of Katharine's nature and prefers to think of it as being lavished not upon him, but upon their future children (p. 246).

Oddly enough, the most healthy balance of passion and friendship seems to be personified in Mary Datchet. Mary loves Ralph deeply, feels intensely drawn to him physically, and shares his interests:

> Purposely, perhaps, Mary did not agree with Ralph; she loved to feel her mind in conflict with his, and to be certain that he spared her female judgment no ounce of his male muscularity. He seemed to argue as fiercely with her as if she were his brother. They were alike, however, in believing that it behooved them to take in hand the repair and reconstruction of the fabric of England (p. 219).

Mary has no doubts about her desire to marry Ralph. Unfortunately, Ralph does not fully return her feelings. This, of course, returns us to the initial issue. How much priority should be given to passion and romance in marriage? The object of Ralph's passion, Katharine, has become engaged to another man, a man she does not love. Ralph, meanwhile, is very fond of Mary Datchet and the chance that they would be compatible is very strong. In a crucial scene, Ralph determines to ask Mary for her hand. When the expression on her face forces him to realize that she loves him with passion, however, he cannot carry through with the proposal. He can accept a practical marriage, but because his passion is reserved for Katharine, he is repulsed when he perceives it in Mary. Mary, for her part, is deeply hurt by Ralph's obvious lack of passion when he finally does propose.

Unlike Mary, Katharine is operating wholly on the assumption that she must be practical in choosing a husband. Her object in marrying consists almost entirely in wanting to be free of the oppressive atmosphere of her parents' house so that she can pursue her study of math and astronomy. Nonetheless, though Katharine's expectations are far from unreasonable, it seems odd to her "not to be happy, when she was supposed to be happier than she would ever be again . . ." (p. 193). Katharine's difficulty is in not knowing whether she ought to expect happiness. Her Aunt Charlotte advises her to *submit* to her husband totally, since women who fail to do so are never happy. Katharine will find happiness, her aunt assures her, in repressing her own desires and allowing her husband to have his own way without question (p. 213). For women of Katharine's class, the marriage of convenience was a time-honored tradition, and the need to adapt to an often loveless union required an almost masochistic submission if friction was to be avoided. How else could a woman share the bed of someone she did not love except by complete self-effacement? Given this tradition, it is not surprising that Katharine finds it difficult to place a very high premium on personal happiness.

Since we presently live in a culture in which romance is highly valued and the idea of a marriage of convenience is repugnant, modern readers may find these notions hard to accept. We can, however, perhaps learn something from taking seriously Ralph Denham's statement that "the risk of marrying a person you're in love with is something colossal" (p. 253). The potential for frustration, disappointment, and disillusionment might be said to increase proportionately with the intensity of passion. A person of whom one has few expectations is not so likely to be disappointing.

Love, of course, means something totally different for each of the four young characters in this novel. For Katharine, love consists in the promise of escape from the oppressiveness of her household and the opportunity to pursue her secret vices, math and astronomy, more openly. For this reason, she is baffled, confused and a little alarmed when she encounters the agony Mary Datchet is suffering in her unrequited love for Ralph Denham. Woolf handles this scene superbly. Mary, who has received Katharine as a visitor, decides that the time has come to enlighten Katharine about the true nature of Ralph's feelings. The scene is a study in discomfort, hesitancy, awkwardness, and tact. Gradually, Katharine becomes aware for the first time of how Ralph feels about her by seeing how Mary feels about Ralph. The two women, who begin the scene as virtual strangers, end it as true friends who have exposed their vulnerabilities, shared pain, and arrived at an understanding of one another.

Katharine, seeing Mary in agony, understands for the first time what love is and how far she is from having such feelings for William Rodney (pp. 270–278).

William Rodney, a paragon of highly civilized Victorian masculinity, is associated throughout the novel with an overscrupulous attention to propriety and conventions. He is a decent man, but rigid and inflexible. He lacks spontaneity and vision, is terribly pedantic, and is incapable of adapting to change. For Katharine, marriage to William Rodney would entail a permanent acceptance of the break between her private visions and desires and her public image and behavior. Her love of math, for example, would remain a guilty secret. Interestingly, both Katharine and William admit that they have a capacity for romance, though they have never felt it for one another. In fact, William is far more suited temperamentally to Katharine's cousin, Cassandra, and very much against his better judgment, he finds himself falling in love with her. William falls in love with Cassandra not only because their interests and tastes coincide, but because she is immensely impressed by the extensiveness of his knowledge and eager to be instructed by him. By contrast, he finds Katharine's reserve and her laconic responses to his discourses distinctly annoying.

Woolf's sensitivity to psychological subtlety is strikingly revealed when Katharine and William discuss breaking their engagement. When Katharine hesitates, William realizes that on some level she does, in fact, love him, and he feels a wave of resentment. Suddenly Katharine, no longer the elusive prey, fetters and encumbers him, and he senses that in the future he will be her master rather than her slave (p. 322). Their basic incompatibility has transformed love into a kind of power game. William is comfortable with Katharine in the role of a suitor courting the unachievable ideal, but he is repulsed when he encounters her vulnerability. In the absence of love, Katharine's appeal consists in her ultimate unattainability.

Most of the confusion which these characters feel results from a contradiction between what they have been taught to seek in a marriage partner and what they are inclined to seek. This problem is greatly exacerbated by the roles which have been forced upon the female characters, so that what they really think and feel is rarely the same as what they profess to think and feel. In Katharine's case, she cannot admit even to herself that her talents and interests are in fact contrary to those she has assumed. Katharine exists in a kind of "no-woman's-land": she can neither accommodate herself to the traditional role of sacrificing her own interests and devoting herself to pleasing the men around her, nor can she assert her independence from these constraints. The result is a schism between her public compliance with social expectations, a part she performs mechanically and unenthusiastically, and her private fantasies and dreams. Katharine is a mystery to others because she is a mystery to herself. Because she is unable to resolve the contradiction between what she privately desires (her "night") and what she is expected to desire (her "day"), she remains an enigma to all who know her. Even Ralph, who loves her, completely misunderstands her. Since she has never shared her private dreams with him, Ralph in fact knows very little about her. His love is based on an imaginary construct, his own vision of an ideal woman.

Fortunately, Ralph is sufficiently reflective and astute to recognize the falseness which is implicit in his perception of Katharine. By questioning the assumptions on which his love is based, he finds he must question the fact of love itself. Consequently, when he has the opportunity to tell Katharine how he feels, he insists that he does *not* love her, and proposes friendship instead. Since Ralph proposes a kind of "ideal" friendship based on total sincerity with one another and no obligations, for the first time in her life Katharine has an opportunity for sharing her private dreams and ideals with a sympathetic listener.

Like Katharine, Ralph is a dreamer who has drawn a sharp distinction between his public life of work, including his obligations to society and family, and his private life of dreams, vision, passion, and ideals. In this they are very similar, and it is from this separation of public and private, and the tension created by it, that the novel takes its title.

As the relationship between Ralph and Katharine develops, they are persistently startled by how little they know of one another. Just as learning makes us more aware of our ignorance, the growing intimacy between Ralph and Katharine exposes all the recesses of personality which have yet to be explored. Their growing relationship is hindered, however, by an element of fear. Because they are beginning to inhabit one another's dream world, worlds which have been previously entirely private, they threaten each other with a profound alteration, nothing less than the disintegration of the barrier between their private and public lives. Perhaps for this reason, they often disappoint one another in person, as dreams are apt to do when exposed to the light of day. Katharine insists that she cannot marry because love is an illusion, because she and Ralph can never be certain of seeing one another clearly (p. 484). Yet when they are apart, they long to be together. Finally, when they share one another's work, when Katharine reads Ralph's poem and Ralph inspects some sheets of Katharine's math, we sense that a crucial resolution has been reached (p. 492).

Concentrating as it does on a set of star-crossed lovers, this novel might not seem to offer a particularly feminist perception of the world. Yet the psychology of love and marriage which the novel explores pivots on the changing needs of women and the unsuitability of traditional marriage in meeting those needs. While a lesser writer might have concentrated on the frustration Katharine feels in being denied the option of pursuing her true interests and talents, Woolf's subject is Katharine's own confusion in the face of these contradictions. Because Katharine has accepted tradition and yielded to the split between her private dreams and her public role, the vague, bewildered unhappiness she experiences engages us as readers and encourages us to acknowledge the tremendous difficulty of change. If political and social change is to be meaningful, Woolf suggests, psychic change must precede it, and that is a very subtle, dangerous, and difficult process, full of obstacles which many women may find impossible to overcome. Even Mary Datchet, who has come farther than most, suffers the loneliness of isolation of a woman in a society which is not yet ready for her. Woolf's feminism, then, is a kind of vantage point from which she assesses the problems women encounter as they attempt to redefine themselves in a society which resists their attempts at every turn. While feminism is often associated with public solutions, Woolf focuses on the private quest.

In *Night and Day*, Katharine ultimately finds a private solution in her relationship with Ralph Denham. In essence, what Ralph and Katharine offer one another is a heady alternative to traditional marriage, an independent partnership in which the need for privacy as well as intimacy would be respected. Katharine is fascinated by Ralph's vision of reforming the traditional relations between men and women, but she must overcome her deeprooted fear of change in order to share his vision. Little by little during the course of the novel, Katharine's inner world is brought out for airing so that, as Winifred Holtby suggests, the dream world becomes "identified with reality," and the "satisfaction of love" is linked with "the discovery of truth."[8] In their mutual vision of a more equal partnership between man and woman, Katharine and Ralph find completion.

In order for these star-crossed lovers to be brought together, however, an outside agency is necessary, and that service is willingly performed by Mrs. Hilbery on her return from Shakespeare's tomb. Throughout *Night and Day*, Mrs. Hilbery is associated with Shakespeare, particularly with the figure of the wise fool, and it is she who orchestrates the comic resolution, re-arranging mismatched couples and creating an ambience of gaiety and emotional honesty.

So far, this discussion of *Night and Day* has focused largely on thematic issues. At this point in her writing career, Woolf had not yet developed the ability to transform her uses of symbol, structure, and style into feminist statements in themselves. We can, however, see the beginning of some of these techniques in her use of a few key images.

The image of the "blot fringed with flame" which Ralph inadvertently draws in his attempt to communicate with Katharine suggests the transformation of the world and its phenomena which love engenders. But perhaps more importantly, this is the first instance we have of Woolf's ability to evoke, through an image, sensations which resist verbal explanation. It is, after all, only when words fail that Ralph finds himself drawing "the blot fringed with flame," and when Katharine sees the drawing, it tells her far more than anything Ralph could say. As such, this image has much in common with certain dream images. It becomes the focus of a cathexis, a concentration of psychic energy, which does not seem warranted by its simplicity.

What, then, accounts for its extraordinary impact on Katharine and Ralph? Of obvious importance is the fact that this image emerges from Ralph's unconscious. Language has failed him and in its place emerges this image, which he draws on a sheet of paper. One could hardly find a better example of what Freud refers to as "condensation," the power of the unconscious to construct a dream image, simple in itself, which has reference to a variety of different emotional situations in the dreamer's life. Such images, because they stand for so many things and suggest such a variety of associations, are far more than simple metaphors or symbols. They ultimately defy analysis because one can never be certain that they have been fully explored.[9] When, for example, Ralph tries to understand "the blot fringed with flame," language seems inadequate and incomplete. At first, when he initially draws it, he is reminded of Katharine's head, but "perhaps the entire universe" as well (p. 487). Later, in his confusion after Katharine has seen his scribblings, he realizes that the image is far more complex:

> He was convinced that it could mean nothing to another, although somehow to him it conveyed not only Katharine herself but all those states of mind which had clustered round her since he first saw her pouring out tea on a Sunday afternoon. It represented by its circumference of smudges surrounding a central blot all that encircling glow which for him surrounded, inexplicably, so many of the objects of life, softening their sharp outline, so that he could see certain streets, books, and situations wearing a halo almost perceptible to the physical eye (p. 493).

Although Katharine's associations with this image are necessarily different from Ralph's, she shares with him the experience of its emotional impact. While she cannot understand the extent to which she is, for Ralph, identified with the image, she does share his vision of a glowing world, a world transformed by the power of love which the image evokes.

This episode in the novel marks a kind of epiphany, a transforming moment of revelation for the two principal characters. Additionally, the episode is one of the first examples of Woolf's ability to offer up an image which draws together everything of importance which has been said or done in the entire course of the novel. This use of symbol in a manner which is associative, elusive, and grounded in the unconscious was, for Woolf, a distinctly feminine innovation. Although some readers of this discussion may object to the association of men with logic, ego, and action while women are associated with vision, expansion of self, and reflection, Woolf consistently saw these distinctions as characteristic of the sexes. Writing in a masculine tradition, she wished us to experience reality differently, and in my view was able to make us do so.

The most famous and memorable of these images is, of course, the lighthouse, and it is worth noting that images of a lighthouse do, in fact, occur in *Night and Day*, although Woolf refrains from making it a key symbol. In this early novel, for the most part the lighthouse seems to represent solidity and tradition. In giving equal emphasis to the birds who are drawn by its light and dash themselves senseless against the glass, however, Woolf is perhaps suggesting the difficulties faced by those who would depart from tradition.

As in all of Woolf's novels, there is also a moment of supreme doubt for one of the characters, an overwhelming sense of "not-being," of the unreality of life and the world. In this novel, it is Katharine who expresses this for us:

With her eyes upon the dark sky, voices reached her from the room in which she was standing. She heard them as if they came from people in another world, a world that was the prelude, the antechamber to reality; it was as if, lately dead, she heard the living talking. The dream nature of our life had never been more apparent to her, never had life more certainly been an affair of four walls, whose objects existed only within the range of lights and fires, beyond which lay nothing, or nothing more than darkness. She seemed physically to have stepped beyond the region where the light of illusion still makes it desirable to possess, to love, to struggle (p. 352).

One is reminded of Rachel Vinrace's experience in *The Voyage Out* when she describes herself as a light which vanishes, leaving the chairs, the tables and other objects to go on, unaffected by the simple accident of her life and death. Similar sensations, of course, are experienced by Mrs. Dalloway and Mrs. Ramsay, and by many other of Woolf's characters. The particular sensation which they feel may have some connection with what Freud referred to as the "oceanic sense," the experience of a loss of personal identity and even of physical being in which one seems to blend with the universe, to experience a "one-ness" which is entirely impersonal.[10]

In *Night and Day*, then, we do see the first rough beginnings of some of the techniques which were to become so characteristic of Woolf's style at her best. In addressing herself to universal social issues, Woolf can avoid preachiness by refraining from simple narrative evaluation of what occurs and instead presenting us with quasi-mystical symbolic equivalents of her approval or disapproval. Instead of saying, "And so Ralph and Katharine ushered in a new and more hopeful age based on mutual freedom and respect of man and woman in equal partnership," she gives us "a blot fringed with flame," a lighthouse, or in her later writings, a man and woman emerging from a taxi. The message is there, but she imparts it subliminally, a technique at which she becomes more and more skilled with each new novel.

Regrettably, in *Night and Day* these strategies account for only a few pages of a five hundred page book. This is a very conventional novel, and not a particularly good conventional novel. As Winifred Holtby sees it, Woolf modeled her novel on Austen but in the course of writing it found that she could no longer uncritically accept Austen's world.[11] The similarities and parallels with Austen's work are certainly striking. Unfortunately, Woolf produced an Austen novel without Austen's sensibility. Woolf is simply unable to spend as much time as Austen does in the drawing room without becoming tedious. As Katherine Mansfield remarked, *Night and Day* is "so long and so tahsome."[12] Nor is the tedium mitigated by the exotic surroundings and presence of death which add intrigue to *The Voyage Out*.

Though her characterizations are memorable, and in the case of Mrs. Hilbery superb and unforgettable, Woolf seems unable to put these characters to good use. The plot is standard: lovers who have chosen inappropriate mates and discover their error in the course of the action. Anyone familiar with Elizabethan and Jacobean plays or the sources of those plays will recognize it. Unfortunately, Woolf does not do much that is new and exciting with the idea. It takes five hundred pages for Katharine to realize that it is stupid to marry someone you do not love and to acknowledge that she does love Ralph. And while the characters are well-developed and interesting, there is nothing sufficiently unusual or appealing in them to make us wish to spend as much time inside their heads as Woolf requires. In addition to being conventional, then, the plot is lifeless and slow-paced. As Holtby rightly notes, there is entirely too much taking of tea.[13] Part of the problem, in Hena Maes-Jelinek's view, is that Woolf "had not yet discovered the form which was to allow her to suggest the social environment of a character through his reaction to it instead of depicting it directly."[14] Nor does the novel ever veer from its simple chronological forward movement. Although the point of view occasionally shifts, it remains primarily that of Katharine and the narrator, and Katharine's point of view simply cannot be sustained for so many pages without becoming monotonous.

Woolf was primarily an experimenter, and her decision to employ traditional novelistic methods was a mistake, though it could hardly have been avoided this early in her career. As Phyllis Rose points out, *Night and Day* "is her attempt to prove herself the master of the classical tradition of the English novel, to create solid characters and place them in realized settings, to have them speak to one another in credible dialogue and to advance the plot through dramatic scenes. It is as though an abstract, expressionist painter felt he must prove himself the master of classical figure-drawing before he discarded the representational." As Phyllis Rose also reminds us, Woolf herself acknowledged these weaknesses years later:

"I can't believe that any human being can get through *Night and Day* which I wrote chiefly in bed . . . But it taught me a great deal, or so I hoped, like a minute Academy drawing: what to leave out by putting it all in."[15] While Woolf does, in this novel, find a means of adapting the age-old institution of marriage to meet the new needs of her characters, she is unable to adapt the traditional structure of the novel to meet her new needs as a writer. David Daiches sums it up thus:

> *Night and Day* demonstrated to Mrs. Woolf herself that the disparity between her matter and her manner was threatening her with inhibition as a novelist altogether. You cannot distill refined essences of time and personality while employing the traditional technique of the novel . . . Woolf wanted to present a distillation of significant ideas about events, which is a very different thing and required a much less rigid form . . . the novel of refined lyrical speculation.[16]

In *Jacob's Room*, Virginia Woolf made remarkable progress toward achieving the form which would foster her vision and not impede it.

III   *Jacob's Room*

> ". . . by the time that I came to compose what
> I think is my finest novel, *No Laughing Matter*,
> in the late 'sixties, I was thoroughly conscious
> that my teacher to whom (after Dickens and
> Dostoevsky) I owed most was Mrs. Woolf her-
> self; it was she who showed me how to pre-
> serve narration with disregard for unity of
> scene or time sequence or angle of vision or
> formal plot. She is, I believe, the master of
> twentieth-century narrative technique."
> (Angus Wilson
> "The Always-Changing Impact of
> Virginia Woolf")

Using what Winifred Holtby terms her "cinematograph technique,"[1] in *Jacob's Room* Woolf gives us an impressionistic biography of the life of a young man, Jacob Flanders, who becomes a casualty of the first World War. Focusing on the theme which was the source of endless fascination for her, the relation of personality to time and death, Woolf's technique in this novel is deliberately and daringly experimental. Throwing aside novelistic conventions, she centers her story on a character who emerges as a composite of other people's more or less fleeting impressions of him. Characters appear and then disappear with no attempt at closure. Some- times we find ourselves in the midst of a social gathering overhearing bits of conversation among people we barely recognize. If we try to patch together a coherent story from these snippets of conversation, the effort is futile. The point of view is constantly shifting, and by no means are these numerous impressions always focused on Jacob. There is, however, a glue that holds this novel together. As Winifred Holtby rightly perceives, everything that happens is in some sense an answer to the over-riding question of the novel, "What is lost when such a young man dies?"[2]

Instead of simply telling a story, as she did in her previous novels, Woolf concentrates on discrete moments, evoking a scene and a given character's response to it without feeling compelled to move the plot forward. Nor is she any longer concerned with an orderly progression of time. Several years pass between chapters one and two, and in the second chapter, Woolf uses the career of Reverend Floyd to indicate that several more years have passed, giving force to her transition by parenthetically informing us that the kitten which Jacob's brother chose as a parting gift from Reverend Floyd is now a very old cat.[3]

Another sharp departure from her previous method is that instead of focusing on Jacob as the main character, Woolf's narrator sets up a variety of scenes, complete in themselves, which Jacob merely intrudes into or passes through. Only rarely do we enter Jacob's mind or see things through his eyes.

As Ralph Freedman notes, the formal paradigm which Woolf perfected in *Jacob's Room* and used in all her novels thereafter is the integration of "social comedy" with "tragic fate." The perceptions of the individual mind occur within a context of the "chorus" of society, and this "chorus" reflects "the tragic dimensions in her novels—dimensions that concern the essence of human life: time and the ending of time or death."[4] One of the important sources of Woolf's form, then, would seem to be the classical Greek drama.

Typically, when Woolf wishes to suggest a given mood or state of mind in Jacob, she refrains from direct description. Instead, the mood of the narrator's descriptions of nature and of the scenes in which Jacob finds himself mirror his state of mind. This decision to approach Jacob by indirection was fortuitous in terms of Woolf's development as a writer since it allowed so many of her strengths to surface for the first time. Her narrator, no longer encumbered by the rigid constraints of a conventional plot, was free to dwell on whatever impressions suited her, without regard for moving the story forward. As Avrom Fleishman says of *Jacob's Room*, "Its characterization of the putative hero as a 'problem' in identity, its narration of a man's life by a synthesis of multiple points of view, its extension of the *Bildungsroman* form into a fitful sequence of unachieved experiences rather than a coherent process—these were innovations as distinctive in the history of fiction as those of *A Portrait of the Artist* had been less than a decade before."[5]

A fascinating example of the ways in which Woolf's new technique better served her objectives as an artist can be found in her handling of a theme which informs all her novels, that of life's ephemerality. As in *The Voyage Out* and *Night and Day*, the mystery of being and not-being becomes central:

> . . . in any case life is but a procession of shadows, and God knows why it is that we embrace them so eagerly, and see them depart with such anguish, being shadows. And why, if this and much more than this is true, why are we surprised in the window corner by a sudden vision that the young man in the chair is of all things in the world the most real, the most solid, the best known to us—why indeed? For the moment after, we know nothing about him.
>
> Such is the manner of our seeing. Such the conditions of our love (p. 72).

Woolf was fascinated by this notion of the fragility of life, especially when measured against the solidity of furniture and rooms. In *Jacob's Room*, for the first time Woolf is able to incorporate this vision into the structure of the novel itself. By maintaining a distance from her main character, by seeing him only briefly and imperfectly through other characters' eyes, and by giving as much or more significance to the scenes which he passes through as to Jacob himself, the novel itself reflects, through its structure and style, the evanescence and frailty of individual human life.

Jacob, Woolf seems to be saying, has no existence except in the minds of those with whom he interacts, and that is true for all of us. While the notion that immortality exists only in the memories of those we have known or influenced is fairly common, Woolf goes beyond this. Life itself is equally ephemeral, and Jacob's shadowy presence in the novel suggests our own shadowy presence in this world. As Jean Guiguet says, "The vagueness, the lack of certainty, the disconcerting quality of this work, and the kind of uneasiness, insecurity and frustration it leaves with the reader, may perhaps be faults in relation to absolute standards in the art of fiction. But in relation to what the author had set out to express, it must be acknowledged that these characteristics are qualities."[6]

Woolf also made a remarkable advance in her use of point of view. Abandoning the traditional method of locating point of view in the narrator or in one or more key characters, Woolf instead employed a rapidly shifting, highly flexible point of view which allowed her to present a given situation obliquely, giving as much credibility to the perspectives of various minor characters as to those around whom the novel revolves. In the first four pages, we shift from the perspective of Betty Flanders to that of Charles Steele, who is painting her, and on to that of Jacob, who is lost.

This novel also differs from her first two in that women and issues related to women, such as marriage, no longer dominate the novel. Significantly, Woolf's decision to de-emphasize women's issues in this novel coincided with the discovery of technical innovations which would dominate her fiction for the remainder of her career. In choosing a male protagonist, Woolf was able to free herself from the "double-focus" which constrained her in the earlier novels. So long as she was primarily concerned with the attempts of Rachel Vinrace and Katharine Hilbery to define themselves as women within a man's world, she was confined by the contours of that world, including the form of the novel. Her intellectual energy was engaged in reacting rather than creating. Jacob frees her from that, allowing her energies to be directed to the creation of new forms of expression. In seeking for the meaning of Jacob's presence and then absence in his world, her perspective is distinctly female. Because she is unable or unwilling to enter Jacob's point of view, the egocentric character of the traditional novel evaporates. In the process, the novel itself becomes fluid, non-linear, and impressionistic, all qualities which Woolf herself viewed as characteristic of the female consciousness.

As Woolf learns to alter the form of the novel to embody her distinctive vision, we become much less aware of her struggle to avoid didacticism. She does not, however, completely abandon the treatment of women's issues on the thematic level. In the course of this novel, we encounter a number of fascinating female characters in subsidiary roles, and Woolf has a point to make about each of them.

Jacob's mother, Betty Flanders, is a charmingly conventional woman. A widow, she grieves daily over her husband Seabrook's death, but is mollified by the courtly attentions of the aging Capt. Barfoot, who is himself married to an invalid. In describing Betty Flanders, the narrator reveals a feminist bias, but the tone is good-natured and entirely unthreatening: ". . . and who shall deny that this blankness of mind, when combined with profusion, mother wit, old wives' tales, haphazard ways, moments of astonishing daring, humour, and sentimentality—who shall deny that in these respects every woman is nicer than any man?" (p. 11). Again, we are aware of Woolf's insistence on the value of characteristics that are traditionally female. Her feminism seems to exist not so much in asserting the rights of women to male prerogatives as in imbuing the non-aggressive sociability of women with new respect and value.

Jacob is Betty's problem child; he is stubborn, disobedient, intractable. Throughout his life, she frets about his behavior, and when he is a grown man, views with alarm rumors of his association with loose women. Betty's wrath, however, is directed not at Jacob but at the women who threaten to corrupt him, as we see in this imaginary confrontation envisioned by the narrator:

> Behind the door was the obscene thing, the alarming presence, and terror would come over her [Mrs. Flanders] as at death, or the birth of a child. Better, perhaps, burst in and face it than sit in the antechamber listening to the little creak, the sudden stir, for her heart was swollen, and pain threaded it. My son, my son— such would be her cry, uttered to hide her vision of him stretched with Florinda, inexcusable, irrational, in a woman with three children living at Scarborough. And the fault lay with Florinda. Indeed, when the door opened and the couple came out, Mrs. Flanders would have flounced upon her—only it was Jacob who came first, in his dressing gown, amiable, authoritative, beautifully healthy, like a baby after an airing, with an eye clear as running water. Florinda followed, lazily stretching; yawning a little; arranging her hair at the looking glass—while Jacob read his mother's letter (p. 92).

Virginia Woolf never comes closer to an explicit description of sex and its ambience than she does here. As she points out in her essay, "Women and Fiction," and in *The Pargiters*, there is hardly a more crucial concern for women than the issue of sex, and yet as a female writer she is blocked by convention from discussing it freely. Sex is perhaps the single most powerful determining force in the lives of her characters, and yet she must modestly skirt the subject whenever it arises. Even in the passage just quoted, Woolf distances herself from what she describes by allowing the act of sex, and Mrs. Flanders' reaction to it, to take place only on an imaginary plane, returning to what actually occurred only when Jacob and Florinda emerge from the bedroom to find a letter from Jacob's mother. Still, considering that Woolf struggled throughout her life with feelings of fear and even disgust about her own sexuality, her candor here is notable. And the fact that despite Mrs. Flanders' horror, Jacob and Florinda emerge from sex looking happy, healthy and satisfied indicates that Woolf was in favor of less restrictive and guilt-laden sexuality.

Florinda threatens Jacob's mother because she represents the nemesis of all the rules of behavior by which Mrs. Flanders governs her own life and the lives of her children. Eschewing modesty and feminine restraint, Florinda sells her body in exchange for the material comforts which only a man can provide. Interestingly, Florinda has no patronymic, which suggests that she has in some sense freed herself from patriarchy at the same time that she makes her living off it.

We first meet Florinda in Jacob's company in the crowd at the burning of Guy Fawkes (p. 74). The usual narrative exposition about who she is and what and where she came from is dispensed with, so that we encounter Florinda as we would in life, as a person who engages our attention and about whom we know nothing. Through the interactions of Jacob and Florinda, however, our understanding of Jacob's character is considerably enhanced. Florinda is a winsome hooker, and Jacob admires her. He even accepts her statement that she is chaste, though he knows on some level that it is not so. The only fault which seriously mars Jacob's appreciation and enjoyment of Florinda is her mindlessness, and he is saddened by the vacancy of Florinda's eyes: "The problem is insoluble. The body is harnessed to a brain. Beauty goes hand in hand with stupidity" (pp. 81–82). Jacob's misogyny, of which this is but one of many examples, must be at least partly blamed on the society which does not allow intelligent, respectable women openly to express their sexuality. As a man, Jacob is not required to be chaste. Most of the women with the background and education to challenge him intellectually, however, are bound by rigid rules in that regard.

Fanny Elmer, an artist's model, differs from Florinda in a number of ways. First, Fanny allows her emotions to take precedence over good business sense. When she falls in love with Jacob, she immediately contrives an excuse for abandoning Nick Bramham, the painter who has kept her, even though Jacob has shown no inclination to return her affection. It is clearly a case of love at first sight, and Fanny's world is transformed. Her impressions of Jacob are revealing: she finds him awkward, childlike and yet majestic, and admires his beautiful voice (p. 117). Gradually, her passion for Jacob is sublimated into a variety of heroic goals. She longs to be well-read and knowledgeable about politics, and determines to learn

Latin (p. 121). She even rushes off to buy a copy of *Tom Jones* because she has heard Jacob recommend it (p. 122). Fanny feels drawn to books on her own behalf, too, but hindered by her lack of training:

> . . . for there is something, Fanny thought, about books which if I had been educated I could have liked—much better than earrings and flowers, she sighed, thinking of the corridors at the Slade and the fancy-dress dance next week. She had nothing to wear (p. 122).

Fanny also differs from Florinda in that she views the educated and well-heeled world of men with a kind of poignant longing which never becomes outright envy because she accepts the impossibility of ever gaining it for herself. Because she knows this, she can view the world of men with bemused appreciation:

> Anyhow, they love silence, and speak beautifully, each word falling like a disc new cut, not a hubble-bubble of small smooth coins such as girls use . . . . And isn't it pleasant, Fanny went on thinking, how young men bring out lots of silver coins from their trouser pockets, and look at them, instead of having just so many in a purse? (p. 117).

In this passage and in others, Woolf manages to convey the dismal lack of educational and economic opportunities available to women without sounding shrill. The poignancy of Fanny's acceptance of "the way things are" and her willingness to accommodate herself to living in a "man's world" reinforce our sense of the unfairness of the female condition far more effectively than if Fanny were to be bitter about her lack of advantages.

Unfortunately, Jacob is scarcely aware of Fanny's existence and soon sets off for a tour of France and Greece. Fanny's love, which is never requited, becomes a source of constant suffering which is made permanently futile by Jacob's death.

In terms of social conventions and expectations, both Fanny and Florinda represent illicit liaisons in Jacob's life. We find a socially acceptable alternative to these women, however, in the person of Clara Durrant, the sister of Jacob's school chum, Tim Durrant. Clara's good-natured ingenuousness charms Jacob, but he has little basis for communication with her. Like all well brought up girls of her time, Clara is inexperienced, poorly educated, and painfully naive. Her life is severely constricted, especially when compared to Jacob's life, and the routine of social obligation which fills her days precludes the development of expertise in any area. She is perpetually pouring out tea for old men and "dowagers in velvet" (p. 123). Although she struggles with learning Italian and improving her skill on the piano, she is unable to gain any real proficiency in either area. Her letters to Jacob are those of a child, so that it is no wonder that he is unable to develop an abiding passion for her. The overly restricted lives of socially acceptable young women, Woolf suggests, drive their male counterparts into the arms of the far more interesting women who live free of such restrictions, though those women must pay for their freedom by permanently eschewing respectability.

When Jacob finds himself in love, the object of his passion is an older woman, a married woman, Sandra Wentworth Williams. Unlike the other women in his life, Sandra fascinates Jacob with her combination of experience and legitimacy. Although relatively uneducated herself, Sandra's sophistication is such that she appears knowledgeable, and Jacob finds in her a complicated sensuality which both excites and challenges him. Like Jacob, Sandra is a romantic, conscious of her own beauty and the "tragic essence" of Greece (p. 142). Sandra is drawn to Jacob and revels in her seductive power. Jacob is dazzled by Sandra's candor, and enjoys returning it. Their encounter is a glorious one, including walks in the Acropolis at night and heightened, impassioned conversations. For the first time, it would seem, Jacob has found a woman who engages him intellectually as well as physically. For Sandra, however, Jacob is ultimately just one more of the numerous suitors who court her with limited success, and his love offering of a volume of Donne's poems is simply placed on the shelf with the other unread volumes of previous would-be lovers.

Not all of the women that Woolf examines in this novel are so directly connected with Jacob. Some of them seem to have been created for the sole purpose of providing an adequately well-rounded vision of the society in which Jacob lives and grows. At times, Woolf offers us a vivid sketch of a character, and then never returns to the same character again. For two pages, we enter the point of view of Mrs. Norman, whose only importance in the novel is that she briefly occupies the same railway carriage as

Jacob. In Mrs. Norman's speculations on how she will defend herself when and if Jacob attacks her, however, she assumes a memorable presence in the novel's fabric (pp. 30–31).

Mrs. Plumer, a don's wife at Cambridge, provides another interesting example. Although she appears only briefly, at a dinner she is giving for a group of undergraduates, she seems to typify the domestic realities of life at Cambridge. Reflecting on her less than welcome obligations as a hostess, Mrs. Plumer examines her role: "It was none of her fault—since how could she control her father begetting her forty years ago in the suburbs of Manchester? and once begotten, how could she do other than grow up cheese-paring, ambitious, with an instinctively accurate notion of the rungs of the ladder and an ant-like assiduity in pushing George Plumer ahead of her to the top of the ladder?" (p. 34).

Mrs. Plumer, then, represents the female underpinning of the great male tradition of learning which is Cambridge. It is she, and many others like her, who support the entire structure through a self-effacement which becomes invidious in the identification of these women with their husbands' ambitions. On the other hand, there are women like Miss Julia Hedge, the feminist, who is just as trapped by her reaction to male prerogatives at Cambridge as Mrs. Plumer is by her sacrifice to them:

Miss Julia Hedge, the feminist, waited for her books. They did not come. She wetted her pen. She looked about her. Her eye was caught by the final letters in Lord Macaulay's name. And she read them all around the dome—the names of great men which remind us—"Oh, damn," said Julia Hedge, "why didn't they leave room for an Eliot or a Bronte?"

Unfortunate Julia! wetting her pen in bitterness, and leaving her shoe laces untied. When her books came, she applied herself to her gigantic labours, but perceived through one of the nerves of her exasperated sensibility how composedly, unconcernedly, and with every consideration the male readers applied themselves to theirs. That young man for example. What had he got to do except copy out poetry? And she must study statistics. There are more women than men. Yes; but if you let women work as men work, they'll die off much quicker. They'll become extinct. That was her argument. Death and gall and bitter dust were on her pen-tip; and as the afternoon wore on, red had worked into her cheek-bones and a light was in her eyes (p. 106).

Like Miss Kilman, the defeated and embittered feminist in *Mrs. Dalloway*, Julia's life is governed entirely by rage and frustration at the inequalities lavished upon her as a woman. This rage locks her into a life of irreprievable misery and warps the free play of ideas, so that her theory about working women is nothing short of batty. Woolf's conviction that the "unfettered mind," free of grievance, forms the necessary basis for a valid act of creation is given force in this portrayal. The only meaningful feminism, in Woolf's view, is that which moves beyond bitterness into a creative vision of a new and more equal partnership between the sexes which will benefit both.

Although Woolf is occasionally didactic in these sketches of women, the novel is not seriously weakened as a result. The inability of these women to become whole psychologically, intellectually, or financially within the context of patriarchy is not, after all, Woolf's theme. Ultimately, all these portraits and interactions are part of a delicately patterned structure which serves to bring into focus the hole in the air that is left when Jacob dies.

Jacob emerges as a character obliquely through the fleeting perceptions of the other characters in the various environments in which he appears. When he is alone, we see him as a stranger might, from a distance. At one point, the narrator offers us short descriptions of the people who are at work in the British Museum. Jacob, who is reading Marlowe, is merely one among others (pp. 105–106). At another point, we find Jacob absorbed in reading the *Phaedrus* in his room (pp. 109–110) or playing chess by himself as Fanny Elmer passes beneath his window (p. 114).

To some extent, Jacob's character is also established through the use of allusion and association. As Beverley Ann Schlack points out, throughout the novel Jacob is linked with Byron, Shelley, Marlowe, and Spenser, all of whom died without realizing their full promise. That his favorite author should be Fielding and that his love-offering to Sandra Wentworth Williams should be a volume of Donne's poems also provide clues to his character,[7] though he never becomes for us fully realized.

The elusiveness and insubstantiality of Jacob's character throughout this novel find a grotesque reinforcement in the final scene. As Jacob's room is described, we suddenly realize that he is dead. It is an alienating experience, and because we know nothing of how he died, or even how he felt about his role as a soldier, his death seems absurd, a pointless sacrifice to the preservation of patriarchy. Our presence in this world, Woolf seems to be saying, is tenuous, a divine trick, and we are fools to think otherwise. When viewed against the solidity of the eighteenth century room in which he has lived, Jacob's life seems ephemeral indeed, just one in a string of lives which have passed within those same four walls.

Woolf's insistence on presenting Jacob only through the eyes of others and her persistent refusal to enter sympathetically into his point of view is responsible for creating this sense of the fragility and unreality of life. Jacob has existed only in the momentary impressions he has made upon others, and because we are not allowed to identify with him, his death offers no catharsis and we are doubly cheated.

Although it is a risky and questionable tactic to seek explanations for fictional practices in an author's biography, it is impossible not to see *Jacob's Room* as in some sense a working out, for Woolf, of her response to her brother Thoby's death. As Quentin Bell points out in his excellent biography of Virginia Woolf, she never fully recovered from the shock of Thoby's death. But more importantly, Woolf was fascinated by those aspects of Thoby's life which remained mysterious to her, namely his experiences at Cambridge and his personal life. Because Virginia loved Thoby so deeply, she felt a kind of awe and admiration for the learning and sophistication he acquired at Cambridge. Yet this same learning created a distance between them. Virginia might be remarkably educated for a young woman of her time, but she would never be a Cambridge Apostle. She was also curious, of course, about sexuality and remarkably naive herself. In this pre-Bloomsbury period, however, a frank discussion of sexuality would have been unthinkable in the Stephen family, particularly between brother and sister. When Thoby quite suddenly died of typhoid fever, Woolf's sense of loss was overwhelming and she was left with an immensity of unanswered questions about who and what he was.[8] *Jacob's Room* is surely, in some sense, an attempt to answer those questions. Woolf needed to analyze, to her own satisfaction, the mixture of fascination, admiration, envy, and perplexity she felt toward her brother, and in so doing she has provided us with a fascinating portrait of the "male mystique" from a female point of view.

If we view *Jacob's Room* as an attempt to come to terms with Thoby's death, then the doubting, detached, speculative stance of the narrator assumes new meaning. This narrator views her protagonist, Jacob, from a distance, and is intrigued and curious, but also mystified, by her subject. Perhaps because this narrator has no answers, she is willing to relinquish her hold on point of view and share it, however briefly, with an enormous variety of characters. There is, as well, no temptation to be didactic since nothing is certain in this world.

Such a narrator does not perceive an ordered, symmetrical reality in which events build toward a final climax and resolution. Only individual moments of perception, detached from the stream of cause and effect, are possible. Hence the breakthrough in style which *Jacob's Room* represents for Virginia Woolf. Because this narrator can no longer believe in the rational ordering of events which the idea of a "story" demands, she offers us instead a series of impressions. Because these impressions are associational rather that logical, the novel achieves its form through a process of "displacement." Just as dreams veil our anxieties and passions by displacing them onto images which are seemingly neutral, the terrible sense of loss which Jacob's death engenders finds expression not through a description of Jacob but through an evocation of the scenes and people associated with him. Although the images which tumble forth, one upon the other, may seem disconnected, they are only superficially so, since the unconscious has an ordering pattern of its own just as valid as that of the conscious, rational mind. Although the narrator often seems to forget Jacob altogether in these rhetorical gambols, everything she says in fact contributes to our sense of the world by which and against which Jacob defines himself.

Not every reader, of course, will find this novel satisfying. Jacob is dead, but did he ever really live? The scattered and only nebulously connected impressions which comprise this novel and the overall elusiveness of Jacob's character create a sense of uneasiness, and it is difficult to judge whether this feeling of something unfulfilled should be viewed as an achievement or a flaw. Phyllis Rose laments that on those rare moments when we are allowed to share Jacob's point of view, it "is scarcely more energetic than that of the snail in 'Kew Gardens.'"[9] And Jean Guiguet maintains that "neither the concentration of chosen moments, nor their interrelatedness by means of structure and tone, nor the network of leitmotivs quite succeed in expressing that indescribable centre which the author has deliberately forbidden herself to formulate."[10]

Still, Woolf's choice of subject served her very well at this point in her career. She could not be didactic about death, and thus was largely free from the strain of trying to avoid sounding preachy. Although there are moments of incisive social commentary in the novel, we never feel that the author has a political design on us.

The importance of this novel in the feminist tradition is that Woolf was able to break free of traditional novelistic constraints and offer a distinctly "female" view of reality which is contemplative, non-linear, non-authoritarian, and non-prescriptive. In choosing to view Jacob from a distance, in an attitude of curiosity and tenderness, as a sister might view a loved and loving brother, Woolf was led to develop a diversity of techniques which were ultimately to become her trademark. Although some of the techniques she employed were used by other writers before her, and many have been used since, Woolf managed to blend them into a style uniquely her own. By filtering her ideas through a variety of points of view and abandoning the omniscient narrator as well as the forward-directed traditional plot which demands a resolution, Woolf was able to offer for the first time a convincingly female vision of the world. This break with the masculine tradition in style marks a turning point in the history of fiction. As Phyllis Rose notes, "She found her own voice, as she says, her style, in *Jacob's Room;* the next stage was to locate her sympathies."[11] In her next attempt, *Mrs. Dalloway*, where we find even more richness in the twelve hours which the novel covers than in the more than twenty years spanned by *Jacob's Room*, these techniques were to serve her well.

IV   Mrs. Dalloway and To the Lighthouse

> There's nothing left of what she was;
> Back to the babe the woman dies,
> And all the wisdom that she has
> Is to love him for being wise,
> She's confident because she fears,
> And though discreet when he's away,
> If none but her dear despot hears
> She prattles like a child at play.
>
> Coventry Patmore,
> from *The Angel in the House*

Virginia Woolf's two most famous and oft-read novels, *Mrs. Dalloway* and *To the Lighthouse*, have a number of points in common. Both novels focus on remarkable, albeit altogether traditional women, Clarissa Dalloway and Mrs. Ramsay, who are experts at elevating domestic skills to the realm of art. Similarities in style also unite these two novels, and for the first time we feel that Woolf has discovered the form and techniques that best suit her aesthetic goals and that she is fully in control of them. In treating Woolf's transformation of polemical material into art, then, there are ample reasons for discussing both novels together.

Virginia Woolf's genteel background certainly gave her some advantages over other women wishing to pursue the profession of writing. She was well-educated and well-read for a woman of her time, socially sophisticated, and had an abundance of leisure time, money, and contacts with influential people. There were, however, certain disabilities in being a well brought up young lady of standing, and Woolf evokes two of them for us in her essay, "Professions for Women," which was written from a talk she delivered to the London/National Society for Women's Service in 1931. In the first place, Woolf had it deeply ingrained in her that her attitude toward men should be consistently sympathetic, supportive, and unassertive. In the second place, the constraints of Victorian modesty with which she was reared dictated that she exclude any reference to physical passion in her writing, and this hypocrisy with regard to a central feature of human experience troubled her throughout her career.

Virginia Woolf's term for the sympathetic, uncritical being she was pressured to become is taken from a highly popular long Victorian poem entitled "The Angel in the House," a few lines of which are quoted at the beginning of this chapter. As Woolf tells us in "Professions for Women," "It was she who used to come between me and my paper when I was writing reviews. It was she who bothered me and wasted my time and so tormented me that at last I killed her."[1] This intelligent but sympathetic, clever but self-effacing model of womanhood was her father's ideal, so we can be sure this exorcism was for Woolf a painful process. Everything in her training urged her to cultivate this paragon:

> She was intensely sympathetic. She was immensely charming. She was utterly unselfish. She excelled in the difficult arts of family life. She sacrificed herself daily. If there was chicken she took the leg; if there was a draught she sat in it—in short she was so constituted that she never had a mind or a wish of her own, but preferred to sympathize always with the minds and wishes of others. Above all—I need not say it—she was pure.[2]

With this shining ideal constantly before her, Woolf found herself stymied when she set about to pursue her profession:

> Directly, that is to say, I took my pen in hand to review that novel by a famous man, she slipped behind me and whispered: "My dear, you are a young woman. You are writing about a book that has been written by a man. Be sympathetic; be tender; flatter; deceive; use all the arts and wiles of our sex. Never let anybody guess that you have a mind of your own. Above all, be pure."[3]

Woolf's response to this personal demon/angel who frustrated and inhibited her as a writer was revolt. Summoning all her courage, Woolf turned on the "Angel" and set about to destroy her: "Had I not killed her she would have killed me. She would have plucked the heart out of my writing."[4]

In a sense, Woolf murders the "Angel" by committing her to paper. The act of creation is an act of control. In creating Clarissa Dalloway and Mrs. Ramsay, Woolf assumes control over the demon which haunts her. If there can be such a thing as a gentle murder, that is what we have here. Both Clarissa Dalloway and Mrs. Ramsay are remarkable women, and far from berating them, Woolf elevates their domestic finesse to the level of art. The ability to create little "moments of perfection" in the routine of daily life and to smooth over the differences which alienate people from one another are obviously valued by Woolf as essential to civilized life. Consequently, Woolf's attitude toward these two fictional creations, insofar as we can ascertain it from the perspectives of the other characters and the narrator, is one of reverence mixed with respect, a certain degree of awe, and occasional good-natured bewilderment.

Neither character, of course, is an altogether perfect example of the traditional womanly ideal. If either were, we would simply have a prose version of Patmore's poem, and Woolf's portrayal could hardly be more different. Patmore's "Angel" is pure sweetness: naive, childlike, and devoted. She has never had an opinion of her own, knows nothing of the sordid world, and is devoted to her husband's happiness. She is like a paper doll—shallow, one-dimensional, and characterless. Woolf's "Angels," on the other hand, are grown-ups. Both Clarissa and Mrs. Ramsay have sophisticated notions of the skill involved in bringing people together amicably and creating a milieu which gives form and harmony to the chaotic events of daily living. In fostering this milieu, they must be capable, and they are, of accurately analyzing the characters and personalities of those around them and being sensitive to individual needs and moods. Like conductors of a symphony, they must be simultaneously aware at all times of both the parts and the whole, of the myriad details that contribute to a moment of perfection and the orchestration of the experience in its entirety.

Although both Clarissa and Mrs. Ramsay are supreme hostesses, they differ from one another in a number of ways. Clarissa, for example, is less than triumphant as a mother. She deeply resents her daughter's attraction to the embittered Miss Kilman, and yet it is clear that there is too much distance and formality in her relationship with Elizabeth to allow them to discuss the problem openly. Clarissa's great failure, in a sense, is her inability to love. With the exception of her relationship with Sally Seton and to some extent with Peter Walsh, Clarissa has never opened herself to the passion and vulnerability of love: thus her virginal quality. She does not particularly love Richard, nor does she appear to love her daughter very deeply. It is perhaps for this reason that the purity of her hatred for Miss Kilman is so satisfying. The emotion is simple, genuine, intense, and because it is hate, it suggests the possibility of love: "She hated her: she loved her. It was enemies one wanted, not friends."[5]

Mrs. Ramsay, on the other hand, is the archetypal mother, so loving and understanding that her children become fiercely protective of her and resentful of their father's tyranny and insensitivity. As Patricia Spacks rightly notes, Mrs. Ramsay's vocation is "taking care of others," but this is "investigated from an aesthetic rather than a moral point of view . . . Mrs. Woolf creates a metaphysics of female altruism; in the process she declares the irrelevance of moralizing about what women should and should not do."[6]

Although Spacks overstates her case in denying a moral perspective, the extent to which Clarissa and Mrs. Ramsay go unjudged is intriguing. One would expect that Woolf, in attempting to rid herself of the "Angel in the House" which threatened her as a writer, would scrutinize such a creature very critically in her fiction. Surprisingly, she takes great care in elucidating everything that makes such women admirable.

The central standard by which both women live is self-sacrifice, and yet, as Spacks suggests, this same sacrifice is shown to provide "rich sources of energy and fulfillment."[7] Both Clarissa and Mrs. Ramsay are artists, masters at supplying form and harmony to experience and making of the moment something perfect and lasting. It is as if Virginia Woolf could exorcize this vision of feminine perfection only by committing it to paper in all its unqualified glory. In creating these "Angels," she assumes control over their magic and in the process asserts her own superiority. A lesser writer, perhaps, would merely attack this vision of traditional feminine perfection, but Woolf seems to have realized that to do so would have the effect not of freeing her from the "Angel" but of trapping her in a mesh of reaction. In creating two "Angels" who are obviously better and more interesting than the people they care for, Woolf is able to free herself of their hold.

Although Woolf succeeded in conquering the "Angel" which hindered her, she was notably unsuccessful in combating the second major obstacle to an authentic rendering of experience—female sexuality. In "Professions for Women," she presents the problem:

I want you to figure to yourselves a girl sitting with a pen in her hand, which for minutes, and indeed for hours, she never dips into the inkpot. . . . And then there was a smash. There was an explosion. There was foam and confusion. The imagination had dashed itself against something hard. The girl was roused from her dream. She was indeed in a state of the most acute and difficult distress. To speak without figure she had thought of something, something about the body, about the passions which it was unfitting for her as a woman to say. Men, her reason told her, would be shocked. The consciousness of what men will say of a woman who speaks the truth about her passions had roused her from her artist's state of unconsciousness. She could write no more. The trance was over. Her imagination could work no longer. [8]

Throughout her professional life, Virginia Woolf grappled with this problem, but was never able fully to resolve it. In *The Voyage Out* and *Night and Day*, we are aware of sexuality only in terms of the exclusivity which couples impose and which is to varying extents resented by the other characters. Sexuality itself is sublimated, most notably in Rachel's fatal fever. In *Jacob's Room*, Woolf comes as close as she ever does to a direct portrayal of the sexual act, but distances herself by shifting the point of view to Jacob's mother and concentrating on the period *after* the characters emerge from the bedroom.

Sex is certainly an important motivating force in *Mrs. Dalloway*, but again it is rendered through the veil of memory and transformed into a kind of romantic idealism. Clarissa's greatest passion seems to have centered on Sally Seton, the wildly charming and reckless friend of her youth:

The strange thing, on looking back, was the purity, the integrity, of her feeling for Sally. It was not like one's feeling for a man. It was completely disinterested, and besides, it had a quality which could only exist between women, between women just grown up. It was protective, on her side; sprang from a sense of being in league together, a presentiment of something that was bound to part them (they spoke of marriage always as a catastrophe), which led to this chivalry, this protective feeling which was much more on her side than Sally's (p. 50).

Clarissa's passion for Sally involved her in an intoxicating process of dreaming, scheming, sharing, and loving which found culmination in a kiss: "Sally stopped; picked a flower; kissed her on the lips. The whole world might have turned upside down" (p. 52). Clarissa never felt this sort of passion for a man. And yet what future was there in her relationship with Sally? Both of them acknowledged "a presentiment of something that was bound to part them." Ultimately, both conceded to the inevitable. Sally married a rich factory owner and settled into the role of a conventional wife and devoted mother to a brood of children. In the process, much of Sally's vitality, independence, courage, and resolution were lost, but there were no obvious alternatives to her choice. Clarissa, too, matter-of-factly put romance behind her and set about choosing the appropriate husband. Yet throughout her life, especially when women confessed some scrape to her, Clarissa did sometimes "undoubtedly then feel what men felt" (p. 47). Only on rare occasions, it would seem, was Clarissa's sexuality called forth.

Sexuality in *To the Lighthouse* is even more attenuated since Mrs. Ramsay sublimates her urges into the art of matchmaking and Lily Briscoe rejects sexuality as a threat to her independence. In *Orlando*, sex is again dealt with more directly but is distanced by the mythical quality of the narrative and by the presence of a character whose life spans four hundred years and who magically changes gender in *medias res*. The later novels, too, acknowledge the existence of sexuality, but tend to consider it from a sociological perspective, concentrating on how sexual needs and repressions affect the social genesis of various characters. Never in Woolf's writing do we have an honest and detailed account of sexual arousal and passion. Woolf obviously perceived this as a disability and yet was unable to conquer the fear of exposure which breaking the conventions would entail.

Woolf's diffidence about sexuality undoubtedly emerges in part from her childhood and adolescent experiences with her two half brothers, George and Gerald Duckworth. Once, when Woolf was a small child, Gerald Duckworth lifted her onto a slab outside the dining room and explored her body. She remembers "resenting, disliking it," and attributes her lifelong shame and fear about her body as deriving, at least in part, from this experience. In the same memoir, Woolf recounts a dream which epitomizes her feelings: "I dreamt that I was looking in a glass when a horrible face—the face of an animal—suddenly showed over my shoulder." From a very early age, then, Woolf connected eroticism with images of horror and disgust.[9]

This connection was reaffirmed when Virginia was about twenty and George Duckworth was in his mid-thirties: "There would be a tap at the door; the light would be turned out and George would fling himself on my bed, cuddling and kissing and otherwise embracing me in order, as he told Dr. Savage later, to comfort me for the fatal illness of my father—who was dying three or four storeys lower down of cancer."[10] Thus, as Woolf adds elsewhere, "the old ladies of Kensington and Belgravia never knew that George Duckworth was not only father and mother, brother and sister to those poor Stephen girls; he was their lover also."[11]

Because of these experiences, sexuality for Woolf was inextricably connected with self-loathing and disgust. Yet, as Phyllis Rose perceives, Woolf's intense shame about her body suggests an intense awareness of it.[12] Ironically, Woolf's need to sublimate her eroticism may have contributed to her extraordinary skill as a writer. In speaking of her shame about her body, Woolf notes that it "did not prevent me from feeling ecstasies and raptures spontaneously and intensely and without any shame or the least sense of guilt so long as they were disconnected with my own body." The rapturous, ecstatic, and often intensely erotic component of Woolf's style, then, may result from the repression of these impulses in her personal life. In Rose's words, "Sensitive to pleasure she prohibited it to herself, or sanitized its source by acknowledging only her responses to nature and impersonal things."[13]

The value Woolf attached to moments of consummate aesthetic pleasure is one of the most pervasive manifestations of this process of sublimation. And as James Naremore points out, "Throughout Mrs. Woolf's work, the chief problem for her and for her characters is to overcome the space between things, to attain an absolute unity with the world, as if everything in the environment were turned to water. This desire for absolute unity can be expressed in both physical and spiritual terms, and in Mrs. Woolf it nearly always has sexual connotations . . . her prose is full of erotic impulses, and sexual themes are major elements in all her books . . . On the other hand, when she does portray sexual emotions, she often injects an element of fear. Her nervous, barely concealed eroticism is, I have tried to indicate, related to the wish to find some permanent, all-embracing union: in effect, to the deathwish."[14]

Phyllis Rose interprets this same tendency more positively when she suggests that "Virginia connects her deepest impulse as a writer with this attempt to see the intruding, destructive, assertive elements of life as a part of a whole. Constructing such 'wholes' would be her equivalent of sexual activity."[15] When Woolf achieves these "wholes," particularly in her transcendent "moments of being," the sensations she evokes have much in common with those normally attributed to sexual consummation. Thus, even though Mark Spilka is correct in saying that one never finds in Woolf's mature fiction "that union of the passions and affections by which adult romantic love usually proceeds," that "there are only predatory passions and respectful affections," it is not quite the "Victorian standoff" that he claims it to be.[16] Harold Fromm hits closer to the mark when he says that Woolf is a decidedly erotic writer who uses a "lyric language of equivalence." In Fromm's opinion, she evokes "manliness" and "womanliness" with a kind of erotic relish, often employing words like "swollen" and "gushed" in her descriptive passages, and in general presenting us with an unspecified eroticism involving all the senses, and like Freud's notion of "polymorphous perversity," not tied to specific sexual acts or erogenous zones. The effect is a presentation of sexuality which is "closer to noumenal than phenomenal. It is a presentation that reveals through lyric imagery that 'jar on the nerves' before it becomes phenomenal, before it is seen as 'masculine' or 'feminine.'" One may be inclined to agree with Fromm, then, that "a reader for whom this is not a sexual voice requires photographs of barnyard copulations, not literature."[17]

One of the complicating factors about sexuality, of course, is that throughout most of history, for women it inevitably has had to lead to marriage, and marriage has in turn entailed a weight of domestic responsibilities which severely curtailed the experiences of women. Woolf resented the limitations which domestic responsibilities imposed on a woman's sphere of activity, and she ponders this issue in *A Room of One's Own*. She wonders why the hypothetical Mary Seton's mother could not have left Mary sufficient money to found a school for women. She soon realizes, however, that a woman who bore thirteen children to a minister of the church, who would not have been allowed to work if she had tried, and who could not have kept her salary if she had (since it belonged legally to her husband), could not possibly have left Mary or any other woman any money.[18]

The predicament of Mary and her mother is mirrored in *Mrs. Dalloway* and *To the Lighthouse*. Clarissa's days are filled with innumerable details of planning and preparation in her eager desire to please others. Mrs. Ramsay must balance the myriad responsibilities of running a household smoothly with the incessant demands for loving attention from her family: "They came to her naturally, since she was a woman, all day long with this and that; one wanting this, another that; the children were growing up; she often felt she was nothing but a sponge sopped full of human emotions."[19] Mrs. Ramsay's dreams, by contrast, extend beyond her life, and she envisions founding a hospital and designing a model dairy. But there is never time. The family must come first.

Significantly, Woolf does not make an issue of these limitations. Both Clarissa and Mrs. Ramsay seem relatively content with the lives they have chosen, and the other characters take it for granted that they are. Peter Walsh bemoans the waste of Clarissa's life, but his dissatisfaction springs from his disappointment at not having been able to claim her for himself. Clarissa, for her part, sometimes yearns for the gaiety which a life with Peter promised, but at the same time continues to be threatened by the loss of autonomy which Peter's need to share everything would involve. In many ways, she would be less independent with Peter than with Richard.

Since Peter Walsh is one of the more attractive characters in the novel, Clarissa's decision to reject him and marry Richard is significant. To be sure, Richard offers Clarissa comfort, security, and respectability, but one can hardly imagine Clarissa being so tiresomely practical as to base her decision on these factors alone.

Peter Walsh is a romantic who is known for repeatedly involving himself in "scrapes" with women. He demands total devotion, wants to share everything with the woman he adores, but soon tires of exclusivity and wants variety. Perhaps because his own emotions are so variable, Peter is jealous as well as noncommittal. Daisy, the object of his passion during the course of this novel, is youthful and therefore easily conforms to his romantic ideal. But his passion for her seems shallow, and even Peter has sufficient self-knowledge, or at least experience, to realize that their relationship might be better left as it is, that if they do marry the glory will fade and they will be forced to cope with disappointments (pp. 238–240).

Peter's spontaneity, combined with his intense affection for women and his unwillingness to be bored in his work or in his life, causes other men to view him with a kind of suspicion. Peter prefers the company of women to that of men, a predilection which is clearly suspect. Even his deity, such as it is, is female. When Peter falls asleep in Regent's Park, the nurse sitting next to him on the bench becomes in his dream the "grey nurse," a mother-figure associated with nature, death, relief, and peace. Instead of a punitive father-god, Peter seeks a mother, one who understands, forgives, and takes one back into herself, into the dark womb. As the Wordsworthian figure of the "solitary traveler," Peter seeks solace in this "nurse," this feminized nature (pp. 85–88).

Peter appeals to the romantic and passionate side of Clarissa's nature and she has moments of profound regret: ". . . all in a clap it came over her. If I had married Peter, this gaiety would have been mine all day! It was all over for her. The sheet was stretched and the bed narrow" (p. 70). Nevertheless, in her cooler moments Clarissa perceives the flaws in this vision. Romantic love, by its very nature, must be either adulterous or impossible. Passionate intensity necessarily fades. Married love, if it is to work, must be a different matter:

> And there is a dignity in people; a solitude; even between husband and wife a gulf; and that one must respect, thought Clarissa, watching him open the door; for one would not part with it oneself, or take it, against his will, from one's husband, without losing one's independence, one's self-respect—something, after all, priceless (p. 181).

Peter cannot accept this need for distance, for the integrity of the self. Unlike Richard, who can allow Clarissa simply to "be," Peter is perpetually critical of her distance, her reserve, her conventionality. Peter's tacit criticism, of which Clarissa is intensely aware, is a perpetual source of pain to her, although she also finds it annoying: "Why always take and never give?" (p. 255). And of course that is precisely the problem with the romantic character which Peter embodies. It is, in essence, narcissistic, and can survive only through sapping the energy of those who encounter it.

In fact, though Clarissa is captivated by Peter's vitality and charm, she fears his tendency to intrude on her privacy. Valuing her independence, Clarissa finds that the sharp distinctions which patriarchy draws between men and women give her breathing space. Peter, who has never been particularly allied with patriarchy, demands her full attention, and Clarissa recoils from this burden of intimacy: "For in marriage a little license, a little independence there must be between people living together day in day out in the same house; which Richard gave her, and she him . . . But with Peter everything had to be shared; everything gone into" (p. 10). Through Clarissa, Woolf explodes a common stereotype in which women are portrayed as being hungry for attention from their husbands and suitors, desiring romance and intimacy above all else. Women like Clarissa, Woolf suggests, value the integrity of the self, and for that a modicum of privacy is essential. Thus, although Clarissa's marriage to Richard is far from ideal, it is clearly preferable to the cloying intimacy of a union with Peter.

The Ramsay marriage, like that of the Dalloways, is only partially satisfying. Although Mrs. Ramsay respects her husband and dedicates her life to serving his needs, his incessant demands on her sympathy wear her down. And few of her own needs are being met in the marriage. Mrs. Ramsay has a kind of crisis when she cannot tell her husband that she loves him, even though he silently demands that she do so: "Was there no crumb on his coat? Nothing she could do for him?" Unable to say the words, Mrs. Ramsay gets out of her predicament by insisting he was right about the weather. Instead of saying she loves him, she defers to his judgment; for him that amounts to the same thing, and he is satisfied (pp. 184–186). Despite these persistent tensions and dissatisfactions, however, the Ramsay marriage is in many ways an inspiration to the other characters in the novel. Perhaps, as Herbert Marder suggests, the Ramsay marriage simply reflects Woolf's own ambivalence. Marriage is a patriarchal institution, with all the corresponding inequity and hollowness, but it is also the ultimate relation.[20]

Woolf's portrait of the Ramsay marriage is heavily influenced, of course, by autobiographical elements. In *A Writer's Diary*, she notes the following plan:

> This is going to be fairly short; to have father's character done complete in it; and mother's; and St. Ives; and childhood; and all the usual things I try to put in—life, death, etc. But the centre is father's character, sitting in a boat, reciting We perished, each alone, while he crushes a dying mackerel.[21]

In a sense, as Ruth Z. Temple maintains, Woolf's employment of Proust's techniques in order to come to terms with her own parents both strengthens and weakens the novel, since her fascination with the processes of memory as they are altered by artistic creativity causes an imbalance. As the novel nears its end, the emphasis shifts from a portrait of the Ramsays to an exploration of the artist's role, symbolized in Lily Briscoe and her painting.[22] Ian Gregor also finds this to be a flaw. In his opinion, in "The Window," the first section of the novel, Woolf has sufficient distance from her childhood experience with her family to give her writing resonance. Then, in "Time Passes," she strips that world of its detail, substituting emptiness and decay for life and vitality. Finally, in "The Lighthouse," the author's questions become so indistinguishable from Lily's that Woolf appears to be casting about for a solution. The solution which is offered, Lily's brush-stroke, is in Gregor's opinion too "technical" to be satisfying.[23] On the other hand, in Woolf's opinion, the writer and the thing written are always connected: "Are not all novels about the writer's self, we might ask? It is only as he sees people that we can see them; his fortunes colour and his oddities shape his vision until what we see is not the thing itself, but the thing seen and the seer inextricably mixed."[24]

It is difficult, certainly, if not impossible, to distinguish autobiographical fact from creative fiction in this novel. Interestingly, by the time she has finished the novel, Woolf's comments in *A Writer's Diary* refer to "Mr. and Mrs. Ramsay" and "Lily Briscoe," while indications that they are portraits of her parents and herself are significantly lacking. Nonetheless, the fictional Mr. Ramsay and Woolf's father, Leslie Stephen, do have a number of characteristics in common. Marder mentions Stephen's "terse judgments" and his habit of chanting poetry to himself. Although Stephen advocated equal opportunities for women, he felt their rightful place was in the home. Above all, he stressed "the importance of domestic life and the integrity of the family." He revered Virginia's mother as a saint which had the dual effect of elevating her and restricting her. Stephen also insisted on the importance of chastity and purity in women. He despised "effeminacy" in literature, however, and therefore viewed with scorn the works of George Eliot and the Bronte sisters.[25]

Her father's values were deeply ingrained in Virginia Woolf, and though she rejected some of them, she was never able to free herself completely from their influence. Throughout her life, she wanted to write honestly about sexuality but could never overcome the psychological barrier against doing so. She did, however, achieve a successful break from her father's code in two important ways. As Marder notes, she opposed his insistence on the morality of literature with a more or less pure aestheticism and substituted her concept of the "androgynous mind" for her father's insistence that the artist's mind is "solidly masculine or feminine."[26] Perhaps because this idea was such an important victory for Woolf over the proscriptive notions of her father, she explored it in great detail, both in her fiction and in her essays:

> Perhaps to think, as I had been thinking these two days, of one sex as distinct from the other is an effort. It interferes with the unity of the mind . . . But the sight of the two people getting into a taxi and the satisfaction it gave me made me also ask whether there are two sexes in the mind corresponding to the two sexes in the body, and whether they also require to be united in order to get complete satisfaction and happiness. And I went on amateurishly to sketch a plan of the soul so that in each of us two powers preside, one male, one female; and in the man's brain, the man predominates over the woman, and in the woman's brain, the woman predominates over the man. The normal and comfortable state of being is that when the two live in harmony together, spiritually cooperating. If one is a man, still the woman part of the brain must have effect; and a woman must also have intercourse with the man in her. Coleridge perhaps meant this when he said that a great mind is androgynous. It is when this fusion takes place that the mind is fully fertilised and uses all its faculties. Perhaps a mind that is purely masculine cannot create, any more than a mind that is purely feminine, I thought.[27]

To the Lighthouse abounds with images and situations which suggest potential androgynous resolutions to the sexual dialectic of the novel. In order to make these resolutions meaningful, however, the sexual dialectic must first be clearly established. During the first part of the novel, the rigidly defined sex roles which Mrs. Ramsay perpetuates are a source of persistent tension, in particular for her children and Lily Briscoe. Woolf seems to suggest that such rigid definition is not only frustrating but dangerous by having Prue die in childbirth, a sacrifice to the female role, and Andrew die in war, a sacrifice to the male role.

Throughout the novel, James and Cam are united in resisting their father's tyranny, while Lily Briscoe fights against the myriad pressures which would force her to conform to the rigidly feminine role which Mrs. Ramsay imposes. Lily provides the foil to a glorification of Mrs. Ramsay's domesticity in her determination not to choose a similar life for herself.

As Marder puts it, Lily "recoils from the muddle of human relations; she fears the confusion of domestic life and immerses herself in an abstract discipline—her art."[28] Her relationship with William Bankes is certainly a form of love, yet for Lily it would be hypocritical to consummate this love in marriage and a family, even though Mrs. Ramsay is willing it. Fortunately, William Bankes is enough of an eccentric not to expect it of her.

Lily admires Mrs. Ramsay and yet she objects to the total sacrifice of self which Mrs. Ramsay's role involves. For her part, Mrs. Ramsay recognizes in Lily something new and perhaps attractive: "There was in Lily a thread of something; a flare of something; something of her own which Mrs. Ramsay liked very much indeed, but no man would, she feared" (p. 157). Yet the integrity of self which Lily sustains through opposing her art to traditional female roles exacts a cost. She can avoid being smothered by domesticity only by distancing herself from other people, denying her sexuality, and sticking rigorously to a discipline at which she does not particularly excel. Thus, while Lily's aversion to Mrs. Ramsay's role is given considerable scope for expression in this novel, we are never incited by the narrator to identify with her point of view.

Despite her personal distaste for domesticity, Lily admires Mrs. Ramsay's capacity to create harmony and form, and it is the dinner party which is Mrs. Ramsay's supreme creative act in this novel. As the meal begins, however, Mrs. Ramsay confronts a cast of characters so locked into their respective roles that she feels unequal to the challenge, bored, and even resentful:

> At the far end was her husband, sitting down, all in a heap, frowning. What at? She did not know. She did not mind. She could not understand how she had ever felt any emotion or affection for him. She had a sense of being past everything, through everything, out of everything, as she helped the soup, as if there was an eddy—there—and one could be in it, or one could be out of it, and she was out of it (p. 125).

Mrs. Ramsay's rather uncharacteristic feelings of enervation here are among the first indications of a loss of vitality and energy which will soon culminate in her death. As the dinner proceeds, however, she is troubled out of her torpor by the inability of her family and guests to begin to communicate on their own:

> Nothing seemed to have merged. They all sat separate. And the whole of the effort of merging and flowing and creating rested on her. Again she felt, as a fact without hostility, the sterility of men, for if she did not do it nobody would do it . . . (p. 126).

Of all the people at the table, only Lily Briscoe is aware of Mrs. Ramsay's distress at this point. But Lily is coping with her own problem, trying to determine how to respond to the ill-mannered taunts of Charles Tansley.

Charles Tansley is thoroughly misogynistic and correspondingly insecure. He is the type, we learn, who if encountered at a picture gallery would demand to know if one liked his tie (p. 16). He thrives on baiting Lily—"Women can't write; women can't paint"—and finds satisfaction in his contempt for the "silliness" of women (p. 129). As Woolf points out in her notes for this novel, she perceives Tansley as the "product of universities" who therefore feels compelled to "assert the power of his intellect."[29] His persistent appeals to feminine sympathy, however, betray the complexity of his feelings about women. He needs to be coddled and admired by the very people toward whom he wishes to feel superior—a classically Oedipal response. Mrs. Ramsay accepts this role without question. It is the social function of women, in Mrs. Ramsay's view, to create bridges among the pinnacles of male egotism. Tansley's insecurity and consequent misogyny present a challenge to her, and she wins his devotion by "insinuating . . . the greatness of man's intellect . . . the subjection of all wives . . . to their husband's labors." He, in turn, becomes a peacock, wishing she could see him "gowned and hooded, walking in a procession" (p. 20). Ironically, while Mrs. Ramsay never ceases in her efforts to promote Tansley's self-esteem, she perceives him as an insufferable prig whose conversation is an endless egomaniacal repetition of the first-person pronoun, "I—I—I" (p. 160).

Lily, who has trouble understanding how Tansley can so effectively degrade her, since he is hardly attractive or superior himself, nonetheless enjoys refusing him solace, thus not fulfilling her traditional social role. As Herbert Marder points out, "Lily's impulse is to retaliate by refusing to perform her part of the contract between men and women, refusing to sooth his injured self-esteem. As a woman, she is instinctively aware of Tansley's extreme discomfort; she is endowed with a sense of social perspective. He, on the other hand, is conscious only of himself. 'He wanted somebody to give him a chance of asserting himself.' "[30]

Once this dialectic of the sexes has been clearly established, Woolf can demonstrate the sacrifices necessary to resolve it. Despite her anger at Tansley's aggressive egotism, Lily is painfully aware of Mrs. Ramsay's silent but desperate plea for help. Before long, her affection for Mrs. Ramsay supersedes her anger at Tansley and she assumes the role of the sympathetic, supportive listener, intent on balming the sore spots of Tansley's ego that she had previously aggravated.

Lily's concession illustrates the negative side of Mrs. Ramsay's code. In putting aside her anger in order to placate Tansley and remove the appearance of tension, Lily is forced into a false position. Like women for centuries past, Lily assumes the role of "reflecting mirror," a role which comes in for sharp criticism by Woolf in *A Room of One's Own*: "Women have served all these centuries as looking-glasses possessing the magic and delicious power of reflecting the figure of man at twice its natural size . . . Whatever may be their use in civilised societies, mirrors are essential to all violent and heroic action. That is why Napoleon and Mussolini both insist so emphatically upon the inferiority of women, for if they were not inferior, they would cease to enlarge."[31] Albeit unwittingly, then, Mrs. Ramsay exemplifies those women who sustain the brutality of patriarchy through self-effacement.

Despite the female sacrifices involved, however, Mrs. Ramsay's capacity to overcome "silliness and spite" and make of the moment something permanent is a high skill which Woolf obviously respects. Isolated individuals are united by her in a profound experience of fellowship and community. At the dinner party, Paul Rayley and Minta Doyle arrive—significantly—with the main dish, the masterful Boeuf en Daube. With the simultaneous arrival of the newly engaged couple and the culinary masterpiece, the moment crystallizes. Perfection is achieved.

Even this moment, however, may have its darker side, as it does for Herbert Marder, who perceives Paul and Minta as sacrificial victims: "The dinner has become a sacrificial meal celebrating social union. Paul and Minta are the victims; Mrs. Ramsay is the priestess. . ."[32] Thus, although Mrs. Ramsay has proven herself masterful at the art of social orchestration, we may be inclined to question the ultimate effect of her power. In bringing Paul and Minta together, and willing their union, Mrs. Ramsay ensures a continuation of the tradition she espouses, but it is a tradition clearly rooted in oppression. Through Lily Briscoe we are made aware of the artifice involved in Mrs. Ramsay's domestic symphony and the sacrifice of personal integrity which it necessarily entails.

In *Mrs. Dalloway*, Peter Walsh provides a similar foil to the sentimental idealization of domestic creativity. While Clarissa's life and personality may be viewed as a work of art by others, Peter sees the waste. Clarissa has sublimated her passions into the trivialities which comprise her life by organizing these trivialities into a ritual which is almost religious in nature. At times this ritual assumes a morbid character. When she returns home from shopping and making arrangements for the party, Clarissa enters her house as if it were a convent, or a morgue:

> The hall of the house was cool as a vault. Mrs. Dalloway raised her hand to her eyes, and, as the maid shut the door to, and she heard the swish of Lucy's skirts, she felt like a nun who has left the world and feels fold round her the familiar veils and the response to old devotions (p. 42).

Although the moment is described as a "flower of darkness" (p. 43), there is a narrowing involved here, a shrinking from life in the world, which is far more a part of Clarissa's personality than the other characters know. Throughout the novel we sense that Clarissa is receding, that the rituals she creates and carries out are death rituals. That Clarissa herself is in some sense conscious of this tendency is indicated by her periodic reflection: "It was all over for her. The sheet was stretched and the bed narrow" (pp. 70, etc.) Even the party which she plans and carries out to perfection has a dark significance. Clarissa perceives the party as an "offering" to life, an opportunity to create life by bringing people together, but as Lucio Ruotolo points out, Clarissa's motives here imply a highly developed awareness of non-life, non-being.[33]

Clarissa shares this awareness with Mrs. Ramsay, and like her, responds to it by becoming a kind of domestic priestess, endowed with the power of investing mundane events with a transforming significance. Both women, to be sure, are masterful within this sphere which has been allotted to them, and Woolf, as their creator, esteems their accomplishments. As Herbert Marder correctly perceives, Woolf's feminism "implied the broadening, not the rejection, of the domestic wisdom traditionally cultivated by women,"[34] and yet the reader is clearly encouraged to see the dark side of this feminine achievement. That neither Clarissa nor Mrs. Ramsay had any opportunity for expanding this wisdom into other spheres may in part account for Mrs. Ramsay's early death and Clarissa's transformation of daily routine into an elaborate ritual of death.

Despite this aura of nihilism, both Clarissa and Mrs. Ramsay appear to accept the status quo, which is fortunate since neither is capable of changing her circumstances. Only in the reactions of Mrs. Ramsay's children and of Lily Briscoe do we have any indication that things may be different in the future. Mrs. Ramsay's daughters see broader prospects than serving men—they have "manliness in their girlish hearts" (p. 14)—although, of course, Prue dies in childbirth very young. But Lily, too, sees new options on the horizon: "Mrs. Ramsay has faded and gone, she thought. We can over-ride her wishes, improve away her limited, old-fashioned ideas" (p. 260).

Since Mrs. Ramsay is largely a portrait of Woolf's own mother, we may find in Lily's reaction a clue to the direction of Woolf's feminism. While Mrs. Ramsay lives, Lily is unable openly to rebel, and she has far too much respect for Mrs. Ramsay's character to urge her to be different. Yet the tension created by her resistance to Mrs. Ramsay stifles her as an artist. As Sally Brett argues, "Lily must, after finding herself, express that self and its experiences in art . . . . (But) feelings of personal inadequacy are extended to her art; the conflict between the Ramsays' way of life and Lily's hoped-for life becomes the conflict between the painting as she sees it and the painting as it is."[35] Only after the mother-figure has died can true purgation occur and freedom be grasped. For Lily, this new liberation is symbolized in the successful completion of her painting; for her creator, Virginia Woolf, in the successful distancing of her mother's influence obtained through committing her to fiction.

Despite these victories over the "Angel in the House," the social matrix within which Woolf's women must continue to live and work is decidedly patriarchal. Woolf was highly critical of patriarchy and its effects and does a fine job of evoking its smothering presence in *A Room of One's Own*, where the narrator picks up a newspaper:

> The most transient visitor to this planet, I thought, who picked up this paper could not fail to be aware, even from this scattered

testimony, that England is under the rule of a patriarchy. Nobody in their senses could fail to detect the dominance of the professor. His was the power and the money and the influence. He was the proprietor of the paper and its editor and its subeditor. He was the Foreign Secretary and the Judge. He was the cricketer; he owned the race-horses and the yachts. He was the director of the company that pays 200 percent to its shareholders. He left millions to charities and colleges that were ruled by himself. He suspended the film-actress in mid-air. He will decide if the hair on the meat axe is human; he it is who will acquit or convict the murderer, and hang him, or let him go free. With the exception of the fog he seemed to control everything. Yet he was angry.[36]

In the Ramsay household, the forces of patriarchy are both pervasive and insidious. Mr. Ramsay, in his reverence for facts, continually forces others to be untrue to their feelings. This leads to a number of ironic situations. Near the beginning of the novel, Mr. Ramsay stuns James by insisting that the long-promised trip to the lighthouse will have to be cancelled because of bad weather. Mrs. Ramsay, in an effort to soothe James' intense disappointment, is forced into an optimism she knows is false and which infuriates her husband. Mr. Ramsay identifies the cause of his irritation as Mrs. Ramsay's "disregard for facts." He needs to believe that she is intellectually naive, and gives no validity whatsoever to the "truth of intuition" with which she counters his "truth of reason." Mr. Ramsay, it would seem, could learn something from Emily Dickinson, although he would undoubtedly dismiss her as silly:

> Tell all the truth but tell it slant—
> Success in circuit lies
> Too bright for our infirm Delight
> The Truth's superb surprise
>
> As lightning to the Children eased
> With explanation kind
> The truth must dazzle gradually
> Or every man be blind—[37]

Mrs. Ramsay would "ease" the truth about the trip to the lighthouse "with explanation kind," while Mr. Ramsay insists upon an immediate acceptance of facts, no matter how brutal their effect.

Part of Mrs. Ramsay's motivation here is a desire to protect childhood because "they will never be so happy again" (p. 91). Mr. Ramsay strongly objects to her saying this, perhaps because of what it implies about Mrs. Ramsay's present state of happiness. As Mrs. Ramsay perceives, ". . . with all his gloom and desperation he was happier, more hopeful on the whole, than she was" (p. 91). Mr. Ramsay, of course, can vent his gloom on his wife and receive sympathy and solace. She, on the other hand, must totally repress her unhappiness. Seeing life as "terrible, hostile, and quick to pounce on you if you give it a chance" (p. 93), Mrs. Ramsay is engaged in a perpetual struggle to keep up a good front. As Phyllis Rose suggests, the deaths of her mother and half-sister Stella so close together conditioned Woolf "to perceive happiness and beauty as a fragile fabric containing a much more substantial world of chaos and pain, explosive, always threatening to break out."[38] Given the intolerable lack of reason, order, and justice in this life (p. 98), one finds solace only in convention (civilization) or death. The flow of Mrs. Ramsay's consciousness reflects a constant movement between these extremes. Like Clarissa, she sometimes has an overwhelming sense of life being over, her female functions having been fulfilled (p. 125). To go on living, a certain amount of self-delusion is necessary, and to achieve this, a certain amount of tampering with the facts may be essential.

Mr. Ramsay's irritation over his wife's lack of respect for facts is ironic given the considerable amount of time he spends engaging in fantasies of personal heroism. While he finds Mrs. Ramsay's inclination to exaggerate annoying, he does not hesitate to envision himself as a reckless and daring leader of men on one fateful expedition after another, most of them inspired by Tennyson (pp. 29, 41, passim). While both Mr. Ramsay's fantasies and Mrs. Ramsay's tendency to exaggerate everything suggest dissatisfaction with things as they are and a desire for some greater and nobler role, he is allowed an indulgence in this regard which she is denied. Mr. Ramsay's intense criticism of his wife is perhaps in part due to a displacement of his embarrassment over his own irrational needs into a criticism of similar qualities in Mrs. Ramsay, qualities he wishes to disown in himself. Mrs. Ramsay's response to this criticism is worth noting:

> To pursue truth with such astonishing lack of consideration for other people's feelings, to rend the thin veils of civilization so wantonly, so brutally, was to her so horrible an outrage of human

decency that, without replying, dazed and blinded, she bent her head as if to let the pelt of jagged hail, the drench of dirty water, bespatter her unrebuked. There was nothing to be said (p. 51).

What we have here is a kind of spiritual rape. The imagery is brutal and violent as everything that Mrs. Ramsay believes in comes under attack. Her response is total defeat, total submission.

One cannot help but wonder at this point about what happens to the anger which is surely generated by such an encounter. In fact, it is transformed, rather horrifyingly if not surprisingly, into a kind of masochistic hero-worship:

> Then he said, Damn you. He said, It must rain. He said, It won't rain; and instantly a Heaven of security opened before her. There was nobody she reverenced more. She was not good enough to tie his shoe strings, she felt (p. 51).

This bears a striking resemblance to the condition explored far more explicitly by Sylvia Plath in "Daddy," the joy in pain which becomes woman's only legitimate response to male domination and control.

The priority which the Mrs. Ramsays of the world assign to masculine vanity has some unfortunate consequences. In her essays and elsewhere, Woolf expresses her belief that this unquestioning acceptance of masculine values is part of what makes war possible. In a sense, then, Andrew's death in the war is partly Mrs. Ramsay's responsibility, as it is the responsibility of all women who do nothing to discourage those values which lead to war. Indeed, from the Marxist point of view, the biological division of roles within families such as the Ramsays is the root of all class structure and exploitation.

This sharp division of roles also exacts a cost on the personal level. In her relationship with her husband, Mrs. Ramsay is perpetually sympathetic, and her highest hope is that she can be sincerely so: ". . . she did not like, even for a second, to feel finer than her husband; and further could not bear not being entirely sure, when she spoke to him, of the truth of what she said" (p. 61). Unfortunately, Mrs. Ramsay can rarely be candid with her husband. Given his insecurity as a historian and his constant need for reassurance, Mr. Ramsay would be shattered were his wife to be honest in her appraisals. She cannot, for example, tell him that she believes his last book *not* to be his best. Her function is simply to soothe his ego, not to encourage him to write better books. Ironically, although the priority Mrs. Ramsay gives to feelings over facts is a constant source of irritation to her husband, Mr. Ramsay is utterly dependent on his wife's reassurances. For her part, Mrs. Ramsay finds that her joy in life is greatly diminished by the amplitude of things about which she must be less than candid (pp. 62–63).

The cost at which Mrs. Ramsay provides this constant solace to her husband is felt keenly by James: "Standing between her knees, James felt all her strength flaring up to be drunk and quenched by the beak of brass, the arid scimitar of the male, which smote mercilessly, again and again, demanding sympathy" (p. 59). Although Woolf rarely comes closer to undisguised polemic than this, she softens the confrontation of masculine aggressiveness with female submission by utilizing James' point of view. Perhaps even more intriguing, however, is the language Woolf employs in describing Mrs. Ramsay's response to her husband's demands. Mrs. Ramsay's "rise" to the occasion is evoked with a panoply of masculine sexual images, so that she meets her husband's demand for sympathy with a kind of phallic aggressiveness:

> Mrs. Ramsay . . . seemed to raise herself with an effort, and at once to pour erect into the air a rain of energy, a column of spray . . . Flashing her needles, confident, upright, she created drawingroom and kitchen, set them all aglow; bade him take his ease there, go in and out, enjoy himself. She laughed, she knitted (pp. 58, 59).

One wonders, of course, how conscious Woolf was of the explicitly sexual nature of her images here. Although the Hogarth Press published the first collected edition of Freud, there is no indication that Woolf was particularly interested in Freud's work, and it seems likely that the modern reader is far more apt to recognize the implications of Mrs. Ramsay's son "standing between her knees, very stiff" than Woolf would have been. Still, the images are there, whether they emerge from the conscious or unconscious mind, and need to be acknowledged.

Annis Pratt, noting this unusual sexual imagery, suggests that Mrs. Ramsay's "erection" is an act of "androgynous creativity" which links her with the lighthouse in its fusion of masculine and feminine.[39] Mrs. Ramsay's "erections" also suggest that her creator did not see her role as entirely "passive." The fact that it is Mrs. Ramsay, rather than her husband, who *confronts* situations and copes with them suggests something about her character which is not entirely obvious. Though a reader, reflecting on this novel, will almost surely view the Ramsays as fulfilling traditional sex roles, it is in fact the case that Mr. Ramsay tends toward the inert, receptive, and passive while Mrs. Ramsay tends toward movement, action, and decisiveness. Intriguingly, Mr. Ramsay has fantasies of dangerous, heroic masculine adventure in contrast to a placid, sedentary, non-heroic life while Mrs. Ramsay's fantasies suggest loss of identity, peace and death in contrast to a life of active giving.

By the end of the encounter in which Mr. Ramsay stands before his wife demanding her sympathy, the image patterns surrounding Mrs. Ramsay's response gradually metamorphose into female sexual symbols: "James, as he stood still between her knees, felt her rise in a rosy-flowered fruit tree laid with leaves and dancing boughs into which the beak of brass, the arid scimitar of his father, the egotistical man, plunged and smote, demanding sympathy" (p. 60). Like the gradual metamorphosis of Daphne into a tree described by Ovid, Mrs. Ramsay is becoming ever more feminine in the face of her husband's relentless masculine aggression. The "flowering fruit tree" suggests a transitional stage, half-male, half-female. Soon, however, Mrs. Ramsay yields completely and gives her husband the satisfaction he desires. Reassured by her sympathy, he leaves her presence:

> Immediately, Mrs. Ramsay seemed to fold herself together, one petal closed in another, and the whole fabric fell in exhaustion upon itself . . . while there throbbed through her, like the pulse in a spring which has expanded to its full width and now gently ceases to beat, the rapture of successful creation (p. 61).

The imagery here is decidedly female, implying as it does the female orgasm, although it also suggests, surely, the complete depletion of resources, the mental, emotional and physical exhaustion which Mr. Ramsay's demands have exacted.

Another aspect of this encounter, which Judith Little points out, is that "Mr. Ramsay has demanded and obtained for himself what he denied to his son; Mr. Ramsay has been soothed 'like a child,' the author remarks in the next sentence; he has received the sustaining assurance of an illusory hope, whereas he would not allow his wife to comfort James with the hope of a trip to the lighthouse." Mrs. Ramsay is in the ironic position of protecting her husband while making him feel that he is protecting her. Because this forms the pattern of their relationship, they cannot share their essentially similar pessimistic outlooks on the world. Although Mrs. Ramsay knows "there is no reason, order, justice: but suffering, death, the poor," she cannot express these feelings because she and her husband are partners in maintaining the illusion that only Mr. Ramsay has the courage to face the stark realities of life.[40]

For Mr. Ramsay, it is also important that he feel confident in his intellectual superiority to his wife, so that when he sees her reading, he must convince himself that she gains nothing from it: "And he wondered what she was reading, and exaggerated her ignorance, her simplicity, for he liked to think that she was not clever, not book-learned at all. He wondered if she understood what she was reading. Probably not, he thought. She was astonishingly beautiful" (p. 182). Mr. Ramsay finds satisfaction in his perception that women's minds in general are "hopelessly vague" (p. 249), and we are reminded of Woolf's point in *A Room of One's Own* that confidence is generated by thinking others inferior to oneself.[41] Because "Women have served all these centuries as looking-glasses possessing the magic and delicious power of reflecting the figure of man at twice its natural size," when a woman criticizes a man, the whole order is threatened. He needs bolstering to go to war, write laws, make speeches, give judgments, and civilize nations.[42] Mrs. Ramsay, in carrying on this tradition finds satisfaction in the notion that men do, in fact, depend on her for encouragement: "Indeed, she had the whole of the other sex under her protection" (p. 13).

One of the consequences of accepting the role of a mirror of men is an uncertain and tenuous identity. At times, Mrs. Ramsay experiences moments of almost total loss of identity. Describing herself as "a wedge-shaped core of darkness" (and this, of course, is how Lily paints her, "a triangular purple shape"), she feels a kinship with the third long stroke of light from the lighthouse. Her physical presence loses its distinctness and blends with nature in a manner very similar to that so often described in Romantic poetry: "It was odd, she thought, how if one was alone, one leant to inanimate things; trees, streams, flowers; felt they expressed one;

felt they became one; felt they knew one, in a sense were one . . ." (pp. 95–97). She becomes profoundly aware, at these times, of the fragility and evanescence of our bodies and the irony that it should be these flimsy physical shells by which others know us (p. 96). The sensation of losing these physical limitations and blending with the environment is one of joy and exhilaration for Mrs. Ramsay: "Losing personality, one lost the fret, the hurry, the stir; and there rose to her lips always some exclamation of triumph over life when things came together in this peace, this rest, this eternity" (p. 96).

Despite Mrs. Ramsay's identification with nature, she does more to create and nurture civilization, nature's antagonist, than any other character. When the candles are lit at her dinner, they create a kind of sanctuary of civilization and order: ". . . they were all conscious of making a party together in a hollow, on an island; had their common cause against that fluidity out there" (p. 147).

Mrs. Ramsay's frequent private escapes into this fluidity can also be seen, of course, as harbingers of her death in which, to use Wordsworth's elegant phrasing, she is "Rolled round in earth's diurnal course, / With rocks, and stones, and trees." Indeed, the sense which the other characters have of Mrs. Ramsay's presence after her death suggests such a blending with the universe.

With Mrs. Ramsay's death, Mr. Ramsay is deprived of essential support and forced to seek it elsewhere. The atmosphere of tension and imbalance created by Mrs. Ramsay's absence is aggravated by the unwillingness of James and Cam, or Lily, to respond to these demands for sympathy and comfort. Nonetheless, the persistent pressure of these demands makes it impossible for Lily to work. In a sense, Lily's position here is representative of the female condition in general which Woolf describes more explicitly in *A Room of One's Own* and *Three Guineas*. The demands of the masculine ego are the nemesis of female creativity. In *To the Lighthouse*, however, Woolf refrains from explanation or analysis. It is up to the reader to determine why Mr. Ramsay affects Lily as he does.

Lily responds to this pressure from Mr. Ramsay by feeling angry at Mrs. Ramsay for giving her entire life to satisfying those demands and then dying and leaving all that need behind. Unwilling to hurt Mr. Ramsay's feelings, however, or wound his vanity, Lily tries to imitate the glowing look of a sympathetic woman, but fails. One is reminded of the Stephen household, after Julia Stephen's death, when Leslie's perpetual groans and demands for sympathy effaced everyone else's grief and were attended to by a train of sympathetic visiting females. When Mr. Ramsay actually groans with need in his plea for sympathy, Lily feels a terrible failure as a woman.

That Lily is able to satisfy Mr. Ramsay's need for sympathy and thus free herself to paint by praising his boots is both humorous and revealing (pp. 229–230). The scene parallels that in which Mrs. Ramsay was able to avoid telling her husband she loved him by submitting to his opinion about the next day's weather. Lily's success with her stratagem, and the genuine sympathy she is able to feel for Mr. Ramsay when the pressure is off, unite her with Mrs. Ramsay, and may suggest as well that a moment of understanding is an adequate substitute for a life-time of self-sacrificing devotion.

This sense of reconciliation is reinforced by a series of perceptions in which Lily increasingly recognizes her kinship with Mrs. Ramsay. For one thing, neither could believe in any grand and perfect answer to the question of what life means: "Instead there were little daily miracles, illuminations, matches struck unexpectedly in the dark . . . Mrs. Ramsay saying 'Life stand still here'; Mrs. Ramsay making of the moment something permanent (as in another sphere Lily herself tried to make of the moment something permanent)" (pp. 240, 241). The point Woolf seems to be making here is that despite their differences, Mrs. Ramsay and Lily Briscoe have an essential element in common, their female consciousness. Both perceive reality as non-linear, non-hierarchical, more process than product oriented. To the extent that this novel has allowed us, as readers, to experience this essentially feminine view of the world, a feminist objective has been achieved.

Through the acknowledgment of all that she shares with Mrs. Ramsay, Lily becomes reconciled with her, and thus freed of her tyranny. This synthesis, and the peace it brings, is represented for Lily in the final consummate stroke which she makes in her painting and which suggests, perhaps, the third long stroke of the lighthouse with which Mrs. Ramsay identifies. And as Allen McLaurin has noted, "Many critics have championed Mrs. Ramsay's vision, some have excused Mr. Ramsay's, but few have seen that the two are complementary and that Lily achieves a successful *aesthetic* fusion of Impressionism and logic in her Post-Impressionist vision: 'She saw the colour burning on a framework of steel; the light of a butterfly's wings lying upon the arches of a cathedral.'"[43] The resolution thus achieved, however, is more than merely aesthetic. The successful fusion of color and steel, light and arches, also symbolizes an androgynous resolution to the sexual dialectic which is one of the novel's major themes.

A similar process of reconciliation is taking place simultaneously in the boat. For most of the journey, tension and hostility prevail as James and Cam form a united resistance to their father's tyranny. With the approaching landing, however, an important change takes place. Gradually, Cam and James begin to feel love and sympathy for Mr. Ramsay *because* they begin to recognize elements of their father in themselves. In doing so, they find freedom from his tyranny. Like Lily, James and Cam are able to conquer the forces which oppress them by recognizing those forces in themselves.

Woolf employs a variety of symbols to heighten this sense of resolution. The lighthouse has been associated throughout the novel with a merging of masculine and feminine, the phallus and the eye. As Marder notes, at times the lighthouse is "erect" and "stark," at other times "misty" and "yielding." As the characters reach it, personal grudges fall away and Mr. Ramsay becomes "reconciled at last with the spirit of his dead wife." Both James and Mr. Ramsay gain what they lack: for James, manhood; for Mr. Ramsay, a freedom from self.[44]

It is odd that Cam should seem almost to fade away in this final scene, but her role has never been large. It is possible that she merely represents the female side of James' character which is absorbed into a more unified identity with the landing at the lighthouse. Simultaneously, of course, Lily makes the final brushstroke which finishes her painting, and throughout the novel it has been the vision of James and Mrs. Ramsay together, a unity of masculine and feminine, which Lily has been trying to achieve.

The ending of this novel, though satisfying in its own way, is also elusive. Whatever resolution takes place does so on a purely suggestive, abstract, almost unconscious level. The automatic response of the reader to Lily Briscoe's statement, "It is finished," might easily be, "*What* is finished?" Our conclusions can be tentative at best. In Marder's opinion, Woolf's tendency to abstract and sublimate whenever the forces in her writing are pushing toward a point to be made springs from an overreaction against her father's moralizing.[45] To be sure, throughout Woolf's work there is an uneasy tension between aestheticism and morality. She persistently maintained that the two could not be reconciled in a work of art and yet her entire career can be seen in some ways as an attempt to do so. Her early novels are marred by a need to explore the issue of the suitability for women of the institution of marriage on the one hand, and yet a fear of answering the question on the other. Beginning with *Jacob's Room*, and certainly in *Mrs. Dalloway* and *To the Lighthouse*, she has learned to subordinate the moral issues by submerging and displacing them in images, symbols and a multitude of points of view.

Woolf's opposition to "moralistic" writing and the strategies she developed to avoid it led to important innovations. Eschewing cause and effect, her concentration on aesthetic synthesis led her to approach characterization and narrative in an entirely new way. She thought of herself as tunneling into "caves" behind her characters through capturing the free play of consciousness. This freed her, as Hermione Lee suggests, "from the unwanted linear structure in which an omniscient narrator moves from point A to B. She arrived instead at a form which could 'use up everything I've ever thought,' giving the impression of simultaneous connections between the inner and the outer world, the past and the present, speech and silence: a form patterned like waves in a pond rather than a railway line."[46] In addition, the point of view floats from character to character, free from the more normal compulsion to locate it in one central controlling consciousness. At times, the point of view is even shared with characters who have no importance in the novel whatsoever. In *Mrs. Dalloway*, for example, Clarissa's party is first described from the point of view of the servants.

The notes which Woolf kept during the process of planning and writing *Mrs. Dalloway* shed considerable light on the function of this constantly shifting point of view. Woolf appears to have envisioned Mrs. Dalloway as a kind of modern tragedy based on the classic Greek model:

> Why not have an observer in the street—at each critical point who acts the part of chorus—some nameless person? . . . Mrs. D. must be seen by other people. As she sits in her drawing room. But there must be a general idea—she must not get lost in detail: her chapter must correspond with his [Septimus]. Question of choruses—that is to say of links between chapters: also, could the scenes be divided like acts of a play into five, say, or six?[47]

This concept of having the scenes in the novel correspond to acts in a play connected by choruses, the structural device of parallel chapters or "acts," and the subordination of detail to more or less universal themes are reminiscent of Aeschylus or Euripides. Intriguingly, these notes occur at the back of her notebook on the *Choephori* of Aeschylus.[48] That Woolf found this compositional strategy challenging and exciting is indicated by another comment in her notes: "The merit of this book so far is in its design, which is virginal—very difficult."[49]

Woolf uses choruses in the form of people who appear briefly and then disappear in the novel to establish moods and bring into focus her major themes. The persistent pendulum swing of the mood of this novel between serenity and apprehension, for example, is reinforced by the responses of a wide variety of characters. In her notes of July 22, 1923, Woolf makes her intention clear as she plans the scene in which Peter falls asleep in Regents Park:

> There should now be a chorus, half of calm and security, the nursemaid and the sleeping baby: [half of?] fear, and apprehension—the little girl who sees Peter W. asleep. There is something helpless and ridiculous about him as well as terrifying; this abandonment to sleep. The child runs away frightened in towards Rezia.[50]

Unless one is conscious of Woolf's intention here, the significance of the juxtaposition of the sleeping infant and the frightened child is easily overlooked. While it is obvious that the child connects Rezia and Peter in some way, unless we approach all the subsidiary characters as also performing the function of choruses, much of the novel's coherence will be missed.

Woolf's conscientious adherence to classical models may also help to explain the rather mysterious passage in *Mrs. Dalloway* which focuses on the old beggar woman whom Peter Walsh passes in Regents Park (pp. 122–124). Peter first becomes aware of the old woman as an incoherent voice, devoid of human meaning, singing "ee um fah um so / foo swee too eem oo—" (p. 122). This ageless, sexless voice reminds Peter of an ancient, battered fountain, in the shape of a woman who has been singing of love and its loss from the beginning of time:

Through all ages—when the pavement was grass, when it was swamp, through the age of tusk and mammoth, through the age of silent sunrise, the battered woman—for she wore a skirt—with her right hand exposed, her left clutching at her side, stood singing of love—love which has lasted a million years, she sang, love which prevails, and millions of years ago, her love, who had been dead these centuries, had walked, she crooned, with her in May; but in the course of ages, long as summer days, and flaming, she remembered, with nothing but red asters, he had gone; death's enormous sickle had swept those tremendous hills, and when at last she laid her hoary and immensely aged head on the earth, now become a mere cinder of ice, she implored the Gods to lay by her side a bunch of purple heather, there on her high burial place which the last rays of the sun caressed; for then the pageant of the universe would be over (pp. 122–123).

The song of the ancient woman, though gibberish on one level, might also be seen as a kind of meta-language which unites all time—past, present, and future—in a harmony of simultaneity. Like a Greek chorus, this fountain voice invests the personal with the universal, while the song itself, in its meaninglessness, evokes a kind of collective unconscious, and may be seen as connected, both psychically and historically, to the glossolalia of Greek oracles and priestesses as well as to the New Testament phenomenon of "speaking in tongues."

Part of the haunting quality of this image of the fountain derives from Woolf's success in linking sublime beauty with eternal sadness. The mood thus created, and the dialectic between ecstasy and tragedy which it sets up, rings through the novel in much the same manner as the leaden circles of sound which issue forth from Big Ben. It was, in fact, in the presence of a similar fountain that the young Clarissa rejected Peter's love (p. 97). It is interesting, as well, that this passage parallels so closely the musings of Septimus a few pages earlier:

He lay very high, on the back of the world. The earth thrilled beneath him. Red flowers grew through his flesh; their stiff leaves rustled by his head. Music began clanging against the rocks up here. It is a motor horn down in the street, he muttered; but up here it cannoned from rock to rock, divided, met in shocks of sound which rose in smooth columns (that music should be visible was a discovery) and became an anthem, an anthem twined round now by a shepherd boy's piping (that's an old man playing a penny whistle by the public-house, he muttered) which, as the boy stood still came bubbling from his pipe, and then, as he climbed higher, made its exquisite plaint while the traffic passed beneath. This boy's elegy is played among the traffic, thought Septimus (p. 103).

The rusty pipe, the elegy, the red flowers, and the notion of a "high" resting place "on the back of the world"; all these images correspond to the passage about the old woman. The major difference, and it is certainly significant, is that Septimus feels compelled to link these lyrical flights with the concrete facts of his daily existence. Desperately trying to retain the connection with the world of fact, a world which people generally can agree upon, he insists that the music he hears is rooted in the sound of a motor horn, while the shepherd's anthem is in fact an old man playing a penny whistle.

Still, the musings of Septimus connect him with the qualities of eternal beauty and suffering which the old woman suggests, as well as with Big Ben and its "leaden circles" of sound, its "visible" music. Though the name itself implies a masculine consciousness and it functions to provide a rigid and perhaps illusory structure to time, Big Ben also suggests contradiction and paradox: its "leaden circles dissolve in the air." (p. 5, etc.). Its striking is like a death knell, preceded by a moment of intense suspense which suggests the heightened consciousness of life which an awareness of death engenders.

The image of Big Ben with its "leaden circles" is also an apt metaphor for the novel's structure, suggesting as it does a central intelligence radiating outward, a "blot fringed with flame," the expanding present moment in which all things, all events and people, though seemingly disparate, are linked, part of an all-encompassing unity, a euphony of life. This structure, which is circular, centered, and encompassing as opposed to linear, progressive, and volitional, represented for Woolf the female consciousness. One could, of course, go on forever proposing potential implications of the Big Ben imagery, and yet it is this very elusiveness, this symbolic openness, that is one of Woolf's greatest strengths. The sounding of Big Ben is endlessly suggestive, and like a "condensed" dream symbol, its significance can never be fully explained.

The image of the lighthouse in *To the Lighthouse* functions in much the same manner. Although stark and clearly "phallic" on one level, the lighthouse, like Big Ben, is paradoxical, contradictory. Mrs. Ramsay clearly identifies with the stroke of light, which suggests that the "eye" of the lighthouse may be identified with feminine consciousness. The movement of the light is circular, like the sound waves of Big Ben, and like the leaden circles, dissolves, displacing darkness only momentarily. Each long stroke of the lighthouse is preceded by a moment of intensity, and the stroke itself, like the sound of Big Ben, is associated with death. And just as Big Ben links events and people in an all-encompassing unity, the lighthouse is the means by which Mrs. Ramsay escapes personality and blends with the universe.

The phenomenological correspondence between Big Ben and the light-house might be seen as existing as well between the old and battered beggar woman Peter encounters and the person of Mrs. McNab, the old lady who cares for the house in the transitional chapter of *To the Lighthouse,* "Time Passes." Like the old "fountain lady," Mrs. McNab is aged and battered, and sings a song which "was robbed of meaning, was like the voice of witlessness, humor, persistency itself, trodden down but springing up again" (p. 197). The similarity of these figures is striking and suggests the importance Woolf attached to their presence. These old women seem to embody in some way all of humanity in its perpetual struggle against time. Their songs, in which language has lost its boundaries and become fluid, suggest the "still, sad music of humanity" with which Wordsworth invests nature in "Tintern Abbey." As such, compared to the "eyeless" and "terrible" nature (p. 203) which prevails when Mrs. McNab leaves, and which has affinities with Shelley's vision in "Mont Blanc," the images of these two old women are reassuring.

The healing and restorative power that Woolf attributes to the "female mystique" in the figures of these two old women assumes even greater clarity when contrasted with her portrait of the death-dealing patriarchal man embodied in the figure of Sir William Bradshaw. Worshipping the goddess of proportion, Bradshaw molds and squeezes all who come under his influence into puppets of the status quo. And as England's most influential doctor of the mind, Bradshaw's power is extensive. As Marder words it, "He has usurped the priest's office but knows nothing of the soul. The social system that honors and advances men like him must be corrupt."[51] By enforcing moderation in all things, Bradshaw destroys spontaneity and imposes a false equilibrium. In enjoining a state of mind which Marder describes as "the surrender of one's feelings" and "blind adherence to convention,"[52] Bradshaw fosters a life-denying conformity. By labelling all dissenting voices as sick, he consolidates his vision in society:

Worshipping proportion, Sir William not only prospered himself but made England prosper, secluded her lunatics, forbade childbirth, penalized despair, made it impossible for the unfit to propagate their views until they, too, shared his sense of proportion—his, if they were men, Lady Bradshaw's if they were women (p. 110).

That Lady Bradshaw's views should form the standard for English women is particularly significant in that she has no views of her own: "Fifteen years ago she had gone under. It was nothing you could put your finger on; there had been no scene, no snap; only the slow sinking, waterlogged, of her will into his. Sweet was her smile, swift her submission" (p. 111). Nor is Lady Bradshaw an anomaly. The narrator characterizes Hugh Whitbread's wife as "almost negligible" (p. 112), the implication being that such men, with their cardboard sterility, their empty manners and rigid observance of social forms, destroy the women who love them. Such men not only are not interested in the truth: they effectively bar its expression. Miss Brush, Lady Bruton's companion, understands this very well and therefore continues to tell Hugh Whitbread, who automatically inquires, that her brother is doing well in South Africa when in fact he has been doing badly in Portsmouth for half a dozen years (pp. 156–157).

The implications of this female capitulation, which Lady Bradshaw so tellingly represents, are explored in this novel not in the obvious terms of her personal losses but in the effect of her submergence on others. Woolf repeatedly asserts, in her essays, that political tyranny begins in the home, and in "Thoughts on Peace in an Air Raid," she maintains that those, like Lady Bradshaw, who have allowed themselves to *become* enslaved must share responsibility for the consequences:

Let us try to drag up into consciousness the subconscious Hitlerism that holds us down. It is the desire for aggression; the desire to dominate and enslave. Even in the darkness we can see that made visible. We can see shop windows blazing; and women gazing; painted women; dressed-up women; women with crimson

lips and crimson fingernails. They are slaves who are trying to
enslave. If we could free ourselves from slavery, we should free
men from tyranny. Hitlers are bred by slaves.[53]

Lady Bradshaw's slavery, in reinforcing her husband's power, allows him
to dominate and manipulate people like Septimus. Bradshaw, having
suffocated his wife, sets out to suffocate the rest of society, and he
exercizes a terrible control.

In illustrating Bradshaw's destructive control, Woolf chooses a male
victim. She could have put Clarissa in Bradshaw's care, but does not. She
was, perhaps, afraid of her own anger, which threatened the integrity of
her fiction and needed to be tempered by a process of transference. Had
Clarissa been subjected to Bradshaw's tyranny, Woolf's polemical intent
would very likely have dominated the novel and created an imbalance. By
having Septimus, as Clarissa's alter ego, suffer the blows of patriarchy,
Woolf can avoid making this the central issue in the novel.

Although Herbert Marder finds Woolf's portrait of Bradshaw a weakness, since he takes on some of the qualities of caricature,[54] this tendency
would be far more pronounced if Clarissa were his victim. And she very
nearly was. In Woolf's " 'Introduction' to *Mrs. Dalloway*," we learn that in
the first version of this novel Septimus did not exist and Clarissa was
either to kill herself or simply die at the end of the party.[55] The increase in
subtlety achieved by transferring the crisis to Septimus and connecting
Clarissa to him psychically instead is admirable. Woolf avoids the pitfalls
of melodrama and yet is able to make her point with great clarity.

Clarissa and Septimus are connected by a remarkable similarity in their
responses to the world. As we learn very early on of Clarissa, "She always
had the feeling that it was very, very dangerous to live even one day"
(p. 11). She shares with Septimus an extreme sensitivity to beauty, a
radical openness to the world and to experience. At times, Clarissa's
openness has a positive effect in allowing her to merge her identity with all
that she sees so that death loses its threat. Clarissa's youthful theory, as we
learn, was that one *lives* in the people and places that surround one, and
that our bodies are very "momentary" compared with this "wide . . .
unseen" part which, because it is so strong, must survive (p. 232).

Septimus is denied this peace in consequence of his sense of "mission,"
his compulsion to assume the world's burden of guilt. While Clarissa's
vulnerability to beauty and sensation allows her to move outward and

blend with the world, Septimus sucks the world into himself. When the Prime Minister's motor car becomes the center of attention, for example, Clarissa can merely appreciate the focus it gives to the scene while Septimus is compelled to displace that focus onto himself (p. 21). And while Clarissa does, like Septimus, experience moments of pure ecstasy in contemplating natural beauty, she is able to carry some of this joy into her contacts with people while Septimus is not. Once again, Woolf's notes for *Mrs. Dalloway* clarify this crucial difference:

> There should be a fairly logical transition in S's mind . . . beauty of natural things. This disappears in seeing people. His sense of their demands upon him: What is his relation to them? inability to identify himself with them . . . He must somehow see through human nature—see its hypocrisy and insincerity, its power to recover from every wound, incapable of taking any final impression.[56]

While Clarissa shares Septimus' insights, she differs from him in her acceptance of human imperfections and her ability to create and share beauty. While Septimus is immobilized by the enormity of his mission to bring truth to the entire human race, Clarissa is capable of confining her activities to the private sphere where a sense of accomplishment is at least possible.

Despite these differences, however, Clarissa and Septimus have a spiritual kinship and are opposed not by each other but by the forces represented in Miss Kilman and Sir William Bradshaw. Both these characters typify worldviews which preclude the state of mind which is open to beauty and joy. In a sense, they represent the female and male foils to Clarissa and Septimus, so that much of the tension in the novel is generated by the dialectical struggle of these opposing forces. Whereas the receptive point of view exemplified by Clarissa and Septimus tends toward "widening" and "dispersing," Miss Kilman and Sir William Bradshaw embody the compulsion toward reductiveness through a process of "narrowing" and "focusing." Woolf's mistrust and suspicion of this tendency may provide some insight into her uneasiness with the cause of feminism. She reacted intensely against any constraint on the free operation of vision. "Programs," like Miss Kilman's "religion" or Sir William Bradshaw's "Proportion" lower the sights, annihilate joy and destroy beauty.

Still, as Clarissa recognizes, the state of "being" as opposed to "non-being" is dangerous. Vulnerability to beauty and sensation creates a state of mind which, in its intensity, is easily thrown off-balance. Septimus suffers because he thinks he is incapable of "feeling" anything, and yet the truth is that he is incapable of *not* feeling, of "non-being." Septimus lives at a constant pitch of emotion from which he has no rest. Because he has lost contact with the *source* of his pain in Evans' death, he is doomed to the experience of unmitigated grief. As Woolf says in her notes, ". . . Septimus should pass through all extremes of feeling—happiness and unhappiness—intensity. Should always remain outside human affairs."[57]

Clarissa is sometimes close to this state of mind herself, but is able to effect a satisfactory compromise with the world of "non-being." Whereas Clarissa, like anyone sensitive to beauty and experience, is capable of perceiving the glorious order behind appearances, the "pattern behind the cotton wool," she does so only during brief moments of vision, or epiphany. Septimus, by contrast, is perpetually and excruciatingly in touch with this vision of the truth behind appearances. Simultaneously aware of reality as other people see it and as it is transformed by his own particular vision, he is unable to reconcile the two. The two layers of reality which he perceives are in perpetual collision—a classic symptom of the schizophrenic mind.

Though both Clarissa and Septimus have experienced similar traumas—Septimus has seen his best friend killed in war; Clarissa has seen her sister killed by a falling tree—Clarissa is able to absorb the experience while Septimus is destroyed by it. Clarissa has a "hardness," a resiliency, which perhaps derives from her sense of social obligation and personal responsibility which Septimus does not have, and as a woman, she is not trapped by egoism to the extent that Septimus is. Clarissa's acceptance of convention is in some sense her salvation, allowing her a retreat from the intensity of "being" into the essential rest provided by periods of "non-being," a rest which is unavailable to Septimus.

Woolf's notes on this novel provide some interesting insights into her conception of Septimus' character:

Question of S's character . . . founded on R? [Roger Fry?] His face. Eyes far apart—not degenerate. Not wholly an intellectual. Had been in the war. Or founded on me? . . . might be left vague—as a mad person is—not so much character as an idea.

That is what is painful to her [Rezia]. . . . becomes generalized—universalized. So can be partly R; partly me . . . He must be logical enough to make the comparison between the two worlds. Why not have something of G. B. in him? The young man who has gone into business after the war: takes life to heart: seeks truth—revelations—some reason: yet of course his insanity. His insensibility to other people's feelings—that is to say he must have the masculine feelings: selfishness: egoism: but has also an extreme insight; and humility.[58]

On one level, then, Septimus is an idealistic young man, sensitive and insightful, who has been pushed over the edge of sanity by experience. His inability to cope is compounded by his masculinity, by an ego which transforms his burden of guilt and grief into a personal responsibility for all the world's woes, so that he envisions himself as a kind of Christ figure. As Woolf's notes suggest, however, the essence of her description of Septimus' psychic disintegration derives from her own experience. A psychoanalyst, Miyeko Kamiya, suggests some similarities in her description of Woolf's periods of breakdown:

The scale of emotions in Virginia Woolf ranged from deepest despondency to highest elation, even ecstasy. Her depression could take the form of despair, loneliness, depersonalization, splitting of personality, nihilism or the sense of "loss of foothold," as amply illustrated by her diary and letters. ". . . life is . . . so like a little strip of pavement over an abyss. I look down; I feel giddy . . ." (Oct. 25, 1920). What might be called hypomanic states are found in the diary, though fewer, in the form of playful exhilaration or excited contentment. [One is reminded of Septimus and Rezia designing hats together shortly before his death.] These moods could be induced by circumstances, but also appeared without any apparent reason: "I am frightfully contented these last few days, by the way. I don't quite understand it" (Sept. 5, 1926). Her feelings of mystical ecstasy, which she called "mountain summit moments" came "spasmodically" (Nov. 16, 1938) and, significantly, after moments of despair (Jan. 26, 1940).[59]

The similarity between Woolf's own experiences and those she ascribes to Septimus in the novel are fascinating, though also ominous. Yet since Septimus shares so many psychic tendencies with Clarissa, Clarissa's ability to endure may suggest some of Woolf's own strategies for psychic survival. As Lucio Ruotolo points out, for both Clarissa and Septimus, a detail often incites flights of creative fancy, but Clarissa, unlike Septimus, has the resiliency to move back and forth between fancy and connectedness.[60]

Both periodically are engulfed in a sense of nihilism—Clarissa through social detachment, Septimus through an inability to forget horror. Both experience a recurring loss of identity, a merging with the forces of timelessness which exist beyond the world of phenomena. When Septimus enters this state, he becomes conscious of the sound of the waves and finds momentary peace. The sensation that he need "fear no more" which he experiences at these moments connects him once again with Clarissa (pp. 211, 58–59). The differences between Clarissa and Septimus are largely a matter of "proportion," which is a very important word in this novel. Septimus' obsession with the profound questions which haunt him and his intense susceptibility to beauty are anathema to the worship of "proportion" and "conversion," as Ruotolo rightly perceives.

Fortunately, Woolf chose to make mental illness and its punishment under patriarchy only one of a number of themes in the novel. If she had not, the subtlety which we so prize in this work would almost certainly have been sacrificed. For the most part, Bradshaw is simply a menacing presence hovering around the edges of the novel. The manifestations of patriarchy within the Dalloway household and among most of their friends are less unsparing, though not altogether benign. Richard Dalloway is a very different and far more pleasant being than he was in *The Voyage Out*. Hugh Whitbread, with his power, his pomposity, and his great good manners, is simply another peg in the power structure. As Sally Seton discerned at an early age, "He represented all that was most detestable in British middle-class life" (p. 110). He performs his duties mindlessly, without reflection, and with never a thought for their consequences.

Ellie Henderson, Lady Bruton, and Miss Kilman represent three types of responses to this total masculine domination of society. Ellie, a spinster, is a leftover in this patriarchal system. Full of fears, poor, aging, lonely, and unable to save a penny, she haunts the corners of Clarissa's party looking for news to tell Edith (pp. 255–157). Lady Bruton, who depends on Richard Dalloway and Hugh Whitbread to write her letters to the *Times* for her, is somehow pitiable, for all her bravado. Full of admiration for the accomplishments of men, Lady Bruton finds her own sex trivial and boring, and calculates her success in life as having "known the ablest men of her day" (p. 169). Alienated from her own sex, Lady Bruton is viewed with tolerant amusement by the men who possess the power she so admires.

Miss Kilman, on the other hand, is possessed by the enemy. Unable to achieve power in the world of men, she dominates and tyrannizes Elizabeth. Although she is ostensibly an "emancipated" woman, Miss Kilman's bitterness, fanaticism, and desire for control ally her with the controllers and exploiters: ". . . all her soul rusted with that grievance in it. . . . For it was not her one hated but the idea of her . . . one of those spectres who stand astride us and suck up half our life-blood, dominators and tyrants" (pp. 16–17). As Clarissa perceives, Miss Kilman invades the sanctity of the private soul. Woolf obviously saw this as one of the dangers in the feminist movement. Political arguments, she felt, were all too often simply justifications for private frustrations, thus betraying a negative egotism. And as Marder perceives, Woolf seems to be saying that, whatever its source, "the desire for power over others always does incalculable harm."[61]

This distrust of causes cannot be separated from an equal aversion for conventional religion and sexual passion, all of which seem somehow connected in Woolf's mind. Clarissa despises organized religion and views sexuality with similar distaste:

> The cruelest things in the world, she thought, seeing them clumsy, hot, domineering, hypocritical, eavesdropping, jealous, infinitely cruel and unscrupulous, dressed in a mackintosh coat, on the landing; love and religion" (p. 191).

This identification of sex with religion, combined with a violent revulsion toward both, tells us a good deal about Clarissa Dalloway and, by extension, Virginia Woolf. As artists, both Clarissa and her creator believe in the individual vision, a vision which is undermined by the conformity which causes, and religion, necessarily impose. For Clarissa, beauty exists in private mystery and ritual, in the old lady coming to her window next door, and not in the tyranny of public ritual which Miss Kilman and Sir William Bradshaw represent.

Nor is Clarissa incorrect in identifying Miss Kilman's religious fervor with sublimated sexuality. The physical attraction which Miss Kilman feels for Elizabeth, because she is unable or unwilling to acknowledge it, is translated into a desire for dominance and control, and the tool Miss Kilman employs to achieve these things is religion. Like sex, Miss Kilman's religion is "clumsy, hot, domineering" (p. 191). Her relation to Clarissa shows a similar pattern: "So now, whenever the hot and painful feelings boiled within her, this hatred of Mrs. Dalloway, this grudge against the world, she thought of God . . . Rage was succeeded by calm" (p. 189). Miss Kilman's cosmic orgasms are a direct result of her fantasy of subduing Clarissa, of reducing her to tears, of humiliating her as she has been humiliated (p. 189). Her monstrous egotism causes her totally to misperceive Clarissa, to view her as someone who feels neither sorrow nor joy and therefore deserves the rape of Miss Kilman's righteous wrath.

The libido, of course, demands expression, and if it is denied the outlet of simple physical passion, its drives are sublimated into other forms. Freud's definition of "sublimation" may be useful here:

> The sexual instinct . . . places extraordinarily large amounts of force at the disposal of civilized activity, and it does this in virtue of its especially marked characteristic of being able to displace its aim without materially diminishing in intensity. This capacity to exchange its originally sexual aim for another one, which is no longer sexual but which is psychically related to the first aim, is called the capacity for sublimation.[62]

One of the most common cultural manifestations of the process of sublimation, as Freud saw it, was the phenomenon of religion. In *Mrs. Dalloway*, the connection of religion with sexuality is suggested by Woolf's portrayal of Miss Kilman, who appears asexual only because these instincts have been sublimated into religious fanaticism. While the language Woolf uses to describe Miss Kilman's attitude toward Elizabeth is the language of a would-be lover, Miss Kilman refuses to acknowledge the sexual component in her desire to possess Elizabeth. Instead, she maintains a tyrannous though unstable hold over Elizabeth through the medium of her religion. Clarissa sees through Miss Kilman's morbid self-righteousness to the lust which motivates her and is disgusted by it.

Sometimes the sublimation of the sexual instincts into religious zeal slides into psychosis. Septimus, for example, identifies with Christ and in fact shows many characteristics in common with one of Freud's own patients. Freud's description of this patient is worth quoting. In establishing a parallel with Septimus, however, it is important to remember that Evans was Septimus' commanding officer, responsible for initiating him into the rites of manhood, and that they had developed a deep affection for one another in the context of that most patriarchal of situations, war:

> As Christ, he could love his father [Evans, in Septimus' case], who was now called God, with a fervour which had sought in vain to discharge itself so long as his father had been a mortal. The means by which he could bear witness to this love were laid down by religion, and they were not haunted by that sense of guilt from which his individual feelings of love could not set themselves free. In this way it was still possible for him to drain off his deepest sexual current, which had already been precipitated in the form of unconscious homosexuality; and at the same time his more superficial masochistic impulse found an incomparable sublimation, without much renunciation, in the story of the Passion of Christ, who, at the behest of his divine Father and in his honour, had let himself be ill-treated and sacrificed.[63]

The martyrdom of Septimus Warren Smith suggests just such a process of guilt, sublimation, and ultimate psychosis.

Clarissa, having rejected religion, must find another outlet for her sexual instincts and appears to have done so in her profound sensitivity to beauty and her ability to create perfect aesthetic "moments." In a sense, Clarissa substitutes social event for sexual event, and one might even see a connection between her "moments of being," of "intense awareness," and sexual climax. It is interesting, as Mitchell Leaska points out, that both Clarissa's marriage to Richard and Septimus' marriage to Lucrezia are characterized by a lack of "relatedness." Clarissa has experienced a culminating love and passion only once in her life, with Sally Seton, and Septimus' love and attraction for Evans is strikingly similar, uniting an intellectual and spiritual bond with a profound eroticism, but accompanied as well by a debilitating guilt. Because Clarissa acknowledges her love for Sally, she is able to incorporate it into her life. While Septimus is unable to do so, his suicide protects the integrity of his passion, an integrity which Clarissa has lost.[64]

The fear and aversion which the notion of lust inspires in Woolf surfaces as well in *To the Lighthouse* where it is complicated by its association with the respectable institution of marriage. This conjunction of lust with a more or less sacred union evokes a strongly ambivalent response in Lily: ". . . the heat of love, its horror, its cruelty, its unscrupulosity . . . while the women, judging from her own experience, would all the time be feeling, this is not what we want; there is nothing more tedious, puerile, and inhumane than this; yet it is also beautiful and necessary" (pp. 154, 155). Later, Lily muses on what it will mean for her to have missed this experience of passion and is reminded of her vision of Paul Rayley when he and Minta Doyle decided to marry:

> It rose like a fire sent up in token of some celebration by savages on a distant beach. She heard the roar and the crackle. The whole sea for miles round ran red and gold . . . And the roar and the crack repelled her with fear and disgust, as if while she saw its splendour and power she saw too how it fed on the treasure of the house, greedily, disgustingly, and she loathed it" (p. 261).

Lily's art becomes for her a shield which protects her from this potential which so powerfully attracts and repels her.

Woolf clearly views sexuality, or at least that instinctive sexuality which she calls lust, as a horrifying and destructive drive which, by its very nature, threatens order and civilization. One cannot but wonder to what extent her disgust springs from her unwilling, though passive, adolescent participation in an incestuous sexual relationship with her half-brother, George Duckworth. Throughout her writings, one has hints that Woolf never recovered from the guilt, shame and humiliation which these encounters engendered. At a very impressionable age, it would seem, sex became identified for Woolf with the violation of a sacred and deep-rooted taboo, with perversion and guilt.[65] There is, of course, great danger in equating fictional attitudes with autobiographical experience, but Woolf's early sexual experiences may shed some light on this persistent theme.

Another characteristic of the sexual instinct which Freud identified and which Clarissa embodies is the connection between sex and death, between *Eros* and *Thanatos*. To be sure, the conjunction of these two forces has long been recognized in western culture, particularly in Anglo-American poetry where "dying" is a frequent metaphor for the experience of orgasm. Nonetheless, Freud was perhaps the first to investigate this connection from a more or less scientific point of view. Noting that many lower animals die after copulation, Freud maintained that "after Eros has been eliminated through the process of satisfaction, the death instinct has a free hand for accomplishing its purpose."[66]

This intimate connection between sexuality and death surfaces again and again in *Mrs. Dalloway*. At one point, the narrator identifies lust with the fascination with which people sometimes view mangled bodies after an accident: "Ah, but thinking became morbid, sentimental, directly one began conjuring up doctors, dead bodies; a little glow of pleasure, a sort of lust too over the visual impression warned one not to go on with that sort of thing anymore—fatal to art, fatal to friendship" (p. 229). When thinking about Peter Walsh begins to arouse erotic feelings in Clarissa, she immediately reminds herself that it is too late, that "the sheet is stretched and the bed narrow" (pp. 69–70).

The most striking moment in this regard comes at the end of the novel when Clarissa learns of the death of Septimus Warren Smith, a man she has never met. Leaving her party, she enters another room where she can be alone. Once there, she becomes Septimus, entering his mind completely and experiencing his death in excruciating detail:

> Up had flashed the ground; through him, blundering, bruising, went the rusty spikes. There he lay with a thud, thud, thud in his brain, and then a suffocation of blackness" (p. 280).

Clarissa respects the integrity and honesty of Septimus, his refusal to accept the sordidness of life. She understands fully Septimus' reaction to Bradshaw, to his kind but unfeeling invulnerability, his absence of passion or vice. It is not surprising to Clarissa, therefore, that Septimus should choose the comforting embrace of death (p. 281).

Emerging from this vision, Clarissa looks up to see the old woman next door performing her nightly ritual of coming to the window, closing the blind, putting out the light, and going to bed. This nightly ritual, which suggests through its imagery of windows, light, and bed, age and approaching death, has a calming effect on Clarissa. On one side of her is the party, a "celebration of life," an "offering;" on her other side is a quiet celebration of death. Life is ritual, neither to be over-valued nor under-valued. For Clarissa, this is a moment of peace, of reconciliation between the forces of life and the forces of death.

In sharing the experience of violent death with Septimus, Clarissa experiences a sudden and powerful synthesis of the dialectic between *Eros* and *Thanatos*. She becomes "violently" alive: "He made her feel the beauty; made her feel the fun" (p. 284). Septimus' suicide ennobles the pain and therefore the beauty of living. To live becomes meaningful because it involves choosing not to die. It is just this pitch of intensity which Peter Walsh recognizes and responds to as he senses Clarissa's imminent appearance: "What is this terror? what is this ecstasy?" (p. 296). When Clarissa does appear, it is the unity achieved through a profound and simultaneous awareness of life and death which makes possible the moment of epiphany suggested by Peter's final comment: "For there she was" (p. 296).

Louise Poresky offers another way of perceiving this ending by comparing it with the mythical experience of initiation: "Mircea Eliade describes an initiation as predicated on a ritual death that involves the initiate's descent into hell. Septimus decends onto Mrs. Filmer's area railings. Also, as Eliade explains, the basic idea of this ritual death is that one life must be sacrificed for the birth of another. Thus, Clarissa emerges from her spiritual vision and rejoins her guests as if newly born into life."[67] And as Steven Cohen suggests, "When the end of a novel coincides with a moment of intense vitality, as in *Mrs. Dalloway*, the tension between the form's completion and the content's implication of perpetual expansion creates the imaginatively attractive paradox of the fictional experience." Our need for an ending, for a resolution, for death, in Kermode's terms, is jarred by this simultaneous reaffirmation of life, of energy.[68]

Woolf's artistic achievement in *Mrs. Dalloway* is prodigious. The uniqueness of her vision and her ability to clothe it in a suitable structure and style are clear indications of her genius. Insofar as this vision involves taking seriously the lives and concerns of women, it is a feminist vision as well, and reflects a way of seeing the world, a mode of perception, that is decidedly female. Her reflective, non-judging narrator, for example, suggests a consciousness which blends assertion with absorption and speculation. Even the point of view is allowed to float free, suggesting a willingness to share authority, to give as much credibility to the perceptions of others as one does to one's own. As Lucio Ruotolo perceives, *Mrs. Dalloway* suggests an aesthetic alternative to the forces of "Conversion" which impose upon Clarissa from every side. Clarissa's rich inner life acts as a foil to her collaboration with repressive social forces, representing a kind of passive resistance. By being married to a man with whom she is not passionately in love, Clarissa avoids the "devouring" aspect of love which male egotism imposes. And through Clarissa, Woolf advocates "the art of understanding other poeple's lives and minds," as opposed to the patriarchal Western tendency "to proselytize and convert."[69]

While patriarchy is clearly viewed as an evil and destructive force throughout the novels and is investigated in great detail in both its personal and public manifestations, Woolf's skill is such that we rarely, if ever, feel preached at. And for the most part, Woolf's themes are the little daily occurrences, the small, private domestic events which are elevated and released from the judgment of triviality with which they are usually invested. This fascination with the daily private lives of women as opposed to the grand dramatic incidents around which the traditional novel revolves again reveals a feminist consciousness. What Woolf considers important and significant is very different from what the prevailing power structure would judge to be so. That Woolf is able to incorporate this feminist vision so successfully into her novels is in large part due to the skill with which she is able to transform opinion into vision, ideology into aesthetic. What she has to tell us, as a feminist, is not simply incorporated into the content of her work, but is embedded in the very structure of the narrative itself. The variety of techniques by which this process occurs is notable. That some of these strategies imitate the work of dreams indicates the subtlety and sophistication of Woolf's skill. Some of the processes by which we protect ourselves from ourselves in life—sublimation, condensation, transference, displacement—complicated processes for which we have only recently had names—are mirrored in Woolf's fiction with uncommon sophistication. The associative, non-linear structure of her novels which replaces plot, the floating point of view, the tentative narrator, the fascination with perception rather than event, the free, non-periodic rush of her sentences: all these characteristics and many more contribute to the embodiment of a vision which is both feminine and feminist in a form and structure perfectly suited to its expression.

V Orlando

> But almost any biographer, if he respects
> facts, can give us much more than another fact
> to add to our collection. He can give us the
> creative fact; the fact that suggests and en-
> genders. Of this, too, there is certain proof.
> For how often, when a biography is read and
> tossed aside, some scene remains bright, some
> figure lives on in the depths of the mind, and
> causes us, when we read a poem or novel, to
> feel a start of recognition, as if we remem-
> bered something that we had known before.
> (Virginia Woolf
> "The Art of Biography")

Orlando is a wonderfully amusing but difficult book, and an anomaly. Nothing quite like it has been written before or since, and consequently it is hard to categorize generically. Is it a biography, a novel, a prose poem? On the title page, we are told it is a biography, and in fact, Woolf lost a good deal of money because booksellers refused to place it on the fiction shelf. But the book conforms to biographical conventions in other ways as well. The narrator offers us the story, in chronological order, of Orlando's life and often refers to the trouble she (or he) is having finding satisfactory documentary evidence. We are never allowed to forget, really, the struggling biographer's presence and may be reminded of a rather similar narrative stance in Carlyle's *Sartor Resartus*.

Certainly, the fact that Orlando's life spans several hundred years, from about 1570 to 1928, through a change of sex, a wife, a husband, and a career in diplomacy and literature, should be a cue that the biographical tradition is also being mocked. In fact, throughout her career Woolf was inclined to think the whole notion of biography absurd, since the essence of a person cannot be captured by recounting "facts," and she expresses that opinion quite frequently in her letters, diaries, and essays. In *Night and Day*, by placing the burden of a biography on Mrs. Hilbery, who could not be more ill-equipped for managing it, Woolf suggests the annoying restrictions implicit in the form, and in *Orlando* and *Flush* (the biography of a dog), she mocks the tradition outright. Still, *Orlando* as "biography" does mark an interesting departure from her previous novels in that it presents an attempt to deal with character directly, and might be seen as a kind of mirror image of *Jacob's Room* in that regard. That Woolf herself turned to serious biography later in her career in *Roger Fry* indicates an ambivalence about the genre which is surprising given the mirth she indulges in at the expense of the tradition in *Orlando*.

In essence, Orlando is a portrait of Woolf's intimate friend, Vita Sackville-West. The photographs which are interspersed with the narrative are all of Vita and her ancestors, and the estate in which Orlando lives bears an intimate resemblance to Knole, the ancestral estate of the Sackville family. Orlando's estate, like Knole, was granted by Queen Elizabeth, and Thomas Sackville, the original owner of Knole, wrote tragedies (*Gorboduc*, etc.) just as Orlando did. Details of the two estates are the same, although mostly exaggerated in the fictional account. Instead of 365 rooms (which Knole in fact has), Orlando's estate is granted 365 bedrooms. The servants' names (Mrs. Grimsditch, et al) are the same as those recorded in the Sackville family history. Vita Sackville-West's poem, *The Land*, which like Orlando's "The Oak Tree" won a prize, is quoted in the novel. Interestingly, the male line in the Sackville family ends about the same year that Orlando changes sex.[1] As for the title of the book, Louise De Salvo notes that in the ambassador's bedroom at Knole there are some late sixteenth or early seventeenth century tapestries by the Flemish artist, Franz Spierincz, depicting scenes from *Orlando Furioso*, which may have provided Woolf with her inspiration for the main character's name.[2]

It is also worth noting, as Frederick Kellerman does, that 1927 and 1928 represented a very happy period in Woolf's life, which is perhaps why *Orlando*, unlike any of her other novels, has its roots in Woolf's *present* rather than her past. Six days before the publication of *Orlando*, Woolf was preparing to testify in court as to the merits of Radclyffe Hall's lesbian novel, *The Well of Loneliness*, and "this was precisely only five days after she had spent a week in France alone with Vita Sackville-West." While *Orlando*, in its celebration of lesbianism and androgyny, is every bit as potentially scandalous as Hall's novel, Woolf avoids these imputations "by the use of fantasy and burlesque as well as by topsy-turvy chronology."[3] Woolf's account of Vita Sackville-West's life takes such liberties with "facts," and is so playful and eccentric, that her critics have had difficulty finding a foothold.

Orlando, then, has many of the elements of biography, but since those conventions are mocked at every turn, isn't it really a novel? It is, certainly, a prose narrative of substantial length, and Orlando is, at least on one level, a fictional personality. The details are *mostly* believable, and the central character certainly grows, changes, and attains a certain degree of self-awareness. We even have a convenient generic category, *roman à clef*, for a novel like this in which the central character is a contemporary historical figure disguised by a fictitious name.

One cannot but notice, however, that *Orlando* differs from the typical novel in a variety of ways. The subsidiary characters are not very fully developed and they tend to disappear and never return. Also, Woolf takes a good deal of license with our sense of credibility, as when she allows Orlando to hobnob with poets of two different centuries. Perhaps, then, considering the intricate and lilting rhythms Woolf is able to achieve in her sentences, and the way in which Orlando's consciousness seems to float from one thing to another, we ought to call this a prose-poem. Or perhaps it would be best just to call it a thing Virginia Woolf wrote. In any case, she apparently had great fun writing it. As Leonard Woolf puts it, "She wrote *Orlando* as a sort of joke, in a way; it was a sort of light relief."[4]

For the purposes of this study, it is Orlando's sexual identity (or lack of it), and the consequences thereof, that is most intriguing. Woolf had been toying with the idea of androgyny and its social implications from her earliest novels, but it was only with *A Room of One's Own*, written during and after the composition of *Orlando*, that she explored this subject in depth. When viewed as a companion piece to *A Room of One's Own*, *Orlando* becomes a fascinating study in the transformation of polemical material into art.

From the very beginning, there is something androgynous about Orlando. When we first meet him, his clothes make it difficult to determine his gender, and on many occasions later on, Woolf (like Carlyle) plays with the significance of clothes and their power to mislead us. Nearly all of the characters in this work are unstable as to gender, and Woolf seems to be suggesting that the sexual self in its uninhibited state is androgynous, that sexual identity should be a happy synthesis of male and female traits: "Different though the sexes are, they intermix. In every human being, a vacillation from one sex to the other takes place, and often it is only the clothes that keep the male or female likeness, while underneath the sex is the very opposite of what it is above."[5]

Still, even in the context of Woolf's celebration of androgyny, she is unable to overcome her intense ambivalence on the subject of sex. In nearly all her novels, and apparently in her life as well, sex seems to ruin everything for Woolf. It is the great "spoiler." In *Orlando*, sexuality is at first a very positive force and is described with a kind of relish and delight. Sasha, the Russian Princess, is ambiguous as to sex, but possesses "extraordinary seductiveness" (p. 37). When Orlando first sees her, his reaction is explicitly sensual: ". . . he did not know whether he had heard her, tasted her, seen her, or all three together . . . Orlando stared; trembled; turned hot; turned cold" (pp. 37, 38). For Woolf, this is an unusually straightforward description of sexual arousal. Later, she is even more graphic: "Hot with skating and with love they would throw themselves down in some solitary reach, where the yellow osiers fringed the bank, and wrapped in a great fur cloak Orlando would take her in his arms, and know, for the first time, he murmured, the delights of love" (p. 45).

The first indication we have that all is not unmitigated bliss is when their embraces cease, and Orlando's thoughts turn immediately to death. Extreme happiness metamorphoses into extreme gloom. "All ends in death" (p. 46), Orlando murmurs, and the connection between sex and death, between *Eros* and *Thanatos*, is once again established, as it ultimately is in all her novels. Soon after, Orlando discovers Sasha in the embrace of a common seaman. Although she is able to convince him that he was "seeing things," the ugliness, cruelty and deceit which Woolf perceived at the core of sexuality has been unveiled. Even though Orlando believes Sasha, he identifies with Othello as he smothers Desdemona in a performance which Orlando and Sasha attend (pp. 56–57). When, therefore, Sasha fails to show up for the planned elopement, we are not surprised, even though the downpour at least creates the possibility that she might not have betrayed him.

If Woolf was ambivalent about love, because of its inseparability from sexuality, she was in absolute horror of lust. In *Orlando*, it is the Archduchess Harriet, who later becomes the Archduke Harry, in whom the "vulture" of lust is embodied. Against his will, Orlando finds himself aroused by the Archduchess, but is simultaneously horrified that a purely physical erotic response is possible:

For Love, to which we may now return, has two faces; one white, the other black; two bodies; one smooth, the other hairy. It has two hands, two feet, two tails, two, indeed, of every member and each one is the exact opposite of the other. Yet, so strictly are they joined together that you cannot separate them. In this case, Orlando's love began her flight towards him with her white face turned, and her smooth and lovely body outwards. Nearer and nearer she came wafting before her airs of pure delight. All of a sudden (at the sight of the Archduchess presumably) she wheeled about, turned the other way round; showed herself black, hairy, brutish; and it was Lust, the vulture, not Love, the Bird of Paradise, that flopped, foully and disgustingly, upon his shoulders (p. 118).

Part of the reason, perhaps, why Woolf found sex so difficult to describe in her novels is that for her it was only admissable when it was interfused with the mystery of love. Sex in its simple, unsublimated form was for Woolf a thing of horror.

The note of genuine aversion in her tone when Woolf discusses lust is an anomaly within the context of *Orlando* as a whole, since the tone otherwise is one of light-hearted mockery. For the most part, Woolf refrains from attacking the objects of her satire directly, preferring to create outlandish situations which reflect obliquely on convention, exposing its absurdities. The character and experience of Orlando are good examples. In the first half of the book, Orlando's masculine gender allows him to pass through a series of adventures—amorous, political, and literary—which would have been denied him as a woman. We need only refer to Chapter Three of *A Room of One's Own*, in which Woolf discusses why Elizabethan women didn't write, to be assured of how lucky Orlando was to be male at this time. It is through these experiences, after all, that Orlando's character is formed.

The receptivity to experience and insight which Orlando's androgynous personality makes possible is brought into focus through Orlando's interaction with the poet and critic, Nick Greene. Nick Greene has all the flaws that Woolf associated with the rigidly masculine personality. He is vain, pompous, crass, egotistical, and vicious toward others in the pursuit of his ambitions. Not surprisingly, when we first meet Green he has nothing but contempt for his contemporaries: Shakespeare, Marlowe, Donne, and later Browne:

Shakespeare, he admitted, had written some scenes that were well enough; but he had taken them chiefly from Marlowe . . . Now all young writers were in the pay of the book sellers and poured out any trash that would sell. Shakespeare was the chief offender in this way and Shakespeare was already paying the penalty. Their own age, he said, was marked by precious conceits and wild experiments—neither of which the Greeks would have tolerated for a moment (pp. 88, 89).

When Nick Greene reappears in the Victorian period, he is remarkably unchanged in all the fundamental ways, although his critical opinions have been altered to accommodate the prevailing spirit of the age and he is now more clearly a part of the literary establishment, having become a knight, a Litt. D., a professor, and a critic (p. 276). Now that three hundred and more years have passed, the Renaissance is to be revered, and his old enemies (Shakespeare, Marlowe, Donne and Browne) held in the highest esteem. True to form, it is the present age which has no writers of value, particularly when compared to the "golden age" of the Renaissance (p. 278).

In a sense, it is Nick Greene's position as the symbolic embodiment of English culture through the centuries that allows Woolf to explicate, by contrast, her own aesthetic opinions. During the Victorian period, for example, Orlando reads something by Greene and realizes that critics in general seem to agree that "one must never, never say what one thought . . . one must always, always write like someone else" (p. 285). In this passage, Virginia Woolf reveals her own frustration with critics too blinded by convention to understand what she was trying to achieve in her experiments with form. In pondering this critical myopia, Orlando ultimately reaches the same conclusion as her creator, namely that tradition and critical acclaim are far less important than the successful achievement of "ecstacy" (pp. 287–288).

If Greene is the incarnation of the masculine English intellectual tradition, the gypsies suggest his nemesis, and by viewing her culture from this totally "other" point of view, Woolf is able to point out a number of absurdities. The gypsies view Orlando with a certain suspicion, but try to protect her feelings by telling her not to be embarrassed that her father is a Duke and that her ancestral home is so huge:

Looked at from the gypsy point of view, a Duke, Orlando understood, was nothing but a profiteer or robber who snatched land
and money from people who rated these things of little worth,
and could think of nothing better to do than to build three
hundred and sixty-five bedrooms when one was enough, and
none was even better than one . . . Nor could she counter the
argument (Rustum was too much of a gentleman to press it, but
she understood) that any man who did now what her ancestors
had done three or four hundred years ago would be denounced—
and by her own family most loudly—for a vulgar upstart, an
adventurer, a *nouveau riche* (p. 149).

The gypsies are also baffled and a little embarrassed by Orlando's hubris
about her heritage when "their own families went back at least two or
three thousand years" (p. 147). This obvious clash in values and all it
suggests about the arbitrariness of the things we elect to prize leads the
biographer to moralize: "No passion is stronger in the breast of man than
the desire to make others believe as he believes . . . It is not love of truth,
but desire to prevail that sets quarter against quarter and makes parish
desire the downfall of parish" (p. 149).

The bareness of Woolf's didacticism here is unusual. One can easily
imagine this sentence in *A Room of One's Own* or *Three Guineas*, but it is
disarming to find it here. It is, however, less disruptive than it might be
because it focuses on such a broad philosophical issue. Woolf is concerned
here not with a particular manifestation of oppression but with the nature
of oppression itself. Only on one other occasion, to my knowledge, does
the narrator make another such bald philosophical assertion and the
subject of this second outburst is the same as the earlier one. Orlando is in
a reflective mood, and although she is not a Christian in the usual sense,
she is musing on her spiritual state. In the midst of these reflections and
without provocation, the narrator slips in an opinion which exists quite
independently from Orlando's thoughts: "Nothing, however, can be
more arrogant, though nothing is commoner, than to assume that of Gods
there is only one, and of religions none but the speaker's" (p. 173).

The satirical mode in which *Orlando* is written certainly lends itself to
such overt moralizing, but in general Woolf is able to avoid it through the
skill with which she employs the technique of indirection. Orlando's
perceptions about the difficulties of being female, for example, carry

considerably more weight than they would otherwise since she has spent so many years as a man. When Orlando dons the cloths of an "Enlightenment" Englishwoman, she immediately begins to experience the restrictions of her sex. Nor can she get excited about protecting her chastity when she has had years of more or less pleasant and carefree sexual experience. As a man, she was free to experience the world in all its variety and to speak about those experiences freely. As a woman, she is forced to be perpetually false to both feeling and experience.

While the sex-change itself may strike the reader as an example of capricious authorial license, disconcerting in its absurdity, it is precisely this disregard for verisimilitude which allows Woolf to explore the full implications of gender imprisonment. Herbert Marder makes an interesting point when he suggests that the series of events leading up to the sex-change represents a ritualistic exorcism of patriarchal values. The ritual begins with the ceremony in which Orlando is awarded the Order of the Bath and elevated to dukedom. In Marder's words, "The whole spectacle . . . is a manifestation of patriarchal absurdity."[6] With the ending of the ceremony, a kind of uprising occurs which might be seen as a reaction to patriarchal political repression. When the disturbance is quelled and everyone goes home, a mysterious woman—apparently of peasant origin—is lifted to Orlando's balcony by means of a rope. Next, Orlando falls into a seven-day sleep, during which a masque occurs. Purity, Chastity, and Modesty appear and plead for secrecy about the mysterious event which is taking place, but they are banished by Truth, which enters to a flourish of trumpets. The parting words of the three feminine virtues betray their alliance, as Marder suggests, "with the repressive forces of 'boudoir, office, law court,' with 'virgins, city men, lawyers, doctors.'" Through the masque, these forces are exorcized, and the entire sequence, beginning with the pompous ceremony, illustrates a movement from repression to freedom.[7]

Nevertheless, although Orlando has been liberated from the tyranny of gender, the English society to which she returns has not. The roles of the sexes are rigidly defined, thereby forcing a disjunction between Orlando's true self and her outward appearance and behavior. Even her clothing restricts her. Unlike others of her sex, Orlando has *known* freedom of movement in the past and is considerably dismayed by her inability to run, to climb, or to play: "Her skirts collected damp leaves and straw. The plumed hat tossed on the breeze. The thin shoes were quickly soaked and mudcaked" (p. 245). Orlando's change of gender allows Woolf, through indirection, to comment far more vividly than would otherwise be possible on the variety of restrictions imposed upon women.

When Orlando returns to England, for example, she is immediately confronted by a passel of lawsuits. While it is to a large extent the English penchant for litigation which is being mocked here, the unfairness of the law as it applies to gender is also exposed:

> The chief charges against her were (1) that she was dead, and therefore could not hold any property whatsoever; (2) that she was a woman, which amounts to much the same thing; (3) that she was an English Duke who had married one Rosita Pepita, a dancer; and had had by her three sons, which sons now declaring that their father was deceased, claimed that all his property descended to them (p. 168).

By embedding her feminist message within the context of the absurdity of the English penchant for litigation and treating the situation comically, Woolf can expose the unfairness of the law as it applies to women without seeming didactic.

The difficulty for Orlando in being a woman is compounded by social decorum and illustrated in her relationship with the Archduke Harry. Orlando's role as a woman is to make the Archduke feel comfortable. The Archduke's role is to continue to press his suit even though Orlando has shown no interest whatsoever. Since modesty precludes that Orlando should show interest even if she felt it, the Archduke can easily assume that she is merely being charmingly coy.

At first, Orlando's hints that she does not wish to pursue the relationship are subtle so as not to wound the Archduke's vanity. Gradually, however, the Archduke's complacency and insensitivity force her into ever bolder maneuvers. When they play "Fly Loo," for example, Orlando openly cheats in the hope that she will so outrage the Archduke that he will abandon her. When he is finally forced by her ever more brazen displays to acknowledge her infamy, he is thoroughly shocked but soon wishes to forgive her, at which point she is forced to put a toad down his shirt (pp. 180–184).

Although the situation which Woolf describes here is wonderfully funny, it captures as well the difficulties of communication between the sexes during this period. There were so many things that men and women could *not* talk about to each other that conversation was inevitably stilted, awkward, and boring, and there was little chance of accurately determining the true nature of another person's feelings.

The difficulty in being a woman which Orlando encounters in the eighteenth century continues into the nineteenth. As Woolf sets the stage for the century, her use of concrete images to evoke moods and ideas is never more stunning. Beginning with the dark cloud which gradually gathers over England, in a very few pages Woolf sums up, through a remarkable collage of images, the spirit of the Victorian age:

> Thus, stealthily, and imperceptibly, none marking the exact day or hour of the change, the constitution of England was altered and nobody knew it. Everywhere the effects were felt. The hardy country gentleman, who had sat down gladly to a meal of ale and beef in a room designed, perhaps by the brothers Adam, with classic dignity, now felt chilly. Rugs appeared, beards were grown and trousers fastened tight under the instep. The chill which he felt in his legs he soon transferred to his house; furniture was muffled; walls and tables were covered too. Then a change of diet became essential. The muffin was invented and the crumpet. Coffee supplanted the after-dinner port, and as coffee led to a drawing-room in which to drink it, and the drawing-room to glass cases, and glass cases to artificial flowers, and artificial flowers to mantelpieces, and mantelpieces to pianofortes, and pianofortes to drawing-room ballads, and drawing-room ballads (skipping a stage or two) to innumerable little dogs, mats, and antimacassars, the home—which had become extremely important—was completely altered.
>
> Outside the house—it was another effect of the damp—ivy grew in unparalleled profusion. Houses that had been of bare stone were smothered in greenery. No garden, however formal in its original design, lacked a shrubbery, a wilderness, a maze. What light penetrated to the bedrooms where children were born was naturally of an obfusc green and what light penetrated to the drawing-rooms where grown men and women lived came through curtains of brown and purple plush. But the change did not stop at outward things. The damp struck within. Men felt the chill in their hearts; the damp in their minds. In a desperate effort to snuggle their feelings into some sort of warmth one subterfuge was tried after another. Love, birth, and death were all swaddled in a

variety of fine phrases. The sexes drew further and further apart. No open conversation was tolerated. Evasions and concealments were sedulously practised on both sides. And just as the ivy and the evergreen rioted in the damp earth outside, so did the same fertility show itself within. The life of the average woman was a succession of childbirths. She married at nineteen and had fifteen children by the time she was thirty; for twins abounded. Thus the British Empire came into existence; and thus—for there is no stopping damp; it gets into the inkpot as it gets into the woodwork—sentences swelled, adjectives multiplied, lyrics became epics, and little trifles that had been essays a column long were now encyclopaedias in ten or twenty volumes (pp. 228–230).

Woolf's attention to the vividly concrete and her complete disavowal of abstract speculation in these pages result in a passage which is remarkable in the brevity with which it captures the flavor and spirit of an entire age. At the same time, Woolf is able to portray the distressing condition of women in Victorian England without sounding didactic since that condition is but one aspect of the age as a whole.

For Orlando, the trials of being female in the nineteenth century are somewhat different, but equally frustrating. Although she has begun to find some enjoyment in the art of feminine wiles, "to resist and to yield" (p. 155), she regards with extreme annoyance the expectation that she should defer to male taste and opinion, however monstrous: "She remembered how, as a young man, she had insisted that women must be obedient, chaste, scented, and exquisitely apparelled. 'Now I shall have to pay in my own person for those desires,' she reflected" (p. 156). Through using a man's point of view to criticize woman's condition, Woolf's perceptions are given resonance. Orlando as a woman, having been a man, is stunned by the ridiculousness of the sexes in their rigidly defined roles. Everyone has a conception about her as a lady which has nothing to do with the reality of her being (p. 162). In her bafflement and desire to be accepted by those around her, Orlando's spirit is ultimately broken and she becomes, for a time, helpless, timid, and forlorn (pp. 244–247).

Still, not all of what happens to Orlando as a woman is negative. The sexual polarization which her male identity created forced the women she encountered into preconceived roles, thus hampering open communication and understanding. As a woman, Orlando gains new insight into why women behave as they do and finds, in consequence, that she loves Sasha even more deeply than she did as a man (p. 161).

At one point, Orlando dresses as a man and accompanies a prostitute to her room off Leicester Square. The "feminine wiles" which this prostitute adopts in order to charm Orlando fall flat, since Orlando the woman recognizes their insincerity. When, however, the prostitute discovers Orlando's sex, she laughs heartily and immediately drops this falseness of manner, thus allowing Woolf to make a point about the hypocrisy which sexual polarization imposes.

That Orlando finally resolves her uneasiness in the feminine role by changing clothes frequently and appearing in the world sometimes as a man and sometimes as a woman is certainly important, particularly since some of these encounters clearly have sexual implications (pp. 220–222). Aside from the obvious approval with which Woolf views androgyny, she seems to indicate an approval of bisexuality as well. By using the metaphor of "changing clothes," Woolf is able to support the idea of bisexuality without naming it as such.

It is in the union of Orlando and Marmaduke Bonthrop Shelmardine, however, that the tensions of the novel are resolved. Both are androgynous—and therefore harmonious—because each understands the other sex intuitively. Their first meeting is one of ecstatic recognition:

"You're a woman, Shel!" she cried.
"You're a man, Orlando!" he cried (p. 252).

Paradoxically, this confusion of gender causes Orlando to feel more fully female: "I am a woman," she thought, "a real woman, at last" (p. 253). And a little later, in their next confrontation, Orlando and Shelmardine continue to be amazed at their compatibility: "For each was so surprised at the quickness of the other's sympathy, and it was to each such a revelation that a woman could be as tolerant and free-spoken as a man, and a man as strange and subtle as a woman, that they had to put the matter to proof at once" (p. 258). With their marriage, Orlando and Shelmardine are, it appears, set to live happily ever after in the bliss of androgynous equilibrium.

As usual, however, Woolf becomes ever more elusive as her narrative moves toward conclusion. In place of verbal resolution, Woolf offers up vivid concrete images to which she clearly attaches a whole complex of meanings. For example, the reader is offered a vision of Orlando bare-breasted before the moon, her pearls gleaming in the light, with Shel at her side and a wild goose springing into the air. This type of ending is characteristic of Woolf. Whereas the traditional novel tends to pull everything in at the end, to resolve conflict and achieve stasis, Woolf's novels offer instead a kind of explosive mystical expansion, rather like the effect achieved by sophisticated fireworks which blaze outward in a series of efflorescences. In ending her novels this way, Woolf offers a "female" alternative to the male tradition of closure. Woolf's objective in these endings seems to be to encourage the reader away from logical, rational resolution and toward a mystical, subconscious understanding, an epiphany of sorts.

Another such image is that of the oak tree, which has surfaced periodically throughout the novel. We have no way of pinning down what the oak tree stands for, what it "means," and yet it functions to anchor the narrative at various points, giving shape to events in the same way that tent pegs function to shape a tent. The oak tree is a constant throughout the three hundred and fifty years which Orlando's life spans, while few other things are. Perhaps even more importantly, the one literary creation which Orlando retains during the ages, which *lasts*, is called "The Oak Tree." That this manuscript is given a symbolic burial at the end of the novel on the top of a hill in the roots of the "actual" oak tree suggests some kind of mystic resolution between nature and art.

The "nature" of art is in fact a major theme in this novel. By making Orlando a writer, Woolf is able to comment, indirectly, on her own difficulties in defining herself against literary tradition:

> Anyone moderately familiar with the rigours of composition will not need to be told the story in detail; how he wrote and it seemed good; read and it seemed vile; corrected and tore up; cut out; put in; was in ecstacy; in despair; had his good nights and bad mornings; snatched at ideas and lost them; saw his book plain before him and it vanished; acted his people's parts as he ate; mouthed them as he walked; now cried; now laughed; vacillated between this style and that; now preferred the heroic and pompous; next the plain and simple; now the vales of Tempe; then the fields of Kent or Cornwall; and could not decide whether he was the divinest genius or the greatest fool in the world (p. 82).

Woolf's narrative stance here is interesting in that we sense the biographer's sympathetic identification with her subject. This breakdown in narrative distance and the effect it has of uniting the subjective with the objective suggests a feminist revision of the biographical tradition. Instead of the detached, objective biographer who is committed to never deviating from the facts, Woolf's biographer empathizes with her subject, speculates on implications and becomes emotionally involved in Orlando's experiences.

Both Orlando and his biographer are deeply engaged, for example, in the attempt to understand the relationship between fact and truth. The biographer, in order to capture the "truth" about Orlando, must move beyond the mere facts to metaphor, and Orlando, as a literary artist, must determine how "free" metaphor can be if it is to remain true to the reality it is meant to evoke:

> "The sky is blue," he said, "the grass is green." Looking up, he saw that, on the contrary, the sky is like the veils which a thousand Madonnas have let fall from their hair; and the grass fleets and darkens like a flight of girls fleeing the embrace of hairy satyrs from enchanted woods. "Upon my word," he said (for he had fallen into the bad habit of speaking aloud), "I don't see that one's more true than another. Both are utterly false" (p. 102).

Orlando's dilemma is also a comment, of course, on Woolf's own difficulties as a literary artist. The tension between the force of literary tradition and the need for a new mode of expression was a persistent challenge to Woolf throughout her career. In *Orlando*, Woolf suggests both the strength of tradition and the fickleness of taste through the endless revision which Orlando's "Oak Tree" must undergo with changes in literary style. When Orlando finds himself under the influence of Sir Thomas Browne, Orlando's experience begins to be recounted in perfect Brownesian style. We are even offered a discourse on the function of memory which one would not be surprised to encounter verbatim in the pages of *Religio Medici* (pp. 78 ff). The importance which Woolf assigns to style and the way in which it determines how we "see" reality is suggested by Orlando's perception upon entering the eighteenth century that "the very landscape outside was less stuck about with garlands and the briers themselves were less thorned and intricate" (p. 113). Clearly, our notion of reality is not determined by what we see but how we see it.

As Jean Guiguet asks, "How, then, are we to judge this book, so intimate and yet so external? If we remain on the purely literary plane we shall see nothing but the artifice, the 'fabulous tapestries.' And *Orlando*, considered thus, is too contrived a book. If the author follows her whim, its wayward wanderings are too cunningly traced, and it seems deliberately devised to mystify the reader, even though it frequently instructs while it entertains him . . . it must be admitted that *Orlando* becomes an esoteric work which can only yield its whole secret to a handful of initiates."[8]

Guiguet is perhaps correct in asserting that certain elements in *Orlando* are too intimate, too deliberately mystifying, to be appreciated by the average reader. But as James Naremore asserts, "Ultimately, *Orlando* is as much about the inner life as any of Virginia Woolf's other novels. The difference is that here she chose to represent a chiefly internal, implicit experience as if it were objective and explicit."[9] It might be fair to say that Woolf has succeeded here in merging granite with rainbow, fact with fancy. And, as Manly Johnson perceives, "The fantastic plot of the novel . . . has a diversionary function similar to that of the style: it is a scintillating, sometimes gaudy cover for Virginia Woolf's investigations into the serious matters of self and sex (both sexuality and gender), life and death, man and nature."[10] There is also some truth in Jean Love's comment that *Orlando* may have served a personal function for Woolf in allowing her to gain the emotional distance she needed from Vita Sackville-West by committing her to paper,[11] just as she achieved emotional distance from her mother by creating Mrs. Ramsay.

The resolution which *Orlando* offers to the question of whether marriage can satisfy a woman's emotional and intellectual needs, a question left unanswered in Woolf's earlier novels, suggests that she has moved into a new phase. Previously Woolf had been prevented from exploring new alternatives to old institutions in her fiction by her determination to avoid overt polemicism. In *Orlando*, her decision to dispense with any and all novelistic conventions which didn't suit her purposes allowed her to revel in all the exciting possibilities of a new way of living. In *To the Lighthouse*, Woolf, as Lily, has her vision: in *Orlando*, she celebrates it. Orlando is as well a liberating and delightful fantasy in which the problems posed in *A*

Room of One's Own are cheerfully resolved in the androgynous characters of Orlando and Marmaduke Bonthrop Shelmardine. The novel is not polemical because it has moved beyond that into a creative, fictional resolution.

VI   The Waves

The writer seems constrained, not by his own free will, but by some powerful and unscrupulous tyrant who has him in thrall to provide a plot, to provide comedy, tragedy, love, interest, and an air of probability embalming the whole so impeccable that if all his figures were to come to life they would find themselves dressed down to the last button of their coats in the fashion of the hour. The tyrant is obeyed; the novel is done to a turn. But sometimes, more and more often as time goes by, we suspect a momentary doubt, a spasm of rebellion, as the pages fill themselves in the customary way. Is life like this? Must novels be like this?

. . . Life is not a series of gig lamps symmetrically arranged; but a luminous halo, a semi-transparent envelope surrounding us from the beginning of consciousness to the end.

Virginia Woolf, from "Modern Fiction"

In *Orlando*, Woolf swam on the surface. In *The Waves*, she plunged to the depths. *The Waves* is a unique literary creation, daringly experimental in style, structure, and theme. Even more than *Orlando*, it defies generic classification. Woolf herself described it as "an abstract mystical eyeless book: a playpoem."[1] The focus of *The Waves*, if it can be said to have one, is the interplay between individual consciousness and the vast, impersonal, and irrational world of phenomena.

Bernard's vision of the "fin in a waste of water" is perhaps the central symbol of this book, suggesting as it does the mystical communion of abstract and concrete, the link between thought and nature. The recurring image of the waves, which blend and then emerge distinct, like the voices of the six characters, functions in a similar manner, suggesting the evanescence of the human attempt to create form out of formlessness. Woolf's ability to present, as Deborah Sitter argues, "both concrete and abstract truths simultaneously" is central. Our perceptions are altered by the coexistence of two states of mind—the factual and the visionary, so that, like Lily Briscoe, we can "feel simply that is a chair, that's a table and yet at the same time it's a miracle, it's an ecstacy."[2]

As Roseanne Rini has suggested, the movement of this novel thematically, structurally, and stylistically is governed by the dialectical principle of expansion and contraction. For the characters, expansion involves a process of moving out of the self—"shedding illusion and confronting reality"—while the process of contraction consists in continually re-creating the self through forging order and meaning out of chaos.[3]

Nature in this book, as in Shelley's "Mont Blanc," is terrifying in its potential impersonality, its complete indifference to human desires and values. The italicized passages, as Frank McConnell perceives, "present a phenomenal world without the intervention of human consciousness, a world of blind things which stands as a perpetual challenge to the attempts of the six monologists to seize, translate, and 'realize' their world."[4] The six characters, then, in a sense represent six attempts to breach the split between consciousness and the world of phenomena. Experience itself is chaotic and achieves form only through language which imposes an arbitrary design. Vision is mystical and wordless, and it is the artist's function to tame this vision within the universe of language. The effect, however, is paradoxical and ultimately frustrating because the act of translating vision necessarily undermines it. A "wordless" vision cannot be caught, finally, in a net of words. It is this dialectic between vision and the compulsive but ultimately futile attempt to articulate it which forms one of the central tensions of *The Waves*.

Through *The Waves*, Woolf was able to make a complete break with literary tradition. There is, in Woolf's own words, "no plot, no comedy, no tragedy, no love interest or catastrophe in the accepted style, and perhaps not a single button sewn on as the Bond Street tailors would have it."[5] The "unscrupulous tyrant" who constrains the writer—masculine literary tradition—has been vanquished. Nevertheless, Woolf's feminism in *The Waves* will not be obvious to the casual reader since it has become so fully submerged in the elements of structure and style. Developing a form in which her own vision of reality could prevail was, for Woolf, a feminist act. As Marshall McLuhan would phrase it, "the medium is the message."

The principle of dialectic informs this novel on nearly every level: in its structure, its themes, and its style. While much of the speculation which conforms to the dialectical model in *The Waves* is abstract and metaphysical, Woolf finds a concrete manifestation of this process in the polarization created by gender. That the issue of gender is significant is indicated by the fact that of the six primary characters, three are male and three are female. It is also true that the ontological strategies that each character develops for coping with existence are in some sense determined by gender. The male characters, for example, have their professions to cling to and consequently do not have to confront the potential chaos and meaninglessness of the universe as directly as the female characters do. Susan, the traditional wife and mother, has nowhere to go when she discovers the limitations of her existence. Bernard, who delights in fatherhood, nonetheless has a rich existence completely apart from that role. Louis shares with Rhoda a lifelong sense of alienation from other people and like her has difficulty maintaining a connection with the physical world, but Louis has his work as a banker to create a sense of meaning and value in his life. Rhoda has nothing.

The issue of gender is significant as well in Woolf's portrayal of Percival. For the six primary characters, this young, handsome athlete and soldier functions as a kind of "muse." Percival is conventional, fully conscious, unreflective, a hero. He does not need to look into mirrors. Frank McConnell does a fine job of summing up what Percival means to the other characters:

> Percival is a "hero" of acclimatization, of the at-homeness in both the world of things and the world of self-awareness whose loss is the creative trauma of the Romantic imagination. He represents in his self-containment, his absolute visibility, the sense which the other characters can never quite attain, or resign themselves to, the sense that "I am (rather than I have) this body" which implies that "I am of (as well as in) this world."[6]

It is, of course, Percival's masculinity that makes this ease and confidence possible. He may be a natural leader, but without the tradition of patriarchy which allows him a Cambridge education and channels him into roles at which he excels, those of the athlete and the soldier, he would be nothing. Susan, it should be noted, possesses many of Percival's characteristics. She is physical, strong-willed, stubborn, and essentially unreflective, a potential hero. Her only option for fulfillment, however, is marriage and a family. Although she pursues these roles with passionate intensity, the time comes when Susan feels "glutted" with natural happiness, and yet finds herself without options. It is during this period of crisis that she thinks yearningly of Percival and experiences a kind of vicarious identification:

> Sleep, I say, sleep. Or I go to the window, I look at the rook's high nest, and the pear tree. "His eyes will see when mine are shut," I think. "I shall go mixed with them beyond my body and shall see India. He will come home, bringing me trophies to be laid at my feet. He will increase my possessions."[7]

At another point, noting that "Life stands round me like glass round the imprisoned reed," Susan recalls her childhood adventure at Elvedon with Bernard: "We ran back panting lest we should be shot and nailed like stoats to the wall. Now I measure, I preserve" (p. 309). For Susan, then, heroism is confined to the fervour with which she embraces domesticity and the realms of memory and fantasy. The larger roles which she imagines are simply unavailable. Denied the possibilitty of heroic exploit herself, she must be satisfied with a fantasy of seeing India and with her vision of receiving trophies from its conquest.

If Percival represents a kind of complete self-containment, consisting of total ease with his body and absolute lack of self-consciousness, then Rhoda is his opposite. Like so many of Woolf's female characters, including Clarissa Dalloway and Mrs. Ramsay, Rhoda's body both imprisons and frightens her, so that she finds a necessary solace in moments of escape in which her physical being dissolves and she has a sense of merging with the universe. While Percival does not need to look into mirrors, Rhoda is terrified of doing so. The normal experiences of a given day are for Rhoda like blows of a sledge-hammer, for they force her out of the comforting realm of pure disembodied consciousness into confrontations which demand an identity she simply does not possess.

While Louis possesses a similarly uncertain and besieged identity, the necessity of pursuing a profession which his masculine role demands adds a structure to his existence which sustains him. Rhoda, finding no structure, seeks a resolution of the perpetual shock of living in death. Rhoda represents, in a sense, the quintessential female response. As a woman,

Rhoda's function in life is limited to the personal sphere, so that she is never called upon to emerge from her autism and act. Ironically, her suicide is perhaps the only act of will she ever engages in, and its function is to remove her from a world in which she had no role. Percival, on the other hand, is killed in that most masculine of activities, war, so that in a sense Percival and Rhoda can be seen as sacrifices to the roles for men and women that society imposes.

Throughout *The Waves*, each character is engaged in a quest for order which, as Michael Payne points out, "takes place concurrently on existential, psychological and artistic planes."[8] Sometimes Woolf illustrates their different strategies in attempting to define the world by cataloguing the varying responses of her characters to a given object. Thus, when Bernard looks at a willow tree, he is compelled to view it in abstract terms: "Its shower of falling branches, its creased and crooked bark had the effect of what remains outside our illusions yet cannot stay them, is changed by them for the moment, yet shows through stable, still, and with a sternness that our lives lack. Hence the comment it makes; the standard it supplies, and the reason why, as we flow and change, it seems to measure." Neville, looking at the same tree, sees, albeit with intensity, "a punt on the river, and a young man eating bananas from a paper bag." As a poet, Neville sees life in terms of sharp, highly-defined images, but his homosexuality and his obsession with imposing order on chaos also determine what he chooses to see, as he looks *through* the tangled branches of the willow tree.

Like Neville, Jinny is obsessed with the physical—with beauty, color, and sensation—but while Neville has recourse to the abstraction of poetry, Jinny must experience sensation and beauty directly, with her body. The process of aging, for that reason, is potentially devastating for Jinny, while Neville can continue to exalt in youth and beauty through poetry even when his lovers become less frequent. Despite her fear of aging, however, Jinny rejoices in the present moment and consequently "made the willow dance, but not with illusion; for she saw nothing that was not there. It was a tree; there was the river; it was afternoon; here we were; I in my serge suit; she in green. There was no past, no future; merely the moment in its ring of light, and our bodies; and the inevitable climax, the ecstacy" (pp. 350–351).

While Jinny takes pleasure and delight in her body, is totally "in" it, Rhoda perpetually seeks escape from hers, from the agony of identity: "Therefore I hate looking-glasses which show me my real face. Alone, I often fall down into nothingness . . . I have to bang my hand against some hard door to call myself back to the body . . . month by month things are losing their hardness; even my body now lets the light through; my spine is soft like wax near the flame of the candle. I dream; I dream" (pp. 204, 205). Thus, the willow as Rhoda sees it "grew on the verge of a grey desert where no bird sang. The leaves shrivelled as she looked at them, tossed in agony as she passed them." Rhoda's desire for solitude, for escape from the pain of identity, determines her response.

Despite these differences, the six characters whose voices we hear throughout *The Waves* are inexorably connected. In a sense, they are all facets of a single unity which has been momentarily shattered into fragments. As children, at least until Jinny kisses Louis and forces him to acknowledge her as separate, as the "other," they have a reassuring sense of connection with their world and with one another. As they grow older, however, their personalities become increasingly distinct: "Louis was disgusted by the nature of human flesh; Rhoda by our cruelty; Susan could not share; Neville wanted order; Jinny love; and so on. We suffered terribly as we became separate bodies" (p. 344).

All six characters undergo a crisis at some point in which their ontological strategies are undermined and threatened. Ultimately, each of them achieves a new level of awareness through a moment of vision, a kind of personal epiphany, which the crisis makes possible. Neville, whose vision of "death and the apple tree" has engendered in him a compulsive need for imposing order on chaos, discovers that he can see chaos and live; he acquires tolerance (pp. 312–314). Louis, who has spent his life suffering the pain of alienation and trying, unsuccessfully, to overcome it, recognizes the futility of his efforts and accepts his separation (pp. 316–317). Susan, the instinctual being, suddenly finds herself "glutted with natural happiness," but accepts that for the most part she is content (pp. 308–309). Jinny, the physical being, discovers with horror that she is aging, but in an act of heroic refusal to give in to age, she "brings the whip down on my flanks" (p. 310). Rhoda, who has never had a strategy for life, finds one in suicide. Bernard, who has agonized over the ephemerality of his phrase-making, his inability to achieve something of permanence, finds courage in his vision of the "fin in a waste of waters" which allows him to accept the overwhelming presence of death, of loss of identity, at the same time that it gives him courage to "fling himself against it."

It is clearly the case, however, that the crises experienced by the female characters are more fundamentally threatening. The capacity which Louis finds to accept his alienation is in part possible because his success as a banker has provided him with an identity which is self-sustaining, while Rhoda, who shares Louis's inability to "belong," has no socially defined identity to support her, and thus chooses suicide. Neville has poetry, Bernard has a job, a family, and a penchant for "phrasemaking." Jinny and Susan, on the other hand, are confined to the realm of the physical, Jinny to her body and Susan to her role of homemaker and mother. For Jinny, then, age presents a far more serious threat than it does to Neville. With the loss of her body's capacity to produce sensation, Jinny stands to lose everything that life has meant for her. Susan, when she recognizes how she has been entrapped by domesticity, must simply accept that entrapment. Her gender precludes, irrevocably, the possibility of a change in direction.

While gender is clearly an important issue in *The Waves*, Woolf is not primarily concerned with the specifics of oppression but with the quest for the undivided personality which oppression obstructs. Gender is an issue insofar as it represents a divisive force in the lives of Woolf's characters, but the novel as a whole consistently progresses, in a dialectical manner, toward a resolution of this conflict and of a variety of other dichotomies as well. The synthesis, in the Hegelian sense, of the gender dialectic occurs at those moments when, through a process of communication, the six characters experience a moment of unified identity. It is notable that these moments always occur when the characters join one another for a meal. One is reminded of Mrs. Ramsay's dinner. Personal differences temporarily vanish, and the integration which takes place suggests a personality which is complex but whole, at peace with itself and with the world, a kind of gestalt. And as Jerry Wasserman points out, when the characters achieve unity, as they do when they are perceived *by others* as a "seven-sided flower," they partake of the peacefulness of the interludes. They become a "thing"—complete and unconscious: "They become, as it were, italicized for the reader."[9]

In the final section of *The Waves*, this resolution through synthesis of the fragmentation imposed by gender finds dramatic expression as Bernard feels the personalities of the other characters merging into his own. First, Bernard experiences a flowing sensation, a merging with the others associated with death: "Was this, then, this streaming away mixed with Susan, Jinny, Neville, Rhoda, Louis, a sort of death? A new assembly of elements? Some hint of what was to come?" (p. 370). Gradually, Bernard loses the capacity to distinguish his personality from theirs. By attributing images and phrases previously associated with the other characters to Bernard, Woolf reinforces the evolution of this unity. By the end of his monologue, Bernard, who has always hated solitude, welcomes it. It is as if through a process of integration with the others he has lost his fear of being alone and has even escaped the compulsion to "make phrases." Like Percival, he has achieved, however temporarily, a state of complete un-selfconsciousness.

Throughout *The Waves*, Woolf's vision seems almost to be racing ahead of her, creating a sense of breathlessness as she struggles to capture what she sees within language. In reading *The Waves*, one senses Woolf's almost palpable excitement as she writes, but there is something vaguely unnerving about it as well, as if she has entered a level of perception beyond the normal confines of accepted reality. Miyeko Kamiya, a psychoanalyst who has studied Woolf extensively, uses Leonard Woolf's testimony to find a correlation between Woolf's creative genius and the periods of mental breakdown which plagued her:

> "I am quite sure," states her husband, "that Virginia's genius was closely connected with what manifested itself as mental instability and insanity. The creative imagination in her novels, her ability to 'leave the ground' in conversation, and the voluble delusions of the breakdowns all came from the same place in her mind." And quoting from her diary of Feb. 7, 1931, he goes on to say, "Here surely is an exact description of genius and madness, showing how terrifyingly thin is the fabric of thought often separating the one from the other." The entry he refers to runs as follows in the diary: ". . . having reeled across the last ten pages [of *The Waves*] with some moments of such intensity and intoxication that I seemed only to stumble after my voice, or almost, after some sort of speaker (as when I was mad) I was almost afraid, remembering the voices that used to fly ahead."[10]

Despite this sense that Woolf is racing after herself in this novel, she did have a plan. In her "notes" for *The Waves*, she makes the following comment: "I have never been able to 'see' for long: hence I only make phrases. That the novel changed when the perspective changed: And I'm not a preacher."[11] Although these notes are somewhat incoherent, it is clear that she felt modern consciousness required a new, more appropriate form for its expression. Given that she did not share the perspective of her Victorian predecessors, she could not share their methods in the art of fiction. As if further to reinforce her determination to break with tradition, she adds, "And I'm not a preacher."

Unlike her father, Leslie Stephen, who insisted upon the morality of literature, Virginia Woolf shunned didacticism and dedicated herself to the attempt to convey moments of vision. Her method for doing so involved a non-linear, almost non-narrative approach. Like a poet, who for the most part is also trying to impart a vision, Woolf's unit is the phrase. "Moments of being" are too evanescent to be contained within sentences, paragraphs, or chapters.

To an extent, then, we are to see Bernard's penchant for phrase-making as a positive value, despite the fact that he seems unable to finish anything or make his living as a writer. Of course the effect of phrase-making is ultimately paradoxical. While it is absolutely necessary to the communication of a vision, it also defeats itself, as it does after the characters share a moment of communion in remembering Percival: "So the sincerity of the moment passed; so it became symbolical; and that I could not stand. Let us commit any blasphemy of laughter and criticism rather than exude this lily-sweet glue; and cover him with phrases, I cried" (p. 360). For Virginia Woolf as writer, there could be no more central concern than the paradox implicit in language, its alternating tendency to aid and then hinder perception.

But beyond this, Woolf's subject was the very nature of consciousness itself and its connection with the unconscious world of phenomena. She was fascinated by the assertion of individual human personality in the context of the vastness and timelessness of the universe. Any given voice, she seems to suggest, is likely to be submerged at any moment. In *The Waves*, she sustains a sense of this context of impersonality by linking the voices of the characters, as they emerge and recede, with the image of the waves. In her note for the "death chapter," she makes her intent clear: "It should be kept simple and large . . . the rhythmic design should dominate the facts. Only one or two scenes."[12]

This notion of the impersonal, timeless, all-encompassing sea, with its connotations of loss of identity in death, of a merging with the universe, recurs throughout Woolf's work. Only in *The Waves* and in two presently unpublished sketches, however, does it form the central motif. In "The

Pool," written in 1929, Woolf explores the fascination of looking into a pool and having one's thoughts blend with the thoughts of all those other people who have also meditated on its banks. The effect is rather like that achieved in "Kew Gardens" where a strange unity is brought about by recording the thoughts of totally unrelated people as they pause at a particular location. The pond becomes a metaphor of universal human consciousness and the action involves the submergence of one's own consciousness in its timeless reality.[13]

In the last fictional piece that Woolf wrote, shortly before her death by drowning, she returns to this theme with a haunting intensity. "The Watering Place" is set in a seaside town which is permeated by the smell of fish. The people who inhabit the town have an unreal quality, a kind of brittleness, like shells. These "shells" gather in a seaside restaurant where fish is consumed in tremendous quantities. Quite suddenly, the focus shifts to the Ladies Lavatory, where two women are talking. Their conversation is trivial, sneering. But gradually, what becomes central is an awareness of the tides and the waves which have entered the lavatory in the form of the water which is foaming and receding in the sinks and waterclosets. The women, fish-like, recede into the background, are "swallowed" by the infinity of the tides by which they are surrounded. They are temporary; the tides eternal. This sketch trails off in an almost stuttering way and was apparently never finished.[14]

This intense awareness of the feebleness of our efforts to achieve uniqueness and leave a lasting impression on the world can be terrifying. The last note which Woolf wrote in her plan for The Waves reveals her perception of the pain and fear which are an integral part of existence: "How strange things are when we see them alone. Oh the infinite torture of human life . . . its passion . . . we must be [illegible] and we must do this and be that and there's no escape—."[15]

The quality of loneliness and of the ultimate futility of our efforts to individualize ourselves is reinforced by Woolf's methods of characterization in The Waves. We never see these characters interacting with other people or going about their daily routines in the context of work or family. This is clearly a deliberate strategy on Woolf's part, since it allows her to break through superficial qualities of character and evoke something closer to the "essence" of personality, the unconscious. Since Woolf associated this intuitive, ego-free response to reality with the female consciousness, her ability to find a form and style for expressing it is a feminist act. The masculine consciousness, in Woolf's view, was too rational, too ego-dominated to be capable of vision. This innovation in the portrayal of character can also be viewed as feminist in that Woolf seems not to be concerned with what people *do* in the world, not with what happens, but with what people *are*, and how, though different, they are united. Like individual waves, they are still part of the sea—showing themselves distinct and then merging once again. Character does not emerge in opposition to nature, then, as it usually does in the masculine tradition, but as one of its multitude of expressions.

It is also worth noting that although Woolf's female characters are locked into sex-determined roles and are not capable of the kind of balanced synthesis which Bernard is able to achieve, they are nonetheless complete in themselves, so that their identities are evolved for us completely without reference to their associations with men. Very few novels in the history of literature so completely disavow the centrality of relations with the opposite sex in exploring female character and experience. Even in novels by women, the lives of female characters are rarely explored with such respect for the wholeness they encompass completely apart from relations with men.

The monologues of *The Waves*, as Phyllis Rose points out, are not "interior monologues" of the sort that depict "a temporal flow and seek to follow the movement of the mind from one thing to another. The monologues in *The Waves* seek to define mental spaces, the structures habitually imposed on experience."[16] In a brilliant essay on Woolf's stylistic innovations in *The Waves*, J. W. Graham explores some of the ways in which she reinforces this sense of small but heroic voices in the wilderness of infinity. For most of the novel, the characters speak in the "pure present" tense ("I go," etc.). As Graham points out, this is an unnatural form for speech or thought, which usually consists in the progressive form ("I am going"). Typically, the pure present is used only in two instances: to indicate an action which is external but with no fixed location in time ("I play ball" or "I teach"); to indicate an internal activity exempt from any fixed duration or location in time ("I believe" or "I feel"). It thus "creates the impression of an act, yet suspends the sense of time in regard to it." This tense, when employed instead of the progressive present, makes acts seem momentary: they "recede into the past even as they occur."[17] The passage evoking Susan's early adult life in the country is a good example:

> I go then to the cupboard, and take the damp bags of rich sultanas; I lift the heavy flour onto the clean scrubbed kitchen

table. I knead; I stretch; I pull, plunging my hands in the warm
inwards of the dough. I let the cold water stream fanwise through
my fingers. The fire roars; the flies buzz in a circle (p. 244).

As Graham points out, action is given an intensity out of proportion to
what is happening. There is a sense of urgency, of "scrutinized" actions.
This tense, which is often employed in lyric poetry, makes actions *seem*
past, while the awareness is present and important.[18] In my view, Woolf's
innovative use of the "pure present" also suggests a feminist revision of the
masculine mode of perception. The intensification of the present moment
which Woolf achieves by using this tense reinforces the potential for
moments of "vision" or "being" which Woolf identified as more commonly
part of the creative province of women than of men. The more usual
progressive tense ("I am going") suggests the tendency Woolf habitually
attributes to her male characters of failing to perceive the richness which is
potentially available in nearly any given moment.

The narrator, too, functions in an unusual manner in *The Waves*. In the
first version of the manuscript, the narrator is omniscient, but in the final
version, as Graham points out, we are left with only the vestige of a
narrative voice. While the use of the word "said" implies a translator,
someone who is at least reporting the speeches and who may also perhaps
be the author of the interludes, this narrator refuses to impose a point of
view, thus forcing the characters (and the reader) to come to grips with the
experience of the novel themselves. The narrative voice seems, in a sense,
to be speaking to itself, while we, as readers, are allowed to eavesdrop.[19]

Many of the recurring images in this novel derive from Woolf's childhood, from those moments of sudden "recognition" or "perception" which
are burned forever upon the memory. While Woolf describes her early
years as consisting largely of what she calls "non-being," or the "cotton
wool" of daily existence, where nothing memorable happens and one is at
a loss to recollect how a given day was spent, this spread of cotton wool
was occasionally interrupted by moments of shock, of sudden and lasting
perception. In "A Sketch of the Past," an autobiographical piece written
late in her career, Woolf recounts three such moments, and the third is
particularly germane to the character of Neville in *The Waves*:

Some people called Valpy had been staying at St. Ives, and had
left. We were waiting at dinner one night, when somehow I

overheard my father or my mother say that Mr. Valpy had killed himself. The next thing I remember is being in the garden at night and walking on the path by the apple tree. It seemed to me that the apple tree was connected with the horror of Mr. Valpy's suicide. I could not pass it. I stood there looking at the grey-green creases of the bark—it was a moonlit night—in a trance of horror. I seemed to be dragged down, hopelessly, into some pit of absolute despair from which I could not escape. My body seemed paralysed.[20]

The description of Neville's experience in *The Waves* is very nearly identical:

He was found with his throat cut. The apple tree leaves became fixed in the sky; the moon glared; I was unable to lift my foot up the stair. He was found in the gutter. His jowl was white as a dead codfish. I shall call this stricture, this rigidity, "death among the apple trees" for ever. There were the floating, pale-grey clouds; and the immitigable tree; the implacable tree with its greaved silver bark. The ripple of my life was unavailing. I was unable to pass by. There was an obstacle. "I cannot surmount this unintelligible obstacle," I said (p. 191).

Both the similarities and the differences in these two accounts are interesting. In both cases, the listener has "overheard" a conversation and thus is not required to put forth a socially acceptable response. While the adults have not been constrained by the impulse to soften the effect of the news on a child, the child, standing alone, can respond with sincerity. In both accounts as well, the apple tree becomes the objective correlative for the horror of death. Somehow, for Woolf, the "grey-green creases" of the bark, which becomes "greaved silver bark" in the fictional account, have a peculiar capacity for evoking a response of sheer horror. The image of the bark, which, though living, has a dead quality about it in its rough and brittle texture, suits Woolf's purpose very well.

In both cases, the listener is paralyzed, "unable to pass." In the fictional account, however, the point is not so much the child's sense of a "pit of despair" as it is in the autobiography, but the recognition of something irrational, "unintelligible" and therefore terrifying. The emphasis has shifted from despair to fear of the inexplicable, of the insanity and irrationality which run through life in the world, and which we try, not always successfully, to keep in abeyance. Also, whereas the reminiscence gives us actual names, Mr. and Mrs. Valpy, and a setting, St. Ives, the fictional account makes the victim anonymous and concentrates instead on an imaginative visual evocation of the suicide itself: "his jowl was white as a dead codfish." The effect, of course, is far more provocative. The actual visual impression of the dead man and the implied connection of his "white jowl" with the moon is powerful and entirely lacking in the autobiographical account. In addition, the presentation of human passion against a backdrop of the natural world, beautiful but entirely indifferent to human destiny, is an important recurring theme for Woolf. Although remarkably similar in content, then, the fictional account shapes the material to increase the shock value of the event and to emphasize the ontological insecurity which springs from the ever-present stream of irrationality and unintelligibility which flows through our existence.

Another experience which Woolf recounts becomes associated in *The Waves* with the character of Rhoda. During one of the intensely monotonous twice-daily walks in Kensington Gardens which Woolf was forced to take as a child, she experienced, inexplicably, another of those moments of "shock": "There was the moment of the puddle in the path; when for no reason I could discover, everything suddenly became unreal; I was suspended; I could not step across the puddle; I tried to touch something . . . the whole world became unreal."[21] In *The Waves*, a puddle evokes the same response in Rhoda. She is paralyzed, unable to cross. Always on the verge of disappearing, of floating away, Rhoda is nearly incapable of retaining a grasp on physical reality, and represents, in a sense, the embodiment in a character of Woolf's childhood revelation of the unreality of the physical world.

These childhood revelations clearly had a profound effect on Woolf's entire development. She had encountered, with a shock, a fundamental truth about the nature of human existence which was to lend its color to everything else she experienced from that day forward. She had glimpsed a piece of the truth through a tear in the cotton wool of daily routine. This "piece" of truth, for Woolf, was also part of an elusive whole as indicated by another comment in the same reminiscence: " . . . one is living all the time in relation to certain background rods or conceptions. Mine is that there is a pattern hid behind the cotton wool."[22] This pattern, it would seem, is never perceivable in its entirety, but is glimpsed by us only in very fragmentary form, in these moments of "vision" with which *The Waves* is permeated.

Perhaps because of the balance Bernard is able to maintain between self and object, reflection and expression, he seems to experience more of these moments of vision and to find them less terrifying than the other characters do. When he perceives himself as simultaneously "one and many" and when he has his vision of the "fin in a waste of water," he is transformed but not paralyzed. Bernard can flow out of himself, as he does on the train, later on when he hears of Percival's death, and again while he is shaving, but then return to identity with relative ease. It is perhaps for this reason that he functions as a kind of focus for the other characters, connecting them and ultimately even incorporating them. The balance he seems to have struck between being and non-being is apparently a healthy one. Still, even though Bernard in many ways combines and balances the tendencies of the other characters, his identity is not stable and definable, but constantly in flux: "There are many rooms—many Bernards. There was the charming, but weak; the strong, but supercilious; the brilliant, but remorseless; the very good fellow, but, I make no doubt, the awful bore; the sympathetic, but cold; the shabby, but—go into the next room—the foppish, worldly, and too well dressed" (p. 357). As Roseanne Rini points out, *The Waves* relies on this perception of Woolf's that character is inconsistent and cannot be isolated.[23] Yet there is a balance about Bernard, no one set of qualities dominating the others, so that he functions to stabilize the other characters.

Given Woolf's consistently feminist point of view, it is obviously significant that her "hero" should be male. As Bernard himself proudly admits, however, "joined to the sensibility of a woman . . . Bernard possessed the logical sobriety of a man" (p. 277). While these stereotypes may chafe, they do in fact represent qualities traditionally assigned to gender, and the point is not so much that these stereotypes exist as that Bernard, as a man, is free to assume those qualities traditionally associated with women if he so desires. On the other hand, the female characters in this novel do not have the option of assuming masculine qualities if they wish to survive. In a society governed by patriarchy, they are dependent on the good will of men and are not free to alter their roles. For that reason, they are denied the flexibility which makes a creative resolution possible for Bernard. Bernard's androgyny is acceptable; in a female character it would represent an act of rebellion.

The final section of *The Waves*, in which Bernard tells the story of his life to a nameless auditor, synthesizes many of the recurring themes. The quest for order in which all the characters are engaged is, especially for Bernard, a process of discovery. As an artist, Bernard has learned the value of a kind of "negative capability" and is able, in a way the other characters are not, to accept the contradiction and paradox which he perceives without feeling compelled to impose a rigid meaning upon it. Although he seeks out patterns throughout *The Waves* with his phrase-making, he never holds fast to any given perception but constantly yields himself up to new meanings in the eternal flux of existence.

In effect, in this final section, Bernard becomes the omniscient narrator. As he addresses himself to his silent dinner companion, the language of *The Waves* for the first time assumes a definite direction, a focus. As narrator, in fact, Bernard seems to function as a kind of mask for Woolf's own voice, while the silent auditor can, without much difficulty, be viewed as an analogous mask for the reader. By using this device, Woolf is able to disguise what is, in essence, a didactic intent, though her themes are so cosmic here that we are rather unlikely to be aware that she has a design on us.

The "message" of *The Waves* which Bernard imparts is more suggestive than determinative. For Bernard, the process of becoming an artist is synonymous with the process of becoming a "self," and it is the unfettered development of this "self," in all its potentiality, that is Woolf's gift of vision to the reader.

The first step for Bernard is sensation ("Then Mrs. Constable raised the sponge above her head, squeezed it, and out shot, right, left, all down the spine, arrows of sensation" (p. 342, etc.). The next step is the perception of identity, for Bernard connected with language, in which he recognizes himself as "separate" and becomes aware of the self/other dichotomy. In the third stage, a kind of unity becomes possible through the discovery of one's connection with others despite this separate identity, followed ultimately by an experience of the collective self, which includes both other people and nature in a profound synthesis of subject and object. It is this last step which Woolf seems to view as so central to a humane vision.

Woolf is apparently saying, then, precisely what John Donne said in more unabashedly didactic language three hundred years earlier, "Ask not for whom the bell tolls . . ." But whereas Donne offers us the perception itself, as a kind of bald revelation, Woolf seems more concerned with the process of arriving at this perception and the importance of doing so. When this resolution is reached, gender becomes meaningless. The collective self is an undivided self, and although gender creates the dialectical energy through which such a resolution is reached, Woolf clearly suggests that we view gender as a means and not an end. For that reason, it is surely accurate to say that feminism and humanism are, for Woolf, indistinguishable.

The quest for resolution in the collective self, however, is not limited to the dialectic of gender. For an artist, and I think Woolf encourages us all to be artists, the process involves a flowing back and forth between a loss of ego boundaries, a blending with the universe in moments of pure vision, and a return to the self in which the experience of vision can be "recollected in tranquillity" in the moment of creativity. The ultimate paradox, of course, is that in attempting to capture the vision in a web of language it is inevitably undermined by the inability of language to communicate what is, in essence, a non-verbal experience. It is the artist's task to stretch the boundaries of language toward a more fruitful communication of such vision. In order to do so, the artist must be both "open" and "self-contained" and must, like Bernard, understand that there are no "true" stories, no neat designs, no wholes except those we create: "Life is not susceptible perhaps to the treatment we give it when we try to tell it" (p. 362). As Roseanne Rini phrases it, "Diversity, inconsistency and disorder lie outside our arbitrary designs."[24]

Given this perception of the arbitrariness of the designs we impose on life, then, Woolf's departure from the traditional novel is significant. The classic novel, with its plot, its characters, its dramatic scenes and "realistic detail," is an illusion, a purely arbitrary form which had lost its capacity, for Woolf at least, to mirror reality truthfully. Just to take one aspect of the novel, characterization, Woolf had to find an entirely new approach. She believed that, in Rini's words, "To render character truthfully the novelist must include a multi-faceted consciousness, a consciousness that may embody many inconsistencies."[25] And as Jean Guiguet states, "We can readily recognize in *The Waves* that favourite subject of Virginia Woolf's: The unity and multiplicity of personality, in its relation with the outside world of things and other people. The originality of this work, the undoubted advance shown over its predecessors, are due to the total elimination of elements alien to that 'reality' which the author is seeking to express.[26] On almost every level, then, *The Waves* is in part a comment on the limitations of the novel in its classic form.

Conceivably, of course, this insistence that all designs are arbitrary can lead to despair, to a virtual stasis in the face of such inimitable chaos. Like Rhoda, one might choose to join chaos and escape the perpetual struggle to oppose it, or like Neville, one might choose to focus on the concrete and easily identifiable, blinding oneself to any truer perception. All six characters in fact represent more or less common strategies for structuring reality, and in that sense it seems possible to see *The Waves* as a comment on us all and by extension on the limitations inherent in our approaches to the world. Once again, Bernard seems to embody the most satisfactory approach. Although he recognizes that any attempt to define reality, any attempt to find meaning, is an illusion, he also recognizes the necessity of illusion. While it is possible, and important, to escape illusion in occasional moments of vision, Bernard recognizes that the truth he glimpses is but a fragment of the greater pattern which eludes him. We must have our illusions to sustain us during the period of time between these brief glimpses of the truth.

Nevertheless, although Bernard seems to represent the ideal synthesis of masculine and feminine, vision and illusion, the ending of *The Waves* suggests that even Bernard's strategy is ultimately futile. Finding "Death" to be his enemy, Bernard resolves to fling himself against it, "unvanquished and unyielding." The final sentence of the book, however—"The waves broke on the shore"—functions to undercut his heroic resolve. Bernard's decision to fling himself against death at the end of *The Waves* is both heroic and absurd; heroic in part because he understands the absurdity. The waves alone will last.

VII   The Pargiters and The Years

The psychologist David McClelland, feeling the need for a distinction between masculine and feminine personality traits that would not be prejudicial to the feminine (as, for example, the oppositions active-passive, independent-dependent are prejudicial), devised an experiment employing two sets of geometrical forms in one of which the figures were closed and in the other open, with their parts unconnected. McClelland found that by and large men preferred the closed forms and women the open ones, and from this geometrical preference he developed a formulation of style: a preference for assertion, for the clearcut and unambiguous, a tendency to impose definite structure and definite limits, characterizes the male personality, while the female concerns itself more with context, prefers to draw no rigid boundaries betwen inner and outer, abhors the definite as a limitation . . . Invoking McClelland's useful formulation, one could therefore characterize the innovations in early twentieth-century novels as a feminization of fiction, and, viewing them in this light, one can perhaps more readily understand how the form of the novel presented itself to Virginia Woolf as a sexual issue.

Phyllis Rose
Woman of Letters

The Pargiters, though never completed, can provide us with considerable insight into Woolf's struggles as a feminist artist. Given her firm though uneasy conviction that the truth of fact and the truth of fiction were incongruous approaches which were fatal in combination, this attempt so late in her career to find some way of combining them in the same work is fascinating. The strategy she developed for doing so is, to my knowledge, unique. Short essays on feminist issues were to be alternated with fictional sketches illustrating their points. The six essays and five fictional chapters which Woolf completed before abandoning the attempt were later incorporated into the "1880" section of *The Years* and provide us with an interesting example of the process by which ideas are transposed into art.

The Pargiters has its roots in a speech delivered to the National Society for Women's Service on January 21, 1931.[1] In this speech, Woolf focuses on the dangers and shortcomings of patriarchal values for both men and women. To illustrate her points, Woolf transports us to the Pargiter living room where several young women are sitting in boredom, restless, but with no outlets for their minds other than the day's trivialities. As an explanation for this relentless tedium, Woolf points out that university education was forbidden to these young women, that no education meant no profession, no way to earn a living, and consequently no money, no experience in the world, and no independence. Virtue, and ultimately marriage, were the only achievements open to them. The unfortunate effect of these restrictions upon the sisters was to engender rivalry, concealment, repression, and guilt.

In her speech, Woolf blames this unhealthy situation largely on the traditions of male authority and fellowship which act to sustain the status quo. Everywhere it is men who make the laws and carry them out, who run the universities, the law courts and the state. In order to embody these notions in concrete reality, Woolf transports us to the rooms of Edward Pargiter at Oxford, where he is in the process of assuming his place in this tradition.

At Oxford, the old values are instilled and sustained in young men through education and a kind of male bonding which creates fellowship and a network of contacts which guarantee power throughout life. Masculine vanity is stroked and encouraged, Woolf tells us, and women's minds are held in contempt. Forced to live in abject poverty, Oxford's women are denied professorships, endowments, and even the use of the library. Oxford requires that women be chaste, sympathetic to their men, and unambitious except for their husbands' careers.

Perhaps to prevent us from being entirely disillusioned by this speech, Woolf provides us with the potential for a new way of relating between men and women in her portrait of Joseph Wright, an Oxford don whose great respect for women stemmed from his reverence for his poverty-stricken mother who worked long and hard to ensure him an education.

Wright blamed the oppression of women on St. Paul and worked hard in his own life to encourage women to assume their rightful place in the order of things. In his own marriage, Wright offered an equal partnership, one which would free his wife from the drudgery of the traditionally assigned roles for her sex. In *The Pargiters*, a character modelled on Joseph Wright was just beginning to emerge when Woolf abandoned her effort.

This speech, then, provided the source for Woolf's attempt to re-invest fiction with an overt polemical intent. Although Woolf originally conceived *The Pargiters* as an essay, a sort of sequel to *A Room of One's Own*, soon after she started writing she went back to the title and inserted the word "novel" with a dash before the word "essay." For Woolf, this was yet another experiment in form, so many of which had been successful. By using fictional sketches to illustrate points made in the essays, she would be illustrating how the woman novelist observes certain facts around her, forms opinions, and then transforms those opinions into the entirely different domain of art. By December 19, 1932, she had completed her first draft of chapter one, comprising six essays and five fictional sketches. Dissatisfied with what she had wrought, however, on February 2, 1933, she decided to omit the essays and incorporate all her material into the fiction. Ultimately, her efforts here became the "1880" section of *The Years*.

Not surprisingly, the intense polemicism of the essays is notably absent in *The Years*. In the attempt to remove any suggestion of didacticism from her art, Woolf added only a certain emotional charge to the description of her characters' lives and a complex system of metaphors and symbols.[2] One cannot but wonder, of course, why Woolf abandoned her effort. On the most obvious level, she must have felt that her attempt to synchronize the truth of fact with the truth of fiction was unsatisfactory, an aesthetic failure. But it is also important, I think, that her polemical purpose in *The Pargiters* required considerable candor and frankness regarding female sexuality, a challenge which she was finally incapable of meeting. This cultural demon, the one requiring that women be chaste, modest, and asexual in demeanor and language, Woolf was never able to defeat:

> The imagination has rushed away; it has taken to the depths; it has sunk—heaven knows where—into what dark pool of extraordinary experience. The reason has to cry "Stop!" The novelist has to pull on the line and haul the imagination to the surface. The imagination comes to the top in a state of fury. "Good

heavens," she cries—"How dare you pull me out with your wretched little fishing line." And I—that is the reason—have to reply, "My dear you were going entirely too far. Men would be shocked" . . . "You see," I go on, trying to calm her, "I cannot make use of what you tell me—about women's bodies for instance—their passions—and so on, because the conventions are still very strong."[3]

Woolf never tried harder than she did in *The Pargiters* to be frank about female sexuality and female oppression. That she ultimately found herself unequal to the task suggests the effectiveness of the social pressure under which she wrote. Although Woolf was a singular innovator in matters of style, she found herself bound by convention in her treatment of eroticism. Nor was she able to follow through with her plan for a straightforward fictional polemic directed toward enlightening her readers about the forms of female oppression. Her aesthetic sensibilities revolted against such obvious didacticism and forced her to abandon the project.

Because *The Pargiters* was abandoned, it exists only in the form of a draft which has the notable advantage of allowing us to view a work in progress, to watch as Woolf struggles to give fictional expression to political conviction. The differences in emphasis between the essays and the fictional sketches reflect Woolf's notions about how material was to be shaped and presented within a given genre. An analysis of *The Pargiters* can therefore yield some useful insights into the tension between Woolf's polemical and aesthetic aims.

For the most part, the essays function as a social and political critique of the events described in the fictional sections. As *The Pargiters* progresses, however, it becomes increasingly difficult to distinguish between the two. Perhaps because Woolf's ultimate goal is effective political and social propaganda, the fictional sketches function more as illustrative parables than aesthetic constructs. Woolf, who was if anything overly sensitive to these matters, must soon have realized the impossibility of combining fiction free from didacticism with didactic essays in the same work. In order to understand the evolution of Woolf's thought on this issue, a closer look at *The Pargiters* and its ultimate transformation into the initial chapter of *The Years* may be useful.

The first essay of *The Pargiters* introduces us to Woolf's purpose. Here we learn that her intention is to discuss the importance of professions for women, and that in order to do so, she wishes to provide us with some historical background. Chapters from her unpublished novel entitled *The Pargiters* will be appropriate for this purpose since she has tried there to give a "faithful and detailed account" of a particular family in the year 1880. Since her account is based on "thousands" of old memoirs, she feels assured of historical accuracy (pp. 8–9).

When we move into the Pargiter living room in chapter one, the situation is very similar to that described by Woolf in her speech to the London/National Society for Women's Service. We find ourselves in a scene of utter boredom as we join the young Pargiter sisters in waiting patiently—and, it would seem, endlessly—for the old tea kettle to boil. When the father, Captain Pargiter, arrives, we are regaled with tedious accounts of the day's trivialities:

> "Eleanor had her music lesson; and I went to Whiteleys"—Milly began, as if she were a child reciting a lesson. "Spending more money?" said her father sharply but not unkindly; "No Papa; I told you; they sent the wrong sheets. I took back the twill sheets and I got unbleached linen instead. They are sending them . . ." (p. 13).

This is the *roman verité* with a vengeance.

In her second essay, Woolf interprets this chapter from a social and political perspective. In doing so, she seems to move away from viewing *The Pargiters* as an aesthetic construct and concentrates instead on a historical critique. Woolf is decidedly not engaged in literary criticism in these essays. Her purpose is entirely polemical, and for that reason, the Pargiter family begins to take shape not as characters in a novel but as embodiments of certain historical realities. We are told, for example, before we have had time to come to our own judgment, that these young women "rouse pity and contempt" in us, and that they do so because "they are young and healthy, and they have nothing to do but change the sheets at Whiteleys and peep behind the blinds at young men going to call next door" (p. 28). By thus imposing a distance between the characters and the reader, Woolf forces us to see these characters as "types." Because the reader is not allowed to explore the Pargiter world vicariously, temporarily withholding judgment, the aesthetic experience is undermined.

These young women, Woolf is at pains to point out, are confined to the drawing room because they are not safe outside. And yet she is unable to identify the danger altogether candidly. She terms it "street love, common love, love in general" (p. 38). All of these terms, obviously, are woefully inadequate and misleading. Sexual harassment hardly deserves the name of "love," no matter how it is modified.

When Woolf attempts to make the experience real to the reader by using specific images, we become aware in other ways of Woolf's uncertainty about who or what to blame. She tells us, for example, that "to be seen alone in Piccadilly was equivalent to walking up Abercorn Terrace in a dressing gown carrying a bath sponge" (p. 37). The image is visually memorable and probably perfectly apt, but it shifts the provocation for sexual harassment to the woman who would be foolish enough to do such a thing and thus weakens Woolf's polemic against masculine sexual aggressiveness. Although Woolf resents the almost total lack of mobility imposed upon women, she seems to accept the inevitability of male intimidation. Her embarrassment about discussing the subject at all is obvious, and her language remains vague and indirect, as exemplified in her inability to be more specific than "street love, common love, general love." Here again we see Woolf struggling, unsuccessfully, with the second devastating caveat of the Victorian "Angel in the House."

Woolf herself may have realized the inadequacy of her treatment of female victimization in this initial chapter, for she never comes closer in all her writing than she does in the second chapter of *The Pargiters* to dealing with the repulsiveness of sexual assault. This chapter, and the essay which follows, represent as well the most successful segment in her effort to combine fictional representation with didactic analysis. Perhaps because the fictional episode is pure story, in the sense that it recounts a single episode limited in time, it does not seem manipulated by the need to function as convincing evidence for the analysis which follows.

In this episode, ten-year-old Rose Pargiter wants to go to the toy store so that she will have some ducks and swans she has seen there for her bath that evening. She is afraid they will be sold if she waits. Rose knows her nurse will not make a second trip to the store and her brother Bobby is busy learning Greek and orders her out. Finally, she decides to go to the store by herself. Sneaking out of the house, she races to the store, enjoying the excitement of being in "the enemy's country." She fantasies that she is on a "deadly mission through hostile territory." Suddenly a man steps from behind a pillar box and smiles queerly at her. She is frightened, but dashes into the toy store. On her way back, however, the man gibbers at her, sucks his lips in and out, and begins to undo his pants. Rose runs for her life, certain the man is pursuing her.

When she reaches home, nobody knows she has been gone, and though she is terrified, she knows better than to tell anyone. Although she is tortured by the recurring vision of this man and unable to sleep, when her sister Eleanor comes to her room, she yawns and pretends to be sleepy. Her experience is too horrible to share, and she is certain that both Eleanor and her father would be very angry with her if they knew what she had seen.

In the third essay, which comments upon this episode, Woolf makes the point that this sort of assault upon young girls is common, and then goes on to discuss its psychological effects. What Rose feels, according to Woolf, is a mixture of fear and curiosity, the sense of something secret and nasty which implicates her and makes her feel guilty and ashamed. In exemplifying Rose's confused reaction, Woolf shows extraordinary insight: the next day, Rose begins to observe her brother Bobby more closely and to hunt for her father's books on "Tropical Diseases," which are illustrated (p. 51).

Woolf sharpens Rose's dilemma by comparing her ignorance about sexuality with her brother Bobby's constantly increasing knowledge. At school, Bobby mingles with other boys from whom he gathers bits and pieces of information about sex. And, of course, he does not need to live in fear of being assaulted by a woman. When he encounters a prostitute, he learns something, but she does not threaten him. At twelve, Bobby knows even more about sex than his much older sisters, but he cannot, of course, share this knowledge. It would be unthinkable for him to tell Rose about the prostitute, nor can Rose tell Bobby about the exhibitionist. Consequently, they become increasingly estranged (pp. 53–56).

Woolf's account of Rose's experience and her subsequent analysis are skillfully handled. Beginning with the specifics of Rose's emotional response, Woolf then places this response within the context of a family with whom it cannot be discussed, points out her difficulties as a writer in even treating the subject, and then presents Rose's experience as emblematic of a much broader cultural oppression. In the process, Woolf musters convincing evidence for the pervasiveness, destructiveness, and injustice of masculine sexual aggression.

When Woolf abandoned her effort with *The Pargiters*, however, and set about to transform this initial material into the "1880" section of *The Years*, she made a number of interesting and significant changes in emphasis. In an effort to rid her novel of overt didacticism, she played down the obviously feminist issues, and built upon those scenes in which gender was largely irrelevant. Instead of opening in the Pargiter drawing room, *The Years* begins with a description of London and then moves to Captain Pargiter at his club and then with his mistress, Mira. Although we soon find ourselves in the drawing room, the opening scenes have acted to deemphasize the enforced triviality and boredom of the Pargiter daughters.

Woolf also makes much less in *The Years* of Rose's experience with the exhibitionist. Although the incident still takes place, without Woolf's convincing and well-wrought analysis it becomes merely one of the almost predictable terrors in a young girl's life. As Phyllis Rose suggests, "the overall impression we get from the book is of a tight-lipped refusal to elaborate, so that the past reverberates hollowly. As a child on her way to the candy store, Rose saw a man exposing himself. As an adult, she still remembers it. But to what end? Woolf scrupulously avoids all examination of effect, as though she might be giving herself away by straying from the facts."[4] In *The Pargiters*, Woolf uses Rose's experience as a nexus for a discussion of male sexual aggressiveness in general. In *The Years*, we are left, right or wrong, to our own conclusions.

With the third chapter of *The Pargiters*, we move to an entirely new setting, with its own peculiar circumstances and problems. Here we are introduced to Edward Pargiter in his rooms at Oxford where he is preparing for exams. Edward wants very much to spend his life at Oxford as a respected don and so works hard at his studies. Edward's tutor has coached him well, prescribing just the right amounts of study, exercise, and relaxation. Mind and body are being maintained in top condition (p. 62).

Edward has come to love and revere the sense of fellowship which his education has engendered. Sitting in his rooms at Oxford, Edward recalls his years at Morley, where he was surrounded by a network of male friends and distinguished himself as an athlete. He feels part of a tradition extending over hundreds of years and concurs with the Headmaster's exhortation that the unity of the school builds "fortitude, self-reliance, intrepidity; devotion to the common weal: readiness for united action and self-sacrifice" (p. 61). Edward's first year at Oxford lacked this fellowship, but he regained it in the second and began to feel ennobled by the magnificence of the tradition and the prestige of the institution.

As with most young men, Edward's concentration is sometimes interrupted by the urgings of sensuality. In this chapter, Edward is unable to maintain his attention while reading Sophocles. The scene between Antigone and Ismene begins to rouse sensual thoughts which he finds distressing and determines to conquer. Although his passion for sports is a means of coping with these feelings, Edward has not been able to escape them entirely. In this case, Edward's strategy is to idealize Antigone and Ismene, seeing them as epitomizing womanhood. This exalted thought ennobles Edward and allows him to overcome his lust (p. 67). When his thoughts then turn to his cousin, Kitty Malone, Edward's fantasies are entirely honorable. It is because of Kitty that he so desires success. She is his inspiration and his goal is to be worthy of her. When he writes her a poem, a love-poem, it is stylized and formal. The conventional phrases and metrical organization protect Edward from dishonorable thoughts.

Before leaving Edward, we are introduced to two of his close friends, Gibbs the sportsman and Jevons the intellectual. There is considerable animosity between these two friends in their competition for Edward's love, and this is flattering to Edward's ego. When Edward indicates his pleasure at accepting Gibbs's invitation to spend the holidays with him, he knows that a scene with Jevons will follow (p. 73). In the absence of women, Woolf makes clear, love triangles still exist.

Because the fiction in this third chapter of *The Pargiters* has become clearly polemical in itself, Woolf's analysis in the fourth essay seems more an extension than a critique. Her treatment of the issue of fellowship and its power, and of the male bonding which takes place during the educational process, could hardly be expressed with greater vehemence than it is in the fictional chapter itself. In discussing Edward's denial of sensuality, however, Woolf gains some critical distance by shifting the point of view from Edward to herself as omniscient narrator-essayist. In the essayist's view, Edward's capacity for idealizing Kitty is made far more simple than otherwise by the fact that they have never been alone together and have only conversed at a matter of half a dozen picnics, receptions, and so on. Edward's poem to Kitty is therefore bad not only because it is affected and sentimental, but because he knows virtually nothing about who Kitty really is. Consequently, "One may be sure that Edward's poem was largely a poem to himself. In his ignorance of her, self-love and self-pity were sure to enter into it . . . because Edward approved of himself for having conquered himself" (p. 83). As Jean Alexander points out, "All intellectuals in Virginia Woolf's novels have arid hearts and pseudo-relationships," from St. John Hirst in *The Voyage Out* to Tansley and Mr. Ramsay in *To the Lighthouse* to Edward in *The Years*, but "scholars are the most hopelessly inhuman."[5]

Edward's repression of his sexuality creates some interesting tensions in his relationship with his friends, Jevons and Gibbs. Whereas Edward's relationship with Gibbs is affectionate but shallow, what he feels for Tony Jevons is far less simple and certainly less shallow. In this instance, Edward's denial of the erotic component in his relationship with Jevons leads him to torture Jevons by pretending to prefer the company of his rival, Gibbs (p. 82). As Sally Sears notes, in the world of *The Pargiters* and *The Years* women eroticize freedom and men eroticize tyranny.[6]

Given the sharp polemicism of this section of *The Pargiters*, it is fascinating to see how Woolf set out to rid her story of didacticism in *The Years*. A number of changes were necessary. Nothing is made, for example, of the "great tradition" and "fellowship" of English education. And because there is no poem to Kitty in *The Years*, there is no comment on academic imitation and false idealization of women, except in the brief and relatively subtle comparison of Kitty with Antigone.

In the fourth chapter of *The Pargiters*, we are introduced to Edward's chosen, Kitty, and her family, the Malones. Professor Malone is the Master of St. Katherine's College at Oxford and is, in fact, engaged in writing a monumental work on the history of that institution. Kitty studies history with the homely, disshevelled, and decidedly poor Miss Craddock, for whom she feels great affection. Kitty perceives that Miss Craddock loves learning for its own sake and finds that inspiring, though she remembers her father's dictum that Miss Craddock shares "the inability of your sex to grasp historical truth" (p. 103). This sentiment is sufficient to cause Kitty to abandon her dream of becoming a historian.

Because of their position in Oxford society, the Malones are a very social family. Consequently, Kitty spends a large part of her time pouring tea for undergraduates whom she considers "uncouth, tongue-tied, rather pink, very awkward" (p. 90). Every day, they come to visit and often stay interminably, ignoring every hint that they should leave (p. 91). They flop down and leap up and don't know how to converse, so that she and her mother must always be filling up the silences with questions about their interests. Kitty, to make things easier, has developed different sets of questions depending on whether the guests are Eton men, Winchester men, or Rugby men (pp. 90–91). In truth, she finds them all dismally boring. Though many of them have gone on to become ambassadors, prime ministers, and so on, Kitty does not share her mother's feelings that she should be grateful for the opportunity to meet them (p. 92). Nothing, in Kitty's view, could be duller than Oxford.

One rather frequent visitor whom Kitty finds less offensive than the others is Edward's friend, Tony Ashton. For the most part, they discuss Edward, whom Kitty suspects is falling in love with her. Tony is far more at ease with her than the other undergraduates are, and Kitty thinks of confiding in him. There is something about Tony, however, which prevents Kitty from trusting him, something "snaky." She senses, for example, that he does not in fact like her, nor does she feel drawn to him (pp. 96–97).

Kitty's happiest days were those rare ones spent with Snap, her mother's nurse, on the Yorkshire moors. There, away from the stilted, confining atmosphere of Oxford, she was able to run wild, to milk cows, gather eggs, and make bread. There she also met George, the farmer's son, who rolled her in the hay and kissed her repeatedly. Though she had gotten into some trouble because of it, this is a fond memory which she often recalls.

In her essay on this chapter, Woolf pursues two strategies. On the one hand, she provides ample background information of the sort that a scrupulous biographer would gather. On the other, she simply makes explicit whatever material was left implicit in the fictional chapter. We learn, for example, that although St. Katherine's College was heavily endowed, the Malones have to be careful about expenses. Because of the endless procession of guests, Kitty and her mother have a great deal of work to do in running the household. Fortunately, Kitty's mother is an excellent manager (p. 107). She dispenses the budget judiciously and skillfully, and since she never receives a penny from the college directly, dresses herself and Kitty on a small income inherited from her father (p. 108). Professor Malone is never aware of any of the problems.

Woolf also addresses the issue of Kitty's sexuality. Because she has been trained in a strict moral code, Kitty has repressed her sexuality almost to the point of extinction. Though she fondly recalls the young farmer's kisses, she knows that was "an appalling crime." For this reason, when her young male visitors clearly admired her, or even proposed, she felt very little physically.

This peculiar vitiation of sexuality leads Woolf to address the question in her essay of whether passion is different in women than in men. Montaigne, she notes, says passion is stronger in women, but repressed. Tennyson says it is weaker. Much had happened, counters Woolf, in the years between their writing, to subdue passion in women. The passion of the Victorian girl was almost gone, having been extinguished by education and restricted by society. The economic position of women alone made illegitimate children unthinkable and sex itself was considered a "furtive, ill-grown, secret, subterranean vice, to be concealed in shame, until by some fortunate chance, a man gave the girl a chance by putting a wedding ring on her finger, to canalize all her passion, for the rest of their married lives, solely upon him" (p. 110). The chance of marriage, moreover, was precarious, given an insufficiency of available males. Kitty, because of her standing, would receive several proposals, but women like Delia Pargiter, though better educated and more intellectual, would receive none. Since sex was denied these women, Woolf notes, their sacrifice to the Empire was considerable (p. 111).

In the fifth chapter of *The Pargiters*, Woolf begins to shape an alternative to the oppression which she has unveiled in the previous chapters. She does so through the introduction of Nelly Hughes, the daughter of a poor man and Miss Craddock's favorite pupil, who is studying to be a doctor. When Kitty is invited for tea at Nel's home, she initially feels uneasy: over-dressed, over-polite, and entirely too tall. Yet she likes this educated, working-class family immensely. Mr. Hughes "ate like a working man . . . had no manners at all; he was by far the nicest man she had ever met" (pp. 131–132). Kitty is impressed by the mutual respect and support of the family members and is amused by the appearance of the Hughes son, Joseph, with wood-shavings in his hair. Kitty senses that this family would have supported her desire to become a farmer. They certainly supported women's rights and the necessity for women to earn their own livings. Kitty also feels confident about expressing her opinions. Even though they may be pounced on, her right to them will be respected and she will be spared Professor Lathom's condescension or Doctor Andrew's rudeness or her father's irony. For their part, the Hughes like Kitty very much, though they regret the way she is being brought up (p. 138).

Given the predominance of feminist issues, and Woolf's directness in expressing them, this chapter might just as well be an essay. Woolf must have realized as much since her writing here remains in very rough form, with few revisions. Even the name of the family Kitty is visiting changes in the middle of the chapter, from Hughes to Brooks. Woolf's obvious intention in this chapter is to expose the oppressiveness of Kitty's circumstances by comparing them with her friend Nel's. Whereas Kitty receives virtually no encouragement in her ambitions, Nel's family is determined that she will succeed, that she will not marry a working-man and bear him ten children in a Yorkshire cottage as her grandmother did. Kitty's response to all this is one of wistful envy:

Oh to be free; to be herself; on her own; to earn her living; to be a farmer; to dig and cook and bake with her own hands; to wash up the tea things in an old serge dress; and then to—the thought did strike her, though probably it was a very wrong and immodest thought—and then to fall in love with Jo, and be the wife of a man with a shaving in his hair who mended hen coops, while she bred pigs in Yorkshire! (pp. 147–148).

When Woolf moves into her sixth essay, it is largely indistinguishable from what precedes it. The essay is devoted to Kitty's reflections on the differences between the Hughes family and her own. Kitty wonders, for example, why it is so hard for her to tell her parents that she wants to be a farmer, and so easy for Nel. She perceives that it has something to do with Mr. Hughes' [or Brooks'] respect for his mother, who was not expected to provide "restful sympathy" to men or to efface herself. Still, she is puzzled by this attitude. Since Kitty has been taught that the laws of conduct for a woman are fixed and permanent, she is thrown off guard by so different a perspective. Kitty had been taught well the importance of striving to be an "ideal woman" like her mother. Without those qualities, a woman was nothing, and "the argument that was most frequently used in Oxford against the higher education of women was that it would unfit them to be women." Women who withdrew their knees from men's hands, or published books, or asked for money or privileges were met with "rudeness, with derision, with rebuffs" (pp. 151–153).

With this sixth essay, *The Pargiters* comes to an abrupt end. Woolf abandoned her attempt at the "novel-essay" and began recasting her material, dropping the essays and trying to unify what remained into what eventually became the "1880" section of *The Years*. That Woolf should have seen the absurdity of trying to continue with her plan is not surprising. Part of Woolf's great talent as an essayist is that she employs fictional techniques to give her ideas force. In *A Room of One's Own*, in *Three Guineas*, and in nearly all of her shorter essays, Woolf develops characters, plots, and dramatic contexts whenever she wants to drive a point home. It would seem that it was inconceivable to her to put forth an argument entirely in the abstract. For Woolf, ideas had always to be embodied in concrete reality, particularly in dramatic situations. Her attempt to create a distinction between essays and fictional chapters in *The Pargiters* was, for this reason, inevitably doomed to fail.

In Woolf's reshaping of the Kitty Malone material for *The Years*, and particularly in her omissions, her views on appropriate fictional content become obvious. Throughout the initial chapter of *The Years*, we are aware of Kitty's dissatisfaction, but it is rarely analyzed. Kitty's malaise is obvious, but we are not certain to what, exactly, it should be attributed. The Oxford undergraduates who wander in and out of the Malone parlor, for example, are not described in sufficient detail to make us feel how burdensome they are to Kitty. Nor does *The Years* include the quasi-friendship which develops between Kitty and Tony Ashton, so that Woolf's interesting exploration of the dynamic between a naive young women and a young homosexual man is lost.

Kitty's sexuality is in general de-emphasized in *The Years*, so that it becomes an issue only in her rejection of the idea of Edward as a suitor and her attraction to Jo, the young man with wood-shavings in his hair. In the *Pargiters* essay, Kitty's vitiated sexuality provides the basis for a discussion of the political, social, moral, and economic reasons for sexual repression in women. In *The Years*, we are aware only of the effects of these repressive forces, and even those are treated with great caution.

Although Woolf retains her vision of an enlightened alternative in *The Years* in her portrait of the Robson family [first the Hughes and then the Brooks in *The Pargiters*], her social and political commentary has been sharply reduced. Only in Kitty's tentative comparisons of the Robsons' views with those of her father and his colleagues do we sense Woolf's own perspective. Whereas all the other dons sneer at Miss Craddock, for example, Mr. Robson obviously respects her.[7] Although the scene at tea is dramatically effective, Woolf has clearly shifted the emphasis from the political implications of the Robsons' way of seeing things to Kitty's growing sensibility. Public outcry has yielded to private vision.

Woolf's modifications in her treatment of Miss Craddock are also interesting. While the relationship between Kitty and Miss Craddock is handled with great skill, Woolf carefully refrains from narrative comment on Miss Craddock's situation. There is less emphasis on her poverty and the contempt of the Oxford dons for her abilities. Kitty's fury at Miss Craddock's treatment has been omitted as well. In general, *The Years* presents us with a Kitty who is far more placid and accepting than the Kitty of *The Pargiters*.

Though we are struck in *The Years* by how boring life is in both the Pargiter and Malone households, the tension created by the analysis of boredom and its causes in *The Pargiters* is lacking. Although we as readers might be expected to supply this analysis on our own, *The Years* makes it difficult to do so. Woolf is so scrupulous in *The Years* about trying to purge her writing of didactic tendencies that she leaves us with a tedium which seems pointless. As readers, we must participate in the unmitigated boredom of the Pargiter drawing room only to leave it for the restive tedium of the Malone household.

Woolf's mistake, in my view, was the decision to turn this material into fiction instead of into a long essay like *Three Guineas*. Because Woolf intentionally constrained her imagination in *The Pargiters* to polemical analysis, the characters are flat and their lives uninteresting. They are like arrows in search of a bow. They have been fashioned for a particular function and suddenly find themselves in a situation in which all the ground rules have been changed. As Hermione Lee perceives, "The characters' reluctance to state anything other than impressions becomes, at length, frustrating. All are tongue-tied . . . and accumulated inconclusiveness has a wearisome effect."[8] The shift from the polemical context of *The Pargiters* to the aesthetic context of *The Years* is, in my view, largely an artistic disaster. A move in the opposite direction, toward an essay enlivened by characters and dramatic confrontations, would almost certainly have been a success.

It might be worthwhile to reiterate the genesis of Woolf's efforts with this material. Her initial intent was to write a sequel to *A Room of One's Own* based on the speech she was writing for the London/National Society for Women's Service.[9] Woolf entitled this project *The Pargiters*, although as her work on it progressed, she altered the subtitle from "An Essay" to "A

Novel-Essay." She perceived this effort, in which fictional sketches would be used to illustrate points made in the essay, as an exciting experiment in form. In September of 1933, she changed the title to *Here and Now.*[10] By the time she had drafted five chapters and six essays, however, Woolf decided to abandon the attempt. The truth of fact and the truth of imagination could not be joined in this manner: granite could not be fused with rainbow.

Her next step, then, was to remove the essays and combine the remaining material into one long fictional chapter which was to become the "1880" section of *The Years.* Woolf never struggled harder than she did with this novel and had grave reservations about its merit to the end. As she later said, "The real novelist can somehow convey both sorts of being [the 'cotton wool' of daily existence and 'moments of vision']. I think Jane Austen can; and Trollope; perhaps Thackeray and Dickens and Tolstoy. I have never been able to do both. I tried—in *Night and Day;* and in *The Years.*"[11] Often, in rereading the novel, she was thrown into the bleakest despair over how bad it was,[12] but then something about it would strike her as good and restore her confidence in its excellence.[13]

While Woolf was in the process of completing *The Years,* an idea was forming for another book, her "war book," which Woolf envisioned as "all the articles editors have asked me to write during the past few years—on all sorts of subjects—Should women smoke: Short skirts: War etc."[14] At first, Woolf did not connect this project with *The Years,* except insofar as she felt it necessary to repress her "preachy" side while she completed the novel. As her work on *Three Guineas* raced ahead, however, she began to be aware of certain connections:

This is the first morning I write, because at twelve, ten minutes ago, I wrote what I think is the last page of *Three Guineas.* Oh how violently I have been galloping through these mornings! It has pressed and spurted out of me. If that's any proof of virtue, like a physical volcano. And my brain feels cool and quiet after the expulsion. I've had it sizzling now since—well I was thinking of it at Delphi I remember. And then I forced myself to put it into fiction first. No, the fiction came first. *The Years.* And how I held myself back, all through the terrible depression, and refused, save for some frantic notes, to tap it until *The Years*—that awful burden—was off me.[15]

Perhaps the reason *The Years* was such a burden to her is that it wanted so much to be a polemical essay. And yet once Woolf had committed herself to writing a novel instead of an essay or a hybrid of the two, she had to be rigorously on guard against any urge to sermonize. Not to have done so would have been an unthinkable violation of her aesthetic principles. Nonetheless, Woolf's struggle to maintain aesthetic purity was terribly taxing, and perhaps for that reason, when she allowed herself to write *Three Guineas*, it came out in a flood:

> Anyhow that's the end of six years floundering, striving, much agony, some ecstacy: lumping *The Years* and *Three Guineas* together as one book—as indeed they are. And now I can be off again, as indeed I long to be. Oh to be private, alone, submerged.[16]

In Woolf's view, then, *Three Guineas* is composed of all the polemical material that had to be repressed in *The Years*. Unfortunately, the quality of *The Years* suffers from the exclusion. As it rambles on through approximately fifty years in the lives of its many characters, no philosophic or thematic thread which would bind the episodes together is readily discernible.

This opinion of *The Years* is, of course, not universal. Hermione Lee finds a philosophical center in Eleanor's chance reading of Dante's lines: "For by so many the more there are who say 'ours' / So much the more of good doth each possess." In Lee's view, "ours" is the alternative to "I": "egotism is combatted, not with the loss of self, but with the interdependence of souls."[17] Perhaps the most positive appraisal of *The Years* is offered by Jane Marcus, and it is worth quoting at some length. Marcus argues that the novel "should be *heard* as an opera for the oppressed, should be participated in by the reader as a modern ritual drama of purification, deriving from Greek ceremonies of the death and rebirth of the year, and at the same time should be read as a realistic anti-fascist novel of the thirties." As Marcus goes on to say, "Operatic, realistic, dramatic, domestic, *The Years* is for me, finally, the female epic. It is Woolf's answer to "The Waste Land" and *Ulysses*, siding with the despised Jews and women of Eliot, bursting with the 'content' she felt Joyce lacked to fill up his form. It is a communal and anti-heroic Odyssey with Nausikaa as its heroine. Eleanor, that militant but non-violent maiden, washes away the sins of a war-torn world. She rises from the tomb—"that Hell"—at Abercorn Terrace—bringing fresh air, light and water out of the Victorian gloom."[18] And in another article, Marcus maintains that Woolf was attempting to write a modern Greek drama in *The Years*, "with the chorus merging into individual heroes and heroines." By dissolving the individual and the authorial voice into the collective voice of the chorus, she was able to offer "a radical response to the aesthetic problem of writing an anti-heroic but deeply historical novel."[19]

Marcus's defense of *The Years* is powerful, sufficiently so to give this reader second thoughts. It is certainly true that many of the stylistic innovations which Woolf perfected in earlier novels are present in *The Years*. For example, the narrative strategy of a "chorus" modeled on the Greek drama, which Marcus discusses, was first used in *Jacob's Room*, and again very successfully in *Mrs. Dalloway*. There are, as well, many similarities with *The Waves* in the theme and structure of *The Years*. As in *The Waves*, each of the characters represents a different ontological strategy. Captain Pargiter is a thorough pragmatist. Edward finds solace in abstraction; Morris in logic. Martin, the youngest Pargiter son, finds meaning in momentary revelations of beauty and harmony through art. Milly chooses blind adherence to convention, while Delia finds definition in political activism. Rose is committed to the heroic and idealistic. Like Bernard in *The Waves*, Eleanor functions as a unifying force, binding these various strategies together into a kind of comprehensive whole, a gestalt of the collective ontology. No single consciousness dominates this novel. Instead, Woolf shapes our sense of reality as something collective, cyclical, reflective, and balanced—in essence androgynous and therefore feminist.

Woolf reinforces the themes of recurrence and the collective consciousness through a complex system of symbol and metaphor. As in *The Waves*, each section of the novel begins with a description of nature in which the various seasons mirror states of consciousness and yet also suggest a pattern of unity and recurrence. Other images and sounds—the crimson and gilt chair, the walrus, the cooing of the pigeons, the bells of St. Paul's—recur throughout *The Years* and function to connect past and present in a series of crystallized moments.

One of the most powerful and yet elusive recurring images in *The Years* is the "blot fringed with flame" or "dot with spokes." Woolf's use of this image suggests her remarkable ability to "condense," in the Freudian sense, a whole variety of emotions, incidents, and objects into a single concrete image. Like Woolf's lighthouse, this symbol is ambiguous and resists any closed and determinate interpretation. Instead it is meant to be suggestive, and in fact functions well to unite Woolf's various themes. On the one hand, it suggests the core of "self," the center of being from which one reaches, spoke-like, out to others. Yet this image is also an apt metaphor for the transformation of fact (the "blot") by vision ("the flame"). One might also see in this image the unification of the various characters (the "spokes") into a single radiating consciousness.

Another key symbol which resists simple definition is Eleanor's final vision in *The Years* of a man and woman climbing into a taxi. For Eleanor, the sight inspires a moment of revelation, of epiphany. Herbert Marder finds in this image a representation of ideal marriage, free from social and historical restrictions, a spiritual union of equals.[20] Surely all these things are suggested, along with much that resists definition. The taxi is a neutral center in which male and female can join together to fulfill a purpose without losing their separate identities. As a vehicle for hire, the taxi represents freedom and mobility as well. And the man and woman who use it illustrate the ideal androgynous union, one which combines partnership with self-definition and independence.

The elusiveness of this final vision is fully in keeping with the structure of *The Years* as a whole. As Marder points out, *The Years* represents an effort to "dramatize a quest" rather than to "manufacture a program." Part of Woolf's purpose was to envision "a system that did not shut out" and her strategy in evoking such a system was to portray the movement from a private to a public vision. Throughout the book, as Marder notes, her characters ask themselves simple fundamental questions about the individual and society: "If we don't know ourselves, how can we know other people? . . . How can we make laws, religions, that fit? . . . [Is] solitude good; [Is] society bad?" Unlike *Three Guineas*, which Marder views as a neurotic failure, *The Years* formulates questions rather than answering them. Marder finds that in this way Woolf is able to achieve her goal of incorporating "millions of ideas but no preaching." In Eleanor's quest for self-knowledge, she achieves not merely an end, but a means, an avenue for social change: "the private Eleanor can say she has had her vision; the public Eleanor, recognizing that vision as a means, must ask, 'And now?'" For the first time in Woolf's novels, Marder maintains, the public and private worlds are reconciled.[21]

James Naremore supports this view when he argues that Woolf was attempting to harmonize two kinds of existence in *The Years:* "on the one hand are the timeless recesses of being, where one feels a loss of personal identity and a communion with nature; on the other hand is the time-bound social world of day-to-day relationships, where people assert their identity and relish their differences. The difficulty presented in *The Years*—and by implication in all of Woolf's novels—is that the two kinds of existence will not "fit," partly because the society will not allow people to translate their private dreams of unity into public relationships. As a result, the characters feel torn between two worlds, doomed if they choose either one exclusively."[22]

Margaret Comstock puts a different interpretation on this dialectic between public and private by insisting that *The Years* is based on Woolf's conviction in *Three Guineas* "that the public and the private worlds are inseparably connected; that the tyrannies and servilities of the one are the tyrannies and servilities of the other." Thus, in her view, *The Years* examines "what it is in the way we live that props up customs or institutions of domination and slavery and lets us see what it would mean to 'live differently.' " And if fascist behavior involves submissive masses adulating a powerful, charismatic figure, then *The Years* is an anti-fascist novel, for "it has no center or central figure around which subordinate elements can be arranged."[23]

Despite Woolf's use of stylistic and structural innovations which served her purposes so well in earlier novels, however, *The Years* remains badly flawed in my view. As the book rambles on through a period of about fifty years, the reader becomes increasingly lost. It is nearly impossible to keep track of all the characters, to remember who did what and when, or even to maintain a sense of the distinct personalities. Although Marcus views this as intentional on Woolf's part and one of the novel's strengths, many readers will find the profusion of characters simply frustrating.

In the immediate Pargiter family alone, there are seven children who appear and then disappear periodically throughout the book, often without leaving any lasting impression. The difficulty the reader encounters in differentiating among some of these characters is exacerbated by the changes which each character undergoes over such a long period of time as the novel attempts to cover. And, of course, there are numerous friends, relatives, and acquaintances, all of whom "walk and strut their hour upon the stage" and then disappear, perhaps to reappear, perhaps not. Trying to keep track of these characters and their contributions is like trying to retain a lasting impression of everyone present at a large cocktail party. As Phyllis Rose says, *The Years* suffers from "Woolf's refusal to define a central character or to shape a narrative, while heaping upon us the kind of detail that demands such a shape."[24]

The Years also suffers, in my view, from its inability to escape its beginnings as an essay/novel. Its scenes and characters are the product of a political vision which is trying desperately not to be obviously political. The result is a novel which is tedious in its attention to trivialities which often seem dwelled upon to no purpose. In *Mrs. Dalloway*, Woolf transformed what we usually think of as trivialities into moments of dazzling vision, but in *The Years*, this transformation rarely takes place. In *Orlando*, which like *The Years* is inspired by a polemical vision and purpose, Woolf is comfortable with this intent so that the novel has an ease and grace which is almost entirely lacking in *The Years*. Nor does *The Years* partake of the humor and whimsy which make Orlando such delightful reading. Instead, as Josephine Schaefer notes, "The reader is oppressed by the mediocrity and dullness of this world."[25]

Woolf's own ambivalence about *The Years* is reflected in the diversity of critical opinion on this book. There are those, like James Hafley, who think it is her best novel.[26] Others consider it a thorough failure. Perhaps, as Woolf herself suggests, *The Years* should not be viewed alone but paired with *Three Guineas* as a single work. Theoretically, at least, that is an attractive idea since the lassitude of *The Years* would benefit from an infusion of the energy and purpose of *Three Guineas*. It is important to remember, however, that Woolf abandoned the concept of the "novel-essay" when she abandoned *The Pargiters*. Ultimately, any novel must stand or fall on its own merits.

VIII   Between the Acts

> Memory and forgetfulness are as life and death
> to one another. To live is to remember and to
> remember is to live. To die is to forget and to
> forget is to die. Everything is so much involved
> in and is so much a process of its opposite that,
> as it is almost fair to call death a process of life
> and life a process of death, so it is to call mem-
> ory a process of forgetting and forgetting a
> process of remembering. There is never either
> absolute memory or absolute death. So with
> light and darkness, heat and cold, you never
> can get either all the light, or all the heat, out of
> anything. So with God and the devil; so with
> everything. Everything is like a door swinging
> backwards and forwards. Everything has a lit-
> tle of that from which it is most remote and to
> which it is most opposed and these antitheses
> serve to explain one another.
>
> Samuel Butler, *Note-Books*

The tension between aesthetic purity and didactic intent which plagued *The Years* is entirely absent from Virginia Woolf's next and last fictional effort, *Between the Acts*.[1] This novel, which explores life as drama, or drama as life, or more particularly the fluid boundary between the two, avoids didacticism by moving beyond polemic to a vision of unity in the dialectical process itself. As we read *Between the Acts*, it soon becomes apparent that every quality implies its opposite: life implies art, love implies hate, unifying implies dispersing. Through drama, these opposites find temporary reconciliation in moments of synthesis, or vision, although these moments soon dissolve leaving meaning to be restructured in a new way.

As in *The Waves* and *The Years*, the characters in *Between the Acts* function on one level as "types" and might even be seen to represent different periods in the genesis of European civilization. Each character has a distinct ontological strategy for investing experience with meaning. Lucy Swithin's spirituality, for example, connects her with the Age of Faith, the Middle Ages, and allows her to perceive patterns which unify the natural and human worlds. Bartholomew's devotion to reason connects him with the Age of Rationality, the eighteenth century, and has the advantage of simplifying his world through the denial of ambiguity. Isa, whose thoughts often assume poetic form, becomes associated with a kind of romantic idealism which is characteristic of several periods but which reached a full flowering with the Romantic poets. Giles is a frustrated "man of action" whose reflections connect him with the pragmatism of the twentieth century. Mrs. Manresa, with her good-natured sensuality, embodies the spirit of the Restoration.

In developing her characters in this way, Woolf is able to connect them with the "history of England" which is the subject of Miss La Trobe's pageant. As the characters watch the pageant unfold, they see, in a sense, themselves. In order better to understand what the play reveals, a closer look at these characters may be useful.

Although Mrs. Swithin represents spirituality, for her Christianity is not a body of doctrine but rather a method, her method, for structuring reality. Although Woolf could not have entered very sympathetically into Mrs. Swithin's affirmation of Christianity, she obviously respected the charitable feelings toward others which Mrs. Swithin derived from her faith. In any case, Mrs. Swithin is far from dogmatic. Her philosophical turn of mind precludes simple certainties: "'But we have other lives, I think, I hope,' she murmured. 'We live in others, Mr. . . . We live in things'" (p. 70).

Mrs. Swithin is by nature reflective with a visionary imagination in which past, present, and future freely intermingle. At times, the transforming power of her vision becomes comic, as when she half-mistakes the maid for a mastodon (p. 9). Given the fluidity of Mrs. Swithin's reflections, the cross which she wears around her neck and frequently touches has a gratifying solidity and seems to function as a kind of bridge which makes possible a smooth transition between opposing realities: "Above, the air rushed; beneath was water. She stood between two fluidities, caressing her cross. Faith required hours of kneeling in the early mornings" (p. 204).

Mrs. Swithin's vision of the unity of all creation gives her an enormous power to soothe and reassure. She immediately recognizes in William

Dodge, for example, a man who is overwhelmed by self-loathing, by unhappy memories, by guilt about his homosexuality. Recognizing his distress, Mrs. Swithin takes him aside and through the power of her vision restores his self-esteem:

At school they held me under a bucket of dirty water, Mrs. Swithin; when I looked up, the world was dirty, Mrs. Swithin; so I married; but my child's not my child, Mrs. Swithin. I'm a half-man, Mrs. Swithin; a flickering, mind-divided little snake in the grass, Mrs. Swithin; as Giles saw; but you've healed me . . ." (p. 73).

The power of women like Mrs. Swithin to heal the wounds of the spirit and create wholeness out of fragmentation was one of the qualities which Woolf most feared would be lost should women simply adopt the male model for success.

If Lucy Swithin represents vision and faith, then Bartholomew, in his devotion to fact and reason, is her opposite. Their views of reality are entirely distinct. As Bartholomew himself says, " . . . she belonged to the unifiers; he to the separatists" (p. 118). Just as Lucy Swithin finds comfort in faith, Bartholomew finds solace in fact. Because the world becomes comprehensible to Bartholomew only through the exercise of reason, he has little tolerance for imprecision: " 'Are we really . . . a hundred miles from the sea?' " asks Isa. " 'Thirty-five only,' her father-in-law said, as if he had whipped a tape measure from his pocket and measured it exactly" (p. 29). Not surprisingly, Bartholomew is most impressed by the scene from the pageant depicting the eighteenth century.

Isa, who goes about muttering snatches of poetry under her breath throughout the day, creates a reality characterized by aesthetic sensibility and passion. Stifled by her role as the wife of Giles, Isa lives more out of this world than in it, so much so that she cannot even follow the plot of the pageant before her. "Did the plot matter? . . . The plot was only there to beget emotion. There were only two emotions: love; and hate. There was no need to puzzle out the plot" (p. 90). And yet, Isa later muses, "Peace was the third emotion. Love. Hate. Peace. Three emotions made the ply of human life" (p. 92). Isa's reality resists the rational ordering of events and of social roles. Instead, her thoughts, which tend to meter and rhyme, are governed by the flux of passion. Her reality is subterranean, a life that is lived on a level beneath social discourse and convention.

Mrs. Manresa, the potential lover of Isa's husband, lives for sensation. Repeatedly described as "the wild child" and the paragon of the "jolly human heart," Mrs. Manresa's passion takes the form of a crude, even vulgar, sensuality. Her animal vitality is not without its beneficent effects, however, in that it allows the other characters to relax and even gives Bartholomew a sense of restored youth (p. 41). She is the "May Queen," the earth mother, a kind of female Bacchus:

> She looked before she drank. Looking was part of drinking. Why waste sensation, she seemed to ask, why waste a single drop that can be pressed out of this ripe, this melting, this adorable world? Then she drank. And the air around her became threaded with sensation. Bartholomew felt it; Giles felt it. Had he been a horse, the thin brown skin would have twitched, as if a fly had settled. Isabella twitched too (p. 56).

Mrs. Manresa's unabashed physicality is like a breath of fresh air amongst the tensions and contradictions of *Between the Acts*.

Giles is a frustrated "man of action." Strongly on the side of masculine authority and tradition, he is deeply offended by what he views as the triviality of feminine preoccupations and is ever eager to take sides with masculine certitude against feminine ambiguity. When, in the course of the pageant, the Victorian constable points his truncheon accusingly at Mrs. Swithin in the audience, Giles triumphs, "taking sides with authority against his aunt" (p. 161). When Mrs. Swithin muses on the view, reflecting that there is something sad in the notion that it will be there when all the people one knows are gone, Giles can barely control his disgust:

> Giles nicked his chair into position with a jerk. Thus only could he show his irritation, his rage with old fogies who sat and looked at views over coffee and cream when the whole of Europe—over there—was bristling like . . . He had no command of metaphor (p. 53).

Anyone familiar with Virginia Woolf will surely find that last sentence rather damning evidence of Giles' limitations. There is no vision without metaphor. It might also be said, of course, that Mrs. Swithin's contempla-tion of the notion of death itself, and what it means to die, is larger and more to the point than the immediate concern of the war. In any case, the juxtaposition of these two views exposes the limitations of the masculine preoccupation with action.

Perhaps the most chilling instance of the ugliness of Giles' repressed anger occurs during one of the Intervals. Kicking a stone up the path, each kick becomes a personified quality: "The first kick was Manresa (lust). The second, Dodge (perversion). The third, himself (coward)" (p. 99). At the top of the path, near the gate, he comes upon a garden snake in the act of trying to swallow a toad. While the snake seems unable to swallow, the toad seems unable to die. Giles is horrified by this "monstrous inversion," this "birth the wrong way round" and crushes both snake and toad with his foot (p. 99). Giles, who "has no command of metaphor," fails to see the parallel with his relationship to Isa, although his action indicates that on some unconscious level he recognizes the tense and anxious stalemate of two opposing forces which characterizes this relationship. Interestingly, Giles finds considerable relief in this act of violence. In a novel about "acting" on all its levels, Giles is like a modern Hamlet who frets and hates and stews in stony silence. Though the object of his anger and frustration is absurdly displaced in this instance, his action provides a much needed outlet for his rage and hate.

The nature of expression, including the variety of forms which it can take, is a central theme in *Between the Acts*. While the most obvious medium for expression is language, communication in fact occurs on a multitude of levels. On one level are "words," which in this novel assume a plastic being, a form and mass which can be handled and shaped at will. After Rupert Haines has spoken to Isa, his words "lie between them like a wire, tingling, tangling, vibrating" (p. 15). When the child who represents "young England" appears on the stage, her words "peppered the audience as with a shower of hard little stones" (p. 78). At other times words are "pellets of information" or even assume flavor, as when the maids can be seen "rolling words, like sweets on their tongues; which, as they thinned to transparency, gave off pink, green, and sweetness" (p. 10).

On the other end of the communication spectrum is a kind of meta-language, a world of non-verbal communication in which the atmosphere itself becomes charged with meaning. When Isa and Rupert Haines are in the same room together, for example, their attraction to one another permeates the atmosphere. Mrs. Haines, who is aware of this emotion which excludes her, must wait till it ends "as one waits for the strain of an organ to die out before leaving church" (p. 6). She determines, in her jealousy, to destroy this emotion, "as a thrush pecks the wings off a butterfly" (p. 6). At another point, Giles and Isa and William Dodge charge the air with their unhappiness, creating an atmosphere of palpable gloom (p. 176). Sometimes, there are visual clues to this wordless language, as when William Dodge studies Isa's face: "Then he saw her face change, as if she had got out of one dress and put on another" (p. 105). Words, then, are only the most obvious, the most graspable, of the measures by which communication takes place.

Woolf's fascination with the nature of expression and the reality behind appearances is also revealed in her exploration of the function of "role-playing" in our lives. In a novel which plays on the notion of "acting," we are encouraged to view the characters of *Between the Acts* as extensions of the pageant they are watching, just as constrained by their roles as the actors before them.

In the pageant, of course, the players are always both themselves and the characters they play. No one can forget for long that Queen Elizabeth is in fact Mrs. Clark of the village tobacco shop (p. 88). The force of the play's illusion is always tenuous, ebbing and flowing like everything else. At times, it very nearly fails altogether: "Then the play began. Was it, or was it not, the play?" (p. 76) The child in the role of young England has forgotten her lines, the gramophone is not working, and the singers are too far away to be heard (pp. 77–78). The illusion breaks and the audience returns to itself.

This quality of illusion bolstered by role-playing is equally characteristic of the audience. " 'Our part,' said Bartholomew, 'is to be the audience. And a very important part too' " (p. 58). What, after all, is a play without an audience except, perhaps, what we are inclined to call reality? Yet the persons in the audience are actors on another level as well, for their cool exteriors are roles, masks for the drama going on within. Giles' controlled face belies the anger and violence which saturate him, and Isa's often rather blank exterior veils the turmoil of passions within.

While the roles we assume and in which we place others limit and entrap us, Woolf suggests, they are nonetheless necessary. Only through assuming a role can life be invested with meaning and purpose. Isa, when she looks at Giles, thinks "my husband; the father of my children." Throughout the novel, only by repeating these phrases over and over like a litany can she conjure up the emotion of love. Only by thus "casting" Giles in the role of husband and father can she summon a positive response to him.

At times, Isa suffers an excruciating awareness of the absurdity of these exterior roles and the hopelessness of her entrapment in them:

> Giles now wore the black coat and white tie of the professional classes, which needed—Isa looked down at his feet—patent leather pumps. "Our representative, our spokesman," she sneered. Yet he was extraordinarily handsome. "The father of my children, whom I love and hate." Love and hate—how they tore her asunder! Surely it was time someone invented a new plot, or that the author came out from the bushes . . . (p. 215).

When Isa looks at Rupert Haines, the "man in the grey suit," she asks herself how her life might have been different had he been placed in Giles' roles as husband and father. Every choice we make in life cancels out an infinite number of other roles which we "might" have played. For all of us, then, the "unacted part" is full of infinite possibility, and it is this sense of potential which Miss La Trobe's play, and Virginia Woolf's novel, help us to envision.

Without drama, Woolf suggests, there is no meaning. The raw energy of life must be shaped and transformed before moments of insight are possible. For this reason, the role of the artist is essential. In *Between the Acts*, this role is assumed by Miss LaTrobe, whose rare happiness occurs only at those moments when she is able to coax her audience, however temporarily, to share her vision.

Structurally, the pageant functions as a kind of heuristic device for exploring the meaning of character and action, of one's role, against the background of history and culture. Individual character can never be entirely free from the historical and cultural sources from which it emerges. The audience in *Between the Acts* is inevitably determined, at least in part, by the history and culture which the pageant represents. This point is brought home forcefully when the players emerge near the end of the play in their various costumes representing the entire course of English history and then turn mirrors on the audience to portray the concept of "present time."

In approximately three hours, the play represents the events of over a thousand years. On one level, we perceive those events as history, but they are also synonymous with "now," with the present moment which rests, like a thin platform, on the events of the past. The present, Woolf makes clear, is never detachable from the past; it is rather the effect of a past which is constantly shifting and changing beneath us. As Woolf has written elsewhere, what one says at a given moment about the past will be different from what one would have said about it a year earlier or a year hence. The present shapes the past, just as the past determines the present. All of this is affected, too, by the fact that in part we "create" the past. The "lady in yellow satin" whose portrait hangs at the top of the stairs is not, in fact, an ancestress, and yet she has become just as much a part of family tradition as the actual ancestor who hangs beside her (pp. 36, 38).

If history is malleable, so is our perception of time. For Mrs. Swithin, who lives in an ever-expanding present moment which ranges freely over past and future, time is largely irrelevant. William Dodge is imprisoned by his unhappy past and consequently is unable to enjoy the present or envision the future. Isa, who is restless and discontented in the present, looks almost entirely forward, envisioning the fulfillment of her various needs.

Woolf repeatedly suggests, however, that behind this elastic medium of time, which each character manipulates in his or her own way, there is an ultimate unchanging pattern. Woolf seems to identify this state of perception with the unconscious mind, so that while these moments of insight, or epiphany, only rarely blossom in the waking consciousness, they can be seen as more or less characteristic of the state of sleep. As one approaches sleep, the boundaries of time and phenomena begin to melt, just as they do during a moment of vision. In *Between the Acts*, the countryside, in its placidity, has the power to evoke in those who survey it a receptive state of mind:

> How tempting, how very tempting, to let the view triumph; to reflect its ripple; to let their own minds ripple; to let outlines elongate and pitch over—so—with a sudden jerk (p. 66).

Once this loss of consciousness has been achieved, the true nature of reality, in which time and roles become irrelevant, is revealed:

"This year, last year, next year, never," Isa murmured. "Tinker, tailor, soldier, sailor," Bartholomew echoed.

He was talking in his sleep (p. 217).

This merging of the individual personality with the timeless and universal is both positive and negative. On the one hand, this freeing of consciousness from the confines of character and ego makes possible the experience of "one-ness" which is the necessary source of vision. On the other hand, this loss of self is inevitably associated with indifference and death:

> Empty, empty, empty; silent, silent, silent. The room was a shell, singing of what was before time was; a vase stood in the heart of the house, alabaster, smooth, cold, holding the still distilled essence of emptiness, silence (p. 37).

As Allen McLaurin perceives, "The image of the vase, a form which encloses nothing and which has no 'content,' illustrates the central theme of Virginia Woolf's art—the emptiness at the heart of life which must be given shape and form."[2]

In *Between the Acts*, no one better understands this emptiness and the importance of investing it with meaning through form than the artist, Miss La Trobe: "This is death, death, death, she noted in the margin of her mind; when illusion fails" (p. 180). No matter how fragile the illusion, it is essential; it is the glue which holds the universe together.

Maintaining this collective illusion requires extraordinary effort on Miss La Trobe's part. Timing is crucial. If the Interval lasts too long, her audience will be impossible to reassemble; they will "split up into scraps and fragments" (p. 122). Like the image of the "blot fringed with flame" which recurs in Woolf's work, Miss La Trobe is the center of consciousness, reaching out to others, aware of their every move. Alienated from her audience by her role as artist and by her lesbianism, she is nonetheless a slave to it, dependent on its response for her sense of self-worth. She is like a teacher with a classroom full of unruly children who knows that in order to hold their attention she must be sympathetic to their tastes and needs. But she is also a "witch," endowed with the magical power to weave a spell, however briefly, which creates unity out of fragmentation:

"Ah, but she was not merely a twitcher of individual strings; she was one who seethes wandering bodies and floating voices in a cauldron, and makes rise up from its amorphous mass a re-created world" (p. 153). The perfect iambic pentameter of the last ten syllables of this quote lend force to this mystic celebration of the artist's role.

Although the reality Miss La Trobe creates is inevitably illusory, the shared vision her art makes possible represents a triumph over chaos, however momentary. Interestingly, whenever the play flags and illusion falters, nature comes to the rescue. When the singers cannot be heard, the cows save the moment with a communal bellowing: "It was the primeval voice sounding loud in the ear of the present moment" (p. 140). When Miss La Trobe tries to "stage" nature, however, her effort fails. Having arrived at "Present Time" in her historical pageant, Miss La Trobe wishes her audience to notice the cows and birds which surround them, to enter the present moment. But although the cows and birds have performed effectively, if accidentally, in the historical scenes, without a drama against which to act, they become merely cows and birds. The point, it would seem, is that without illusion, without a strategy for structuring reality, the universe loses meaning. The process, Woolf implies, is dialectical. Life is the necessary source of drama while drama invests the chaos of life with meaning, and in the interplay between life and drama a kind of reinvigoration takes place. Cows moo, and planes fly over, but instead of destroying the play's illusion, these interruptions continue, and perhaps even rescue, the play. Chance and circumstance have their place in the orderly world of art.

In her earlier novels, Woolf would probably have found some way of suggesting that the continuing patriarchy is the *reason* why airplanes fly over and darken the pageant with harbingers of war, but she does not do so in *Between the Acts*. As Ann Wilkinson points out, Woolf has succeeded here in virtually eliminating time-bound polemic from her fiction.[3] It is no longer particular issues which matter, but rather a loosening up and acceptance of the dialectical process itself. In the universal ebb and flow, all such issues are contained, and as each quality interacts with its opposite, moments of synthesis or vision become possible in which the "pattern behind the cotton-wool" is temporarily revealed.

Like Woolf after she finished a novel, Miss La Trobe crashes into depression and despair when the performance is over. Chaos and darkness hide the light of her vision, as if it had never been. As Bartholomew rightly perceives, Miss La Trobe's need is for darkness, coarse language, and a drink at the pub (p. 203), not well-meant but unsatisfying praise for her performance. No one, for the moment, can dispell her sense of failure and despair, and yet out of that despair, as she sits by herself in the pub, she begins once again to envision, to create (p. 210).

In *Between the Acts*, Woolf's awareness of the dialectical process of history and culture as well as individual personality and action finds its fullest realization. As we read through this novel, its structure mirrors, brilliantly, the interplay of life and art, conscious and unconscious, time and timelessness which is Woolf's theme. Thus we have the emblematic image of Giles and Isa with which the novel ends:

> Left alone together for the first time that day, they were silent. Alone, enmity was bared; also love. Before they slept, they must fight; after they had fought, they would embrace. From that embrace another life might be born. But first they must fight, as the dog fox fights with the vixen, in the heart of darkness, in the field of night.
>
> Isa let her sewing drop. The great hooded chairs had become enormous. And Giles too. And Isa too against the window. The window was all sky without colour. The house had lost its shelter. It was night before roads were made, or houses. It was the night that dwellers in caves had watched from some high place among rocks.
>
> Then the curtain rose. They spoke. (p. 219).

Jane Marcus reads this scene, and the novel as a whole, as indicating "how fully Woolf saw the source of the violence of war in the violence of human sexuality."[4] Yet, as Nancy Bazin perceives, "The union of the eternal male and the eternal female makes possible the eternal renewal," even though "the story that follows always seems to be the same: reintegration is always followed by disintegration." The inevitability of disintegration leads Bazin to view *Between the Acts* as Woolf's version of Eliot's "The Wasteland."[5] Nevertheless, to my mind there is a quietly positive acceptance of this dialectic on Woolf's part. The final encounter between Giles and Isa has a primeval quality in its association with the dark and primitive forces of passion which antedate civilization, its structure and its roles. And their encounter suggests as well the necessity of structuring that passion through the drama of human confrontation, the struggle to define and express oneself which is the basis of all creativity.

It is worth noting that although the ending is forceful, an examination of the manuscript indicates that Woolf may not have been entirely satisfied with it, at least initially. The final pages of the first typescript exist in several versions, and it is often difficult to tell where one begins and another ends. In general, in the versions which were deleted from the final manuscript, Woolf seems to place more emphasis on the dilemma of searching for a meaning which is no sooner grasped than it is shattered by contradiction. Life, she suggests, is a continuous process of finding and losing definition:

> They sat in their shell [the house] looking out at the pageant. Then as if they had been waiting, the stars came out. Aldebrana [sic], betelgeuse, cassiopeia. The little heads of the man and the woman showed black against the sky.
>
> It was as if another act were beginning; denuded, scaled, stark, and bare.
>
> "Is a play a failure," said Isa, "if we don't know the meaning? And why are we forced to act our parts?" "Is a play a failure," they asked each other, without coming closer, as they watched the first night of a new age take its place irrevocably, with them in the parts of hero and heroine who [sic] had given them their parts irrevocably as hero and heroine, "is a play a failure, when we don't know the meaning, but do know that we have to act our parts?"[6]

Here the emphasis is on the future and on Giles and Isa as emblematic figures who must create that future and usher in the new age. Interestingly, while all Woolf's previous novels have moved toward a resolution of their tensions in a vision of androgyny, that is not the case here. Giles and Isa represent forces which are deeply opposed, yet it is only through the interaction of such opposing forces, Woolf suggests, that a regenerative creative energy can be released. Equally important is the fact that Giles and Isa are equals in their struggle. No longer does the masculine point of view predominate and smother the feminine. And because they are equals, there is hope that an appropriate balance can be found.

In all of Virginia Woolf's work, form and meaning are at some point indistinguishable, but never more so than in *Between the Acts*. The structure, in its evocation of the ebb and flow of reality on all its levels, is the meaning. As Phyllis Rose perceives, "The qualities that make Woolf's work distinctive—the leaching away of authorial presence, the lyric grace, the fragmentariness and richly random development—are more prominent here than ever before. Stylistically, *Between the Acts* is the quintessential Woolf novel."[7] And as Lotus Snow points out, Lily's private vision of order which concludes *To the Lighthouse* here becomes a public, universal vision in Miss La Trobe's perception of the pattern of recurrence "in seasons, in civilizations, in the drama of individual lives." Consequently, "the distance between the two novels measures the growth of Virginia Woolf's vision of a design that endures."[8]

Woolf, as author, has achieved her lifelong goal of the androgynous mind, unfettered by private grievance of any sort. Thus freed, she is able to replace polemic with dialectic and concentrate her energy on the power of art to shape reality and forge meaning from chaos. In the process, her message about the importance of vision—a message which has reverberated throughout her novels—emerges more clearly than ever before.

Conclusion

It should not surprise anyone that Mrs. Woolf was severe in her obituary notice of the generation [the thirties]; she had not liked their work when she first commented on it in 'A Letter to a Young Poet' in 1932, and their writing since then had pleased her no better. She had wanted beauty and fine language, and they had given her politics and polemics, and so in 1940 she was prepared to dismiss the entire generation as casualties of history.

Samuel Hynes, *The Auden Generation*

In reviewing Woolf's career as a writer, one can watch the development of her ability to "get her genius expressed whole and entire."[1] From the very beginning, Woolf resisted the constraints of an artistic tradition which she found unsuitable to the expression of her vision and set about to metamorphose new forms from the old. Although she despised "preachiness" in novels and firmly believed that the artist's mind had to be "unfettered by grievances" in order to create, she was a true feminist in that she insisted throughout her career on the legitimacy and importance of a view of reality which was distinctly feminine. As she struggled to create the style and structures capable of conveying that perspective, she exposed in the process the limitations and one-sidedness of the masculine perspective which had dominated literature for so long.

In her first two novels, *The Voyage Out* and *Night and Day*, the challenge she faces is obvious as she struggles—largely unsuccessfully—against the constraints of characterization and plot development. Her narrator is of the standard omniscient type, and there is nothing creative in her use of point of view. The rich associational quality which is so characteristic of her later novels and which conveys a concentric rather than a linear view of reality is almost entirely lacking. Even her sentences lack the lyric grace of those in her later works, and because her vision is not embedded structurally, when she explores feminist issues she must do so on the overt level of thematic content.

The issue at stake, in both novels, is the question of whether a woman's needs, in the broadest sense, can be satisfactorily fulfilled within the context of marriage. Because traditional marriage so narrowly circumscribes the freedom of women, it is viewed as an oppressive and even suffocating institution. The issue in these novels is whether marriage can be changed to foster a union of equal partners. More broadly, can the vision of two individuals prevail against the force of social tradition, or will they be swallowed by it? The issue, significantly, is left unresolved. Whether or not this is viewed as a weakness in these novels, Woolf's ultimate evasiveness is a salient characteristic of her style. As Woolf developed as a writer, she was able to transform this evasiveness into an obvious artistic strength, since it spurred her to create situations and envisage symbols which, in their ambiguity, have enormous suggestive power. In these early novels, however, she has not yet developed a form and style which fit the contours of her imagination.

Jacob's Room represents a breakthrough in this regard. Perhaps because she distanced herself from women's issues by choosing a male protagonist, Woolf was able to distill and consolidate certain stylistic innovations far better suited to the uniqueness of her vision. The conventional plot evaporates, point of view becomes diffused over a wide spectrum of characters, and images begin to take on a rich associative power. These techniques, and the new possibilities opened up by them, were to serve Woolf well in her next two novels.

It is interesting that the two novels generally considered to be Woolf's best revolve around two women, Clarissa Dalloway and Mrs. Ramsay, who are very traditional in terms of their values and expectations, and yet do not seem particularly thwarted by their roles in life. On the contrary, both, in their respective ways, are remarkably attractive and even majestic beings, geniuses in the art of graceful living. On the overt level, Woolf's feminism takes the form of placing supreme value on the civilizing influence of these women. Traditional feminine skills are invested with a new credibility and importance.

For the most part, however, Woolf's feminism is veiled, having undergone a series of fictional transformations, or sublimations, which act to distinguish the fictional work from the unveiled exposition of convictions set forth in the essays. Woolf's feminist values have not been dismissed in *Mrs. Dalloway* and *To the Lighthouse*. They are merely disguised. When art serves as the vehicle for polemic, in order to be effective the polemical material must become an integral part of the aesthetic. Failure to integrate it successfully results in a jarring conflation of the expository and expressive styles. Through the use of sophisticated rhetorical strategies which served to embed her feminist values, Woolf was able to express her views without sacrificing aesthetic integrity.

The action of *Mrs. Dalloway*, unlike most other novels, covers only one day, but it is a day loaded with rich associations from the past so that the most seemingly trivial action becomes the touchstone for a new understanding. This emphasis on perception, connection, and association represents a distinct departure from the masculine fictional tradition. The notion of what constitutes an event has been redefined. Clarissa's day, though outwardly relatively uneventful, is punctuated by a series of perceptual "events" which constitute the action of the novel.

Very often these perceptual events are clustered around a visual or auditory image, such as the chiming of the London clocks or most notably, the lighthouse. The connection between these symbols and the thing or things symbolized is far from simple, and it is this capacity to "leave the ground," as Leonard Woolf phrased it,[2] that is responsible for the haunting power of Woolf's symbolic flights. By tending toward the associational (female) rather than the logical (male) in her use of symbols, Woolf gains a resonating quality which few writers can equal.

Another technique employed by Woolf to great advantage here might be termed her "floating point of view." Throughout *Mrs. Dalloway* we pass almost imperceptibly, in a rocking, back and forth motion, from Clarissa's consciousness to those of the other characters. As Suzanne Ferguson points out in her discussion of Woolf's novels as part of the Impressionist tradition, the narrator has only a selective, sporadic omniscience, and is frequently unable to tell us the absolute "truth" of the characters' experiences. And because the narrative voice and the thoughts of the characters often become indistinguishable, the reader is able to both evaluate characters and sympathize with them at the same time.[3] Through the use of this technique, Woolf is able to offer an alternative to the typically more egocentric narrative style of traditional novels.

As we pass from consciousness to consciousness, past and present mingle freely, and the reader, like the spirit Ariel, floats from one to the other of these personalities in a sea of consciousness punctuated by the chiming of the London clocks. As David Daiches perceives:

> The whole novel is constructed in terms of the two dimensions of space and time. We either stand still in time and are led to contemplate diverse but contemporaneous events in space or we stand still in space and are allowed to move up and down temporally in the consciousness of one individual. If it would not be extravagant to consider personality rather than space as one dimension, with time as the other, we might divide the book quite easily into those sections where time is fluid and personality stable or where personality is fluid and time is stable and regard this as a careful alternation of the dimensions.[4]

Personality does not seem locked in a mortal combat with time as it does in the traditional novel. Death does not loom as a threat upon the horizon; it is ever-present, inseparable from life. Consequently, the fear of death, in Woolf's novels, is indistinguishable from the fear of life. This way of looking at death is characteristically female, arising as it does from a mode of life which is traditionally domestic, inward-turning, and self-contained as opposed to the goal-oriented masculine world of competition and advancement.

These, then, are some of the techniques evolved by Virginia Woolf in *Mrs. Dalloway* which transform the traditional novel into a vehicle far more suitable for the accurate rendering of female consciousness. In *To the Lighthouse*, these same techniques are employed, but with new innovations. As Eric Auerbach notes, " . . . the exterior events have actually lost their hegemony, they serve to release and interpret inner events, whereas before her time (and still today in many instances) inner movements preponderantly function to prepare and motivate significant exterior happenings."[5]

Traditionally, the writer of fiction has defined the mark a character will leave on his or her world by the character's reaction to dramatic crises. In Woolf's novels, by contrast, random, trivial occurrences are exploited in and for themselves, so that in Auerbach's words, "in the process something new and elemental appeared: nothing less than the wealth of reality and depth of life in every moment to which we surrender ourselves without prejudice."[6] One reason why Woolf's innovation here is so important is that the daily lives of women are given new credibility. Typically, in earlier novels, since women were barred from participation in the affairs of the world, their interest for us as characters has derived primarily from their management of relationships with male characters. One need only consider the Bennet sisters or Emma Woodhouse or Jane Eyre or Dorothea Brooke to see that this is true. Woolf, then, makes an emphatic contribution to the portrayal of women in fiction through her insistence on the richness and importance of non-dramatic reality.

Again, this reflects a feminist consciousness. An emphasis on action and event has given way to an elevated exploration of consciousness itself, so that the most trivial of incidents, because it serves as a catalyst for a wealth of perceptual associations, assumes an importance equal to the most notable events. In the process, Woolf dignifies the seemingly non-eventful lives of women. For perhaps the first time, women *as* women are the subject of fiction.

In Woolf's next work of fiction, *Orlando*, she largely avoids the difficulty of transforming polemic into art by dispensing with verisimilitude and envisioning a world in which feminine dissatisfaction has found a solution in androgyny. As we follow Orlando's life between the years of about 1570 and 1928, through a change of sex, a wife and husband, and a career in diplomacy and literature, we become increasingly aware of the pleasure Woolf is taking in undercutting our expectations as readers of conventional novels. Orlando's sex change does, however, serve Woolf's feminist aims. As a woman, Orlando remembers the freedom and mobility that was hers when she was a man and so is able to comment with considerable credibility on the restrictions and difficulties she suffers in her life as a woman. At least in part a portrait of Woolf's intimate friend, Vita Sackville-West, *Orlando* is also the most joyfully outrageous book Woolf was ever to write.

Woolf's "abstract, mystical, eyeless book,"[7] *The Waves*, followed *Orlando*. Daringly experimental in form, it explores the interplay between individual consciousness and the vast, impersonal, irrational world of phenomena. All of the techniques evolved by Woolf over the years find full expression in this remarkably controlled composition. The dialectical interplay between what might be termed the collective unconscious and the individual human personality, Woolf's primary theme here, is evoked through the alternating presence of the impersonal interludes with the chorus of the characters' voices and the elusive vision of the "fin in the waste of water" which Bernard experiences.

It is interesting that Woolf would return to this theme shortly before her death in 1941. In a haunting unpublished sketch entitled "The Watering Place," which was probably Woolf's last effort in fiction, the narrator describes a gathering of people at a seaside town. Just as the smell of the sea permeates the town, the people in turn become inseparable from the sea. They have an unreal, brittle, toy-like quality, like shells that have been cast upon the shore. These shells gather in a restaurant permeated by the smell of fish, which is consumed in tremendous quantities. As the sketch progresses, we move to the Ladies Lavatory where two women are talking. Their conversation is trivial, sneering. But gradually what becomes central is the presence of the tides and the waves as the narrator's attention moves to the water which is foaming and receding with a rush of sound in the sinks and water closets. The two women, fish-like, recede into the background. They are temporary; the tides eternal.[8]

This sketch trails off in an almost stuttering way and was apparently never finished. It would seem that the sound of the waves followed Woolf everywhere—even into restrooms. Yet, whereas *The Waves* ends in a defiance of death, as Bernard flings himself against it, in this sketch death is master. Humanity, and especially women, have been reduced to fish: smelly, cannibalistic, mindless, and above all mortal. Life stinks of death, and the eternal, impersonal tides, though terrifying, offer a kind of cleansing solace.

If there is a single unifying theme in everything Woolf wrote, this dialectic between human personality and the vast, impersonal, timeless "other" is surely it. The theme surfaces in all her novels, but in *The Waves* it is the controlling concept. Perhaps this is why Leonard Woolf thought *The Waves* was her greatest book: "I think it has all the marks of great literature. Whether any of the others are on the same level I rather doubt."[9] Yet *The Waves* is a difficult novel, both to read and to discuss, partly because the language of criticism, as it relates to novels, is not well-adapted to its unique structure and style. The usual methods for approaching character, plot, themes and structure simply do not apply. And since the focus of the novel is on the human dilemma in the broadest sense, *The Waves* would seem to resist definition as a feminist novel. The issue is a complicated one, largely because Woolf's feminism in *The Waves* is not nearly so much a matter of the subject she has chosen as it is of her method itself, which in its departure from convention offers an entirely new mode of perceiving. In *The Waves*, Woolf's feminism is so thoroughly embedded in the internal structure of her narrative, in the *way* she renders reality, that it is almost no longer recognizable as such.

For that reason, Woolf's next attempts, *Flush* and *The Pargiters*, are surprising in their sharp departure from this visionary mode. *Flush*, a biography of Elizabeth Barrett Browning's dog, is a lighthearted, largely tongue-in-cheek account of Miss Barrett's early adult years and her ensuing relationship with Mr. Browning. In *The Pargiters*, however, Woolf returns to a serious intent which is nonetheless startling in its departure from certain aesthetic principles which had guided her work so far.

Ignoring her steadfast conviction that fact and fiction represent two different kinds of truth which it is fatal to combine, she set out to write a "novel of fact" in which feminist polemical essays would alternate with fictional chapters illustrating her ideas. Only seven years before, Woolf had written, ". . . it is fatal for anyone who writes to think of their sex . . . it is fatal for a woman to lay the least stress on any grievance; to plead even with justice any cause; in any way to speak consciously as a woman."[10] Yet that is precisely what she set out to do: to increase awareness of the oppressed condition of women and to encourage change in that regard. Although the project failed, it is fascinating that so late in her career Woolf felt inclined to abandon certain of her most tenaciously held aesthetic principles in an effort to make fiction serve more directly as a vehicle for polemic. This attempt and failure illustrate the tremendous tension between the need to enlighten and the requirements of aesthetic integrity with which Woolf struggled throughout her career.

Woolf salvaged the scraps of her effort by incorporating the fictional material, with some changes, into the "1880" section of *The Years* and using the non-fiction chapters as the core of her second long feminist essay, *Three Guineas*. In my opinion, *The Years* is a less than satisfying novel. Woolf did not relinquish her goal of incorporating "facts as well as the vision. And to combine them both. I mean, *The Waves* going on simultaneously with *Night and Day*."[11] Unfortunately, these two purposes seem to jar in *The Years*, which lacks the impressive vision of her earlier works and yet fails to make a coherent or convincing case for greater female participation in the world. In her effort to sidestep overt didacticism, Woolf leaves us with a feminism which, because it is still present in highly truncated form, seems merely vitiated. Although there is a wealth of excellent material in *The Years*, it never jells. The novel is loosely structured, lacks the humor and whimsy of earlier novels, and does not, finally, manage to cohere.

In *Between the Acts*, Woolf's final novel, one senses movement toward a new resolution. Ideas are generated by the process of dialectic which informs this novel on a variety of levels. Every quality implies its opposite, and through the interaction of these opposites, experience is invested with meaning. Yet there is an overall pattern as well. All contradictions—life and art, love and hate, time and timelessness, unity and fragmentation—are shown to be part of a unified reality which can be glimpsed in moments of vision.

As in *The Waves*, Woolf's feminism in *Between the Acts* is more apparent in how reality is perceived than in what she has to say about it. Experience is not linear but cyclical. Time and personality are fluid. The sexual dialectic, which has been such an important theme in all her novels, is equally apparent here, but is presented somewhat differently. The male characters, in their devotion to reason and action, lack vision, but their perspective no longer dominates and smothers the female perspective as it has in previous novels. The men in this novel have no power over the women, so that Lucy Swithin's spirituality, Mrs. Manresa's sensuality, and Isa's romantic idealism are equally viable and independent perspectives. The autonomy of the female perspective is important, for it allows a struggle among equals, and the struggle is essential. Through struggle, creative energy is released, life finds definition, and moments of synthesis are achieved. Giles and Isa love and hate, hate and love. Before they embrace, they must fight. But from that struggle, new life may emerge.

As in earlier novels, androgyny represents a resolution of the sexual dialectic. In *Between the Acts*, the androgynous perspective is embodied in Miss La Trobe, the director of the pageant. The androgyny of Miss La Trobe sets her apart from her audience and is essential to her function as an artist. She is the "other," but from her perspective of isolation, she can manipulate character and scene to bring moments of "vision" to the others. The role of the artist is therefore essential to the creation of a vision of reality which can be shared.

If the role of the artist is to create a new reality by transforming the familiar through the shaping power of vision, then Virginia Woolf is a great artist. Throughout her career, she struggled against a literary tradition that ran counter to her vision. As she says in "Women and Fiction," ". . . both in life and in art the values of a woman are not the values of a man. Thus, when a woman comes to write a novel, she will find that she is perpetually wishing to alter the established values—to make serious what appears insignificant to a man, and trivial what to him is important. And for that, of course, she will be criticized . . ."[12] Nevertheless, Virginia Woolf remained true to her values. In the process, she developed a style uniquely her own which has allowed all of us to perceive reality in a new way.

Notes

Introduction

1. Virginia Woolf, "The New Biography," in *Granite and Rainbow* (New York and London: Harcourt, Brace, Jovanovich, 1958), p. 154.

2. Mitchell A. Leaska, ed., *The Pargiters*, by Virginia Woolf (New York and London: Harcourt, Brace, Jovanovich, 1977), p. 9.

3. Friedrich Engels, "Letter to Kautsky," in *Marxism and Art: Writings in Aesthetics and Criticism*, ed. Berel Lang and Forest Williams (New York: David McKay Co., 1972), p. 13.

4. Engels, in *Marxism and Art*, p. 49.

5. Mao, from *On Literature and Art*, in *Marxism and Art*, p. 117.

6. Virginia Woolf, "Women and Fiction," in *Granite and Rainbow* (New York and London: Harcourt, Brace, Jovanovich, 1958, 1959), pp. 79–80.

7. Virginia Woolf, *A Room of One's Own* (New York and Burlingame: Harcourt, Brace, and World, 1927, 1957), p. 72.

8. Woolf, *A Room of One's Own*, pp. 62–64.

9. Woolf, *A Room of One's Own*, pp. 77.

10. Miyeko Kamiya, "Virginia Woolf: An Outline of a Study on her Personality, Illness and Work," *Confinia Psychiatrica* 8 (1965), p. 195.

11. Virginia Woolf, "Phases of Fiction," typescript, Monks House Papers (MH/B7b), p. 63, the University of Sussex Library.

12. John Keats, "Letter to George and Tom Keats," (Dec. 21–27, 1817), in *English Romantic Writers*, ed. David Perkins (New York: Harcourt, Brace, and World, 1967), p. 1209.

13. Woolf, *A Room of One's Own*, p. 108.

14. Herbert Marder, *Feminism and Art: A Study of Virginia Woolf* (Chicago: University of Chicago Press, 1968, 1974), p. 1. (For the context of the quote, see *A Writer's Diary*, ed. Leonard Woolf (New York: Harcourt, Brace, Jovanovich, 1953, 1954), p. 284.

15. Marder, p. 23.

16. Virginia Woolf, *Three Guineas* (New York: Harcourt, Brace, Jovanovich, 1938, 1966), p. 170.

17. Virginia Woolf, *Mrs. Dalloway* (New York: Harcourt, Brace, and World, 1953), p. 16.

18. Berenice Carroll, "'To Crush Him in Our Own Country': The Political Thought of Virginia Woolf," *Feminist Studies* 4 (1978), 104.

19. Marder, p. 175.

20. Virginia Woolf, "The Introduction," in Articles, essays, fiction, reviews, vol. 2, dated 1925, The Berg Collection, the New York Public Library.

21. Woolf, "The Introduction," p. 19.

22. Barbara Hill Rigney, "The Sane and the Insane: Psychosis and Mysticism in *Mrs. Dalloway*," in her *Madness and Sexual Politics in the Feminist Novel: Studies in Bronte, Woolf, Lessing and Atwood* (Madison: University of Wisconsin Press, 1978), p. 43.

23. Berenice Carroll, "'To Crush Him in Our Own Country': The Political Thought of Virginia Woolf," *Feminist Studies* 4 (1978), 99–131.

24. David Daiches, *The Novel and the Modern World* (Chicago: University of Chicago Press, 1960), p. 195.

25. Lucio P. Ruotolo, "Clarissa Dalloway," in *Virginia Woolf*, ed. Thomas S. W. Lewis (New York: McGraw-Hill, 1975), p. 39.

26. Woolf, "Women and Fiction," p. 81.

27. Virginia Woolf, "Scenes from the Life of a British Naval Officer," unpublished typescript, 10 pp., Monks House Papers (MH/B9d), the University of Sussex Library.

28. Woolf, "Women and Fiction," p. 81.

29. Sydney Janet Kaplan, "Virginia Woolf," in her *Feminine Consciousness in the Modern British Novel* (Urbana: University of Illinois Press, 1975), p. 82.

30. Geoffrey Hartman, "Virginia's Web," in his *Beyond Formalism* (New Haven and London: Yale University Press, 1970), p. 71.

31. Virginia Woolf, "Introduction to *Mrs. Dalloway*," in *Virginia Woolf*, ed. Thomas S. W. Lewis (New York: McGraw-Hill, 1975), p. 36.

32. Daiches, p. 189.

33. Virginia Woolf, Diary (1897), The Berg Collection, the New York Public Library.

34. Virginia Woolf, Autograph notebook (1906 and 1909), visit to Italy and Greece, Manuscript no. 61837, the British Library.

35. Virginia Woolf, "Monday, Tuesday—The Diary," unpublished sketch, Monks House Papers (MH/B9e), the University of Sussex Library.

36. Virginia Woolf, "What the Telescope Discovered," "Incongruous/Inaccurate Memories," "A Scene from the Past," and "The Telescope," Monks House Papers (MH/B9j and k; MH/B10e and f), the University of Sussex Library.

37. Kamiya, p. 198.

38. Roger Poole, *The Unknown Virginia Woolf* (Cambridge University Press, 1978), pp. 66–67.

39. Ellen Hawkes [Rogat], "A Form of One's Own," *Mosaic* 8, No. 1 (Fall, 1974), pp. 80–84.

40. Sigmund Freud, "'Civilized' Sexual Morality," in *The Complete Psychological Works of Sigmund Freud*, Vol. 9 (London: Hogarth Press, 1959), p. 187.

41. Freud, "Transference," in *The Complete Psychological Works*, Vol 16 (1963), pp. 443–444, and "A Case of Hysteria," in *The Complete Psychological Works*, Vol. 7 (1953), p. 116.

42. Freud, "The Work of Displacement," in *The Complete Psychological Works*, Vol. 4 (1953), p. 305.

43. Freud, "Jokes, Dreams, and the Unconscious," in *The Complete Psychological Works*, Vol. 8 (1960), pp. 163–164.

44. Freud, "The Means of Representation," in *The Complete Psychological Works*, Vol. 4, (1953), pp. 322–323.

45. Freud, "The Work of Condensation," in *The Complete Psychological Works*, Vol. 4 (1953), p. 279.

46. Freud, "On Dreams," in *The Complete Psychological Works*, Vol. 5 (1953), p. 652.

47. Freud, "The Work of Condensation," in *The Complete Psychological Works*, Vol. 4 (1953), p. 283.

48. James Naremore, "Nature and History in *The Years*," in *Virginia Woolf: Revaluation and Continuity*, ed. Ralph Freedman (Berkeley, Los Angeles, London: Univ. of California Press, 1980), p. 242.

The Voyage Out

1. Virginia Woolf, *The Voyage Out* (New York and London: Harcourt, Brace, Jovanovich, 1920, 1948), p. 19. (All further references to page numbers in the text will correspond to the 1948 printing.)

2. Herbert Marder, *Feminism and Art: A Study of Virginia Woolf* (Chicago and London: University of Chicago Press, third impression, 1974), p. 53.

3. Elizabeth Heine, "The Earlier *Voyage Out*: Virginia Woolf's First Novel," *Bulletin of Research in the Humanities* 82 (1979), 294, 303.

4. Virginia Woolf, "The Symbol," Monks House Papers (MH/A24e), the University of Sussex Library.

5. James Naremore, *The World Without a Self: Virginia Woolf and the Novel* (New Haven and London: Yale University Press, 1973), p. 22.

6. Mitchell A. Leaska, "The Death of Rachel Vinrace," *Bulletin of Research in the Humanities* 82 (1979), 331.

7. Leaska, 337.

8. Virginia Woolf, "On Being Ill," in *The Moment and other Essays* (New York: Harcourt, Brace, 1948), p. 14.

9. Naremore, p. 245.

10. Alice van Buren Kelley, *The Novels of Virginia Woolf: Fact and Vision* (Chicago and London: University of Chicago Press, 1971, 1973), pp. 5, 32.

Night and Day

1. Winifred Holtby, *Virginia Woolf: A Critical Memoir* (Chicago: Cassandra Editions, Academy Press, Ltd., 1978), pp. 81–84.

2. Jane Marcus, "Enchanted Organs, Magic Bells: *Night and Day* as Comic Opera," in *Virginia Woolf: Revaluation and Continuity*, ed. Ralph Freedman (Berkeley, Los Angeles, London: University of California Press, 1980), p. 99.

3. Herbert Marder, *Feminism and Art: A Study of Virginia Woolf* (Chicago: Univ. of Chicago Press, 1968, 1974), p. 22.

4. Virginia Woolf, *Night and Day* (New York: Harcourt, Brace, Jovanovich,

1948), p. 265. (All following page references in the text will correspond with this edition.)

5. Holtby, p. 91.

6. Margaret Comstock, "'The Current Answers Don't Do'; The Comic Form of *Night and Day*," *Women's Studies* 4 (1977), pp. 165–167.

7. Marder, p. 34.

8. Holtby, p. 93.

9. Sigmund Freud, "The Work of Condensation," *The Complete Psychological Works of Sigmund Freud*, Vol. 4 (London: Hogarth Press, 1953), pp. 279–304.

10. Freud, "Civilization and its Discontents," in *The Complete Psychological Works*, Vol 21, pp. 64–65, 72.

11. Holtby, pp. 87–91.

12. Quentin Bell, *Virginia Woolf: A Biography*, Vol. 2 (New York: Harcourt, Brace, Jovanovich, 1972), p. 69.

13. Holtby, p. 97.

14. Hena Maes-Jelinek, "Virginia Woolf," in *Criticism of Society in the English Novel Between the Wars* (Paris: Société d'Editions "Les Belles Lettres," 1970), p. 119.

15. Phyllis Rose, *Woman of Letters: A Life of Virginia Woolf* (New York: Oxford University Press, 1978), p. 96.

16. David Daiches, *The Novel and the Modern World* (Chicago: University of Chicago Press, 1960), p. 196.

Jacob's Room

1. Winifred Holtby, *Virginia Woolf: A Critical Memoir* (Chicago: Cassandra Editions, Academy Press, Ltd., 1978), p. 117.

2. Holtby, p. 116.

3. Virginia Woolf, *Jacob's Room* and *The Waves* (New York: Harcourt, Brace, Jovanovich, 1923, 1959), p. 22. (All page references which follow in the text will correspond with this edition.)

4. Ralph Freedman, "The Form of Fact and Fiction: *Jacob's Room* as Paradigm," in *Virginia Woolf: Revaluation and Continuity*, ed. Ralph Freedman (Berkeley, Los Angeles, London: University of California Press, 1980), p. 127.

5. Avrom Fleishman, *Virginia Woolf: A Critical Reading* (Baltimore: Johns Hopkins University Press, 1975), p. 46.

6. Jean Guiguet, *Virginia Woolf and Her Works*, trans. Jean Stewart (London: Hogarth Press, 1965), p. 225.

7. Beverley Ann Schlack, *Continuing Presences: Virginia Woolf's Use of Literary Allusion* (University Park: Pennsylvania State University Press, 1979), pp. 40–46.

8. Quentin Bell, *Virginia Woolf: A Biography* (New York: Harcourt, Brace, Jovanovich, 1972), pp. 27, 68–70, 97–100.

9. Phyllis Rose, *Woman of Letters: A Life of Virginia Woolf* (New York: Oxford University Press, 1978), p. 108.

10. Guiguet, p. 373.

11. Rose, p. 94.

Mrs. Dalloway and To the Lighthouse

1. Virginia Woolf, "Professions for Women," in *The Death of the Moth and Other Essays* (New York: Harcourt, Brace, Jovanovich, 1942, 1972), pp. 236–237.

2. "Professions for Women," p. 237.

3. "Professions for Women," p. 237.

4. "Professions for Women," p. 238.

5. Virginia Woolf, *Mrs. Dalloway* (New York: Harcourt, Brace, and World, 1925, 1953), p. 266. (All following page references in the text will correspond with this edition.)

6. Patricia Meyer Spacks, *The Female Imagination* (New York: Avon Books, 1972, 1975), p. 134.

7. Spacks, p. 141.

8. "Professions for Women," p. 240.

9. Virginia Woolf, "A Sketch of the Past," in *Moments of Being*, ed. Jeanne Schulkind (New York: Harcourt, Brace, Jovanovich, 1976), p. 69.

10. Virginia Woolf, "Old Bloomsbury," in *Moments of Being*, p. 160.

11. Virginia Woolf, "22 Hyde Park Gate," in *Moments of Being*, p. 155.

12. Phyllis Rose, *Woman of Letters: A Life of Virginia Woolf* (New York: Oxford University Press, 1978), p. 17.

13. Rose, p. 17.

14. James Naremore, *The World Without a Self: Virginia Woolf and the Novel* (New Haven and London: Yale University Press, 1973), pp. 242–243.

15. Rose, pp. 15–16.

16. Mark Spilka, "On Mrs. Dalloway's Absent Grief: A Psycho-Literary Speculation," *Contemporary Literature* 20 (1979), 335.

17. Harold Fromm, "Virginia Woolf: Art and Sexuality," *Virginia Quarterly Review* 55 (1979), 447, 452–453, 459.

18. Virginia Woolf, *A Room of One's Own* (New York and Burlingame: Harcourt, Brace, and World, 1958, 1975), pp. 20–23.

19. Virginia Woolf, *To the Lighthouse* (New York: Harcourt, Brace, and World, 1927, 1955), p. 51. (All further page references in the text will correspond with this edition.)

20. Herbert Marder, *Feminism and Art: A Study of Virginia Woolf* (Chicago and London: University of Chicago Press, 1968), p. 53.

21. Virginia Woolf, *A Writer's Diary*, ed. Leonard Woolf (New York: Harcourt, Brace, Jovanovich, 1954), p. 75.

22. Ruth Z. Temple, "Never say 'I': *To the Lighthouse* as Vision and Confession," in *Virginia Woolf*, Twentieth Century Views, ed. Claire Sprague (Englewood Cliffs, N.J.: Prentice-Hall, 1971), pp. 90–100.

23. Ian Gregor, "Spaces: *To the Lighthouse*," in *The Author in His Work; Essays on a Problem in Criticism*, ed. Louis L. Martz and Aubrey Williams (New Haven: Yale University Press, 1978), pp. 387–388.

24. Virginia Woolf, "George Moore," in *The Death of the Moth and Other Essays*, p. 157.

25. Marder, pp. 11–14.

26. Marder, pp. 15–17.

27. *A Room of One's Own*, pp. 100, 102.

28. Marder, p. 56.

29. Virginia Woolf, "Notes for Writing," Holograph notebook, p. 12, the Berg Collection, the New York Public Library.

30. Marder, p. 42.

31. A Room of One's Own, pp. 35–36.

32. Marder, pp. 44, 45.

33. Lucio P. Ruotolo, "Clarissa Dalloway," in Virginia Woolf, ed. Thomas S. W. Lewis (New York: McGraw-Hill, 1975), p. 47.

34. Marder, p. 35.

35. Sally Alexander Brett, "No, Mrs. Ramsay: Feminist Dilemma in To the Lighthouse," Ball State University Forum 19, No. 1 (1978), 53.

36. A Room of One's Own, pp. 33–34.

37. Emily Dickinson, The Complete Poems, ed. Thomas H. Johnson (Boston and Toronto: Little, Brown, and Co., 1960), p. 506 (Poem #1129).

38. Rose, p. 15.

39. Annis Pratt, "Sexual Imagery in To the Lighthouse: A New Feminist Approach," Modern Fiction Studies 18, No. 3 (Autumn, 1972), 417–431.

40. Judith Little, "Heroism in To the Lighthouse," in Images of Women in Fiction, ed. Susan Koppelman Cornillon (Bowling Green, Ohio: Bowling Green Popular Press, 1972), pp. 238–241.

41. A Room of One's Own, p. 36.

42. A Room of One's Own, pp. 35–37.

43. Allen McLaurin, Virginia Woolf: The Echoes Enslaved (Cambridge University Press, 1973), p. 184.

44. Marder, pp. 146–147.

45. Marder, p. 15.

46. Hermione Lee, The Novels of Virginia Woolf (London: Methuen, 1977), p. 93.

47. Virginia Woolf, "Holograph notes, unsigned, dated Nov. 9, 1922–Aug 2, 1923," 13 pp. At back her Choephori of Aeschylus (ed. by A. W. Verrall), the Berg Collection, the New York Public Library.

48. "Holograph notes, unsigned, dated Nov. 9, 1922–Aug. 2, 1923."

49. "Holograph notes, unsigned, dated Nov. 9, 1922–Aug. 2, 1923."

50. "Holograph notes, unsigned, dated Nov. 9, 1922–Aug. 2, 1923."

51. Marder, p. 49.

52. Marder, p. 48.

53. Virginia Woolf, "Thoughts on Peace in an Air Raid," in The Death of the Moth and Other Essays, p. 245.

54. Marder, pp. 48–50.

55. Virginia Woolf, "'Introduction' to Mrs. Dalloway," in Virginia Woolf, ed. Thomas S. W. Lewis, p. 36.

56. "Holograph notes, unsigned, dated Nov. 9, 1922–Aug. 2, 1923, 13 pp. Entries for July 22 and Aug. 2, 1923.

57. "Holograph notes, unsigned, dated Nov. 9, 1922–Aug. 2, 1923, 13 pp. Entry for Nov. 19, 1922.

58. 'Holograph notes, unsigned, dated Nov. 9, 1922–Aug. 2, 1923, 13 pp. Entry for Nov. 19, 1922.

59. Miyeko Kamiya, "Virginia Woolf: An Outline of a Study of her Personality, Illness, and Work," Confinia Psychiatrica 8 (1965), 195–196.

60. Ruotolo, p. 46.

61. Marder, p. 24.

62. Sigmund Freud, *The Complete Psychological Works of Sigmund Freud*, Vol. 9 (London: Hogarth Press, 1959), p. 187.

63. Freud, "An Infantile Neurosis—Part IX: Recapitulations and Problems," *The Complete Psychological Works*, Vol. 17, p. 115.

64. Mitchell Leaska, *The Novels of Virginia Woolf: From Beginning to End* (New York: John Jay, 1977), pp. 106–115.

65. Quentin Bell, *Virginia Woolf: A Biography* (New York and London: Harcourt, Brace, Jovanovich, 1972), p. 43.

66. Freud, "The Ego and the Id—Part IV: The Two Classes of Instincts," *The Complete Psychological Works*, Vol. 19, p. 47.

67. Louise Poresky, *The Elusive Self: Psyche and Spirit in Virginia Woolf's Novels* (Newark: University of Delaware Press, 1981), p. 122.

68. Steven Cohen, "Narrative Form and Death: *The Mill on the Floss* and *Mrs. Dalloway*," *Genre* 11 (1978), 128.

69. Lucio Ruotolo, "*Mrs. Dalloway:* The Journey Out of Subjectivity," *Women's Studies* 4 (1977), 174–177.

Orlando

1. Frank Baldanza, "Orlando and the Sackvilles," *PMLA* 70 (March, 1955), 274–279; David Bonnell Green, "Orlando and the Sackvilles: Addendum," *PMLA* 71 (March, 1956), 268–269.

2. Louise De Salvo, "A Note on the Orlando Tapestries at Knole House," *Virginia Woolf Miscellany* 13 (1979), pp. 3–4.

3. Frederick Kellerman, "A New Key to Virginia Woolf's *Orlando*," *English Studies* 59 (1978), 139, 145.

4. Leonard Woolf, "Transcript of BBC Interview, Feb. 1, 1965," p. 9, Leonard Woolf Papers (II/7b), the University of Sussex Library.

5. Virginia Woolf, *Orlando* (New York: Harcourt, Brace, Jovanovich, 1928, 1956), p. 189. (All following page references in the text will correspond with this edition.)

6. Herbert Marder, *Feminism and Art: A Study of Virginia Woolf* (Chicago and London: University of Chicago Press, 1968), p. 112.

7. Marder, pp. 110–116.

8. Jean Guiguet, *Virginia Woolf and her Works*, trans. Jean Stewart (London: Hogarth Press, 1965), p. 279.

9. James Naremore, *The World Without a Self: Virginia Woolf and the Novel* (New Haven and London: Yale University Press, 1973), p. 191.

10. Manly Johnson, *Virginia Woolf* (New York: Frederick Ungar, 1973), p. 78.

11. Jean O. Love, "*Orlando* and Its Genesis: Venturing and Experimenting in Art, Love, and Sex," in *Virginia Woolf: Revaluation and Continuity*, ed. Ralph Freedman (Berkeley, Los Angeles, London: University of California Press, 1980), p. 218.

The Waves

1. Virginia Woolf, *A Writer's Diary*, ed. Leonard Woolf (New York: Harcourt, Brace, Jovanovich, 1953, 1954), p. 134.

2. Deborah Sitter, "The Debate of *The Waves*," *Durham University Journal* 37, No. 1 (Dec., 1975), 125.

3. Roseanne Rini, "Transcendent Perception in Virginia Woolf's *The Waves*," unpublished essay, The Ohio State University, pp. 6–7, 36.

4. Frank D. McConnell, "'Death Among the Apple Trees': *The Waves* and the World of Things," in *Virginia Woolf*, ed. Claire Sprague (Englewood Cliffs, N.J.: Prentice-Hall, 1971), p. 126.

5. Virginia Woolf, "Modern Fiction," in *The Common Reader* (New York: Harcourt, Brace, and World, 1925, 1953), p. 154.

6. McConnell, p. 123.

7. Virginia Woolf, *Jacob's Room* and *The Waves* (New York: Harcourt, Brace, and World, 1923, 1959), p. 295. (All following page references in the text will correspond with this edition.)

8. Michael Payne, "The Eclipse of Order: The Ironic Structure of *The Waves*," *Modern Fiction Studies* 15, No. 2 (Summer, 1969), 209–218.

9. Jerry Wasserman, "Mimetic Form in *The Waves*," *Journal of Narrative Technique* 9 (1979), 47–48.

10. Miyeko Kamiya, "Virginia Woolf: An Outline of a Study on her Personality, Illness, and Work," *Confinia Psychiatrica* 8 (1963), p. 199.

11. Virginia Woolf, "The Waves. Holograph notes, unsigned, dated June 15, 1930–Jan. 30, 1931," 1 vol., 22 pp., The Berg Collection, The New York Public Library.

12. Woolf, "The Waves. Holograph notes."

13. Virginia Woolf, "The Pool," Unpublished Sketch, Monks House Papers (MH/B9c), the University of Sussex Library.

14. Virginia Woolf, "The Watering Place," Unpublished Sketch, Monks House Papers (MH/A28), the University of Sussex Library.

15. Woolf, "The Waves. Holograph notes."

16. Phyllis Rose, *Woman of Letters: A Life of Virginia Woolf* (New York: Oxford University Press, 1978), p. 209.

17. J. W. Graham, "Point of View in *The Waves*: Some Services of the Style," in *Virginia Woolf*, ed. Thomas S. W. Lewis (New York: McGraw-Hill, 1975), p. 96.

18. Graham, pp. 97–98.

19. Graham, pp. 98, 108.

20. Virginia Woolf, "A Sketch of the Past," in *Moments of Being*, ed. Jeanne Schulkind (New York: Harcourt, Brace, Jovanovich, 1976), p. 71.

21. Woolf, "A Sketch of the Past," p. 78.

22. Woolf, "A Sketch of the Past," p. 73.

23. Rini, p. 37.

24. Rini, p. 38.

25. Rini, p. 39.

26. Jean Guiguet, *Virginia Woolf and Her Works*, trans. Jean Stewart (London: Hogarth Press, 1965), pp. 286–287.

The Pargiters and *The Years*

1. Virginia Woolf, "Speech before the London/National Society for Women's Service, January 21, 1931," in *The Pargiters*, ed. Mitchell A. Leaska (New York: Harcourt, Brace, Jovanovich, 1977), pp. xxvii–xliv. (What follows is a summary of Woolf's points in that speech. All following page references in the text which refer

either to the speech or to the text of *The Pargiters* will correspond with this edition.)

2. Mitchell A. Leaska, "Introduction" to *The Pargiters*, pp. xvi–xvii.

3. Woolf, "Speech before the London/National Society for Women's Service," pp. xxxviii–xxxix.

4. Phyllis Rose, *Woman of Letters: A Life of Virginia Woolf* (New York: Oxford Univ. Press, 1978), p. 215.

5. Jean Alexander, *The Venture of Form in the Novels of Virginia Woolf* (Port Washington, N.Y. and London: Kennikat Press, 1974), p. 4.

6. Sally Sears, "Notes on Sexuality: *The Years* and *Three Guineas*," *Bulletin of the New York Public Library* 80 (Winter, 1977), 211–220.

7. Virginia Woolf, *The Years* (New York: Harcourt, Brace, and World, 1937, 1965), p. 69. (All following page references in the text will correspond with this edition.)

8. Hermione Lee, *The Novels of Virginia Woolf* (London: Methuen, 1977), pp. 194, 195.

9. Virginia Woolf, *A Writer's Diary*, ed. Leonard Woolf (New York: Harcourt, Brace, Jovanovich, 1953, 1954), pp. 161–162.

10. *A Writer's Diary*, p. 204.

11. Virginia Woolf, "A Sketch of the Past," in *Moments of Being*, ed. Jeanne Schulkind (New York and London: Harcourt, Brace, Jovanovich, 1976), p. 70.

12. *A Writer's Diary*, pp. 225, 230, 234, 257–258, 261, 262, 263, 265.

13. *A Writer's Diary*, pp. 215, 230, 252, 257, 263, 268.

14. *A Writer's Diary*, p. 253.

15. *A Writer's Diary*, p. 276.

16. *A Writer's Diary*, p. 284.

17. Lee, pp. 194, 195.

18. Jane Marcus, "Pargeting 'The Pargiters': Notes of an Apprentice Plasterer," *Bulletin of the New York Public Library* 80 (1977), 416, 435.

19. Jane Marcus, "Some Sources for *Between the Acts*," *Virginia Woolf Miscellany* 6 (1977), pp. 1–2.

20. Herbert Marder, *Feminism and Art: A Study of Virginia Woolf* (Chicago: University of Chicago Press, 1968), p. 129.

21. Marder, pp. 170–174.

22. James Naremore, *The World Without a Self: Virginia Woolf and the Novel* (New Haven and London: Yale University Press, 1973), pp. 258–259.

23. Margaret Comstock, "The Loudspeaker and the Human Voice: Politics and the Form of *The Years*," *Bulletin of the New York Public Library* 80 (Winter, 1977), pp. 253–254.

24. Rose, p. 213.

25. Josephine O'Brien Schaefer, "The Vision Falters: *The Years*, 1937," in *Virginia Woolf*, ed. Claire Sprague, Twentieth Century Views (Englewood Cliffs, N.J.: Prentice-Hall, 1971), p. 135.

26. James Hafley, "*The Years*," in *Virginia Woolf*, ed. Thomas S. W. Lewis (New York: McGraw-Hill, 1975), pp. 113–124.

Between the Acts

1. Virginia Woolf, *Between the Acts* (New York: Harcourt, Brace, Jovanovich, 1941, 1969). All following page references in the text will correspond with this edition.

2. Allen McLaurin, *Virginia Woolf: The Echoes Enslaved* (Cambridge University Press, 1973), p. 54.

3. Ann Y. Wilkinson, "A Principle of Unity in *Between the Acts*," in *Virginia Woolf*, ed. Claire Sprague, Twentieth Century Views (Englewood Cliffs, N.J.: Prentice-Hall, 1971), pp. 145–154.

4. Jane Marcus, "Art and Anger," *Feminist Studies* 4 (1978), 92.

5. Nancy Topping Bazin, *Virginia Woolf and the Androgynous Vision* (New Brunswick, N.J.: Rutgers University Press, 1973), p. 207.

6. Virginia Woolf, Between the Acts, Typescript of end of projected longer version, with variant ending, paginated 190–238, with author's manuscript corrections, unsigned and undated, 60 pp., The Berg Collection, the New York Public Library. All typescripts have currently been edited by Mitchell A. Leaska and published as *Pointz Hall*. New York: University Publications and John Jay Press, 1983.

7. Phyllis Rose, *Woman of Letters: A Life of Virginia Woolf* (New York: Oxford University Press, 1978), p. 237.

8. Lotus Snow, "Visions of Design: Virginia Woolf's 'Time Passes' and *Between the Acts*," *Research Studies* 44, No. 1 (March, 1976), 34.

Conclusion

1. Virginia Woolf, *A Room of One's Own* (New York and Burlingame: Harcourt, Brace, and World, 1927, 1957), p. 72.

2. Leonard Woolf, "Transcript of BBC Interview with Malcolm Muggeridge," (Feb. 1, 1965), Leonard Woolf Papers (II/76), p. 11, the University of Sussex Library.

3. Suzanne Ferguson, "The Face in the Mirror: Authorial Presence in the Multiple Vision of the Third-Person Impressionist Narrative," *Criticism* 21 (1979), 244–248.

4. David Daiches, *The Novel and the Modern World* (Chicago: University of Chicago Press, 1960), p. 203.

5. Eric Auerbach, "The Brown Stocking," in *Virginia Woolf*, Twentieth Century Views, ed. Claire Sprague (Englewood Cliffs, N.J.: Prentice-Hall, 1971), p. 8.

6. Auerbach, p. 88.

7. Virginia Woolf, *A Writer's Diary*, ed. Leonard Woolf (New York: Harcourt, Brace, Jovanovich, 1953), p. 134.

8. Virginia Woolf, "The Watering Place," unpublished sketch, Monks House Papers (MH/A28), the University of Sussex Library.

9. Leonard Woolf, "Transcript of BBC Interview," p. 11.

10. Woolf, *A Room of One's Own*, p. 108.

11. Woolf, *A Writer's Diary*, p. 191.

12. Virginia Woolf, "Women and Fiction," in *Granite and Rainbow* (New York and London: Harcourt, Brace, Jovanovich, 1958, 1975), p. 81.

Bibliography

Primary Works—Virginia Woolf

"Autograph notebook." (1906 and 1909), visit to Italy and Greece. Manuscript no. 61837, the British Library.

Between the Acts. New York: Harcourt, Brace, Jovanovich, 1941, 1969.

"Between the Acts." Typescript of end of projected longer version, with variant ending, paginated 190–238, with author's manuscript corrections, unsigned and undated. 60 pp. The Berg Collection. The New York Public Library. All typescripts have currently been edited by Mitchell H. Leaska and published as *Pointz Hall.* New York: New York University Publications and John Jay Press, 1983.

The Captain's Death Bed and Other Essays. New York: Harcourt, Brace, Jovanovich, 1950.

The Common Reader. New York: Harcourt, Brace, and World, 1925, 1953.

The Death of the Moth and Other Essays. New York: Harcourt, Brace, Jovanovich, 1942, 1970.

The Diaries of Virginia Woolf. 5 vols. New York: Harcourt, Brace, Jovanovich, 1977–1984.

"Diary." Holograph notebook, unsigned, dated Jan. 4, 1897–Jan. 1, 1898. The Berg Collection. The New York Public Library.

Flush: A Biography. New York: Harcourt, Brace, Jovanovich, 1933, 1961.

Granite and Rainbow. New York and London: Harcourt, Brace, Jovanovich, 1958.

A Haunted House and Other Stories. New York: Harcourt, Brace, and World, 1921, 1944, 1972.

"Incongruous/Inaccurate Memories." Unpublished sketch. Monks House Papers (MH/B9K). The University of Sussex Library.

"The Introduction." In articles, essays, fiction, reviews, vol. 2, dated 1925. The Berg Collection. The New York Public Library.

"Introduction to *Mrs. Dalloway.*" In *Virginia Woolf,* ed. Thomas S. W. Lewis. New York: McGraw-Hill, 1975, pp. 35–37.

Jacob's Room and The Waves. New York: Harcourt, Brace, and World, 1923, 1950 (*Jacob's Room*), 1931, 1959 (*The Waves*).

The Letters of Virginia Woolf. 6 vols. New York: Harcourt, Brace, Jovano-
vich, 1975–1980.
The Moment and Other Essays. New York: Harcourt, Brace, Jovanovich,
1948.
Moments of Being. Compiled and edited by Jeanne Schulkind. New York
and London: Harcourt, Brace, Jovanovich, 1976.
"Monday, Tuesday—The Diary." Unpublished sketch. Monks House
Papers (MH/B9e). The University of Sussex Library.
Mrs. Dalloway. New York: Harcourt, Brace, and World, 1925, 1953.
"Mrs. Dalloway." Holograph notes, unsigned, dated Nov. 9, 1922–Aug.
2, 1923. 13 pp. At back her: Choephori of Aeschylus. The Berg
Collection. The New York Public Library.
Night and Day. New York: Harcourt, Brace, Jovanovich, 1920, 1948.
"Notes for Writing." Holograph notebook. The Berg Collection. The
New York Public Library.
Orlando. New York: Harcourt, Brace, Jovanovich, 1928, 1956.
The Pargiters. Ed. Mitchell A. Leaska. New York and London: Harcourt,
Brace, Jovanovich, 1977.
"Phases of Fiction." Typescript. Monks House Papers (MH/B7b). The
University of Sussex Library.
"The Pool." Unpublished sketch. Monks House Papers (MH/B9c). The
University of Sussex Library.
A Room of One's Own. New York and Burlingame: Harcourt, Brace, and
World, 1929, 1957.
"A Scene from the Past." Unpublished sketch. Monks House Papers
(MH/B10e). The University of Sussex Library.
"Scenes from the Life of a British Naval Officer." Unpublished sketch.
Monks House Papers (MH/B9d). The University of Sussex Li-
brary.
The Second Common Reader. New York: Harcourt, Brace, and World, 1932,
1960.
"Speech before the London/National Society for Women's Service, Jan.
21, 1931." In *The Pargiters.* Ed. Mitchell A. Leaska. New York:
Harcourt, Brace, Jovanovich, 1977, pp. xxvii–xliv.
"The Symbol." Unpublished sketch. Monks House Papers (MH/A24e).
The University of Sussex Library.
"The Telescope." Unpublished sketch. Monks House Papers (MH/B10f).
The University of Sussex Library.
To the Lighthouse. New York: Harcourt, Brace, and World, 1927, 1955.
Three Guineas. New York: Harcourt, Brace, Jovanovich, 1938, 1966.
The Voyage Out. New York and London: Harcourt, Brace, Jovanovich,
1920, 1948.
"The Watering Place." Unpublished sketch. Monks House Papers (MH/
A28). The University of Sussex Library.

"The Waves." Holograph notes, unsigned, dated June 15, 1930–Jan. 30, 1931. 1 vol. 22 pp. The Berg Collection. The New York Public Library.
"What the Telescope Discovered." Unpublished sketch. Monks House Papers (MH/B9j). The University of Sussex Library.
A Writer's Diary. Ed. Leonard Woolf. New York: Harcourt, Brace, Jovanovich, 1953, 1954.
The Years. New York: Harcourt, Brace, and World, 1937, 1965.

Secondary Material

BOOKS

Albright, Daniel. *Personality and Impersonality: Lawrence, Woolf and Mann.* Chicago: University of Chicago Press, 1978.
Alexander, Jean. *The Venture of Form in the Novels of Virginia Woolf.* Port Washington, N.Y. and London: Kennikat Press, 1974.
Apter, T. E. *Virginia Woolf: A Study of Her Novels.* London and Basingstoke: Macmillan, 1979.
Bazin, Nancy Topping. *Virginia Woolf and the Androgynous Vision.* New Brunswick, N.J.: Rutgers University Press, 1973.
Beja, Morris, ed. *Virginia Woolf: To the Lighthouse.* London: Macmillan and Co., Ltd., 1970.
Bell, Quentin. *Virginia Woolf: A Biography.* New York: Harcourt, Brace, Jovanovich, 1972.
Bennett, Joan. *Virginia Woolf: Her Art as a Novelist.* Cambridge University Press, 1949.
Blackstone, Bernard. *Virginia Woolf: A Commentary.* London: Hogarth Press, 1949.
Daiches, David. *Virginia Woolf.* Norfolk, Conn.: New Directions, 1942.
Dickinson, Emily. *The Complete Poems.* Ed. Thomas H. Johnson. Boston and Toronto: Little, Brown, and Co., 1960.
DiGaetani, John Louis. *Richard Wagner and the Modern British Novel.* Farleigh Dickinson University Press. London: Associated University Presses, 1978.
Ellman, Mary. *Thinking About Women.* New York: Harcourt, Brace, Jovanovich, 1968.
Firestone, Shulamith. *The Dialectic of Sex: The Case for Feminist Revolution.* New York: Bantam Books, 1970.
Fleishman, Avrom. *Virginia Woolf: A Critical Reading.* Baltimore: Johns Hopkins University Press, 1975.

Flynn, Elizabeth Ann. "Feminist Critical Theory: Three Models." *Dissertation Abstracts International* 38, 1978, 4842A.

Freedman, Ralph, ed. *Virginia Woolf: Revaluation and Continuity.* Berkeley, Los Angeles, London: University of California Press, 1980.

Freud, Sigmund. *The Complete Psychological Works.* 24 vols. London: Hogarth Press, 1950–59.

Gorsky, Susan Rubinow. *Virginia Woolf.* Boston: Twayne Publishers, 1978.

Guiguet, Jean. *Virginia Woolf and Her Works.* Trans. Jean Stewart. London: Hogarth Press, 1965. Originally appeared in French in 1947.

Hafley, James. *The Glass Roof: Virginia Woolf as Novelist.* New York: Russell and Russell, 1963.

Heilbrun, Carolyn G. *Toward a Recognition of Androgyny.* New York, Evanston, San Francisco, London: Harper and Row, 1973.

Holtby, Winifred. *Virginia Woolf: A Critical Memoir.* Chicago: Cassandra Editions, Academy Press, Ltd., 1978.

Hynes, Samuel. *The Auden Generation: Literature and Politics in England in the 1930s.* London, Sydney, Toronto: The Bodley Head, 1976.

Johnson, Manly. *Virginia Woolf.* New York: Frederick Ungar, 1973.

Kaplan, Sydney Janet. *Feminine Consciousness in the Modern British Novel.* Urbana: University of Illinois Press, 1975.

Kelley, Alice van Buren. *The Novels of Virginia Woolf: Fact and Vision.* Chicago and London: University of Chicago Press, 1971, 1973.

Lang, Berel, and Forrest Williams. *Marxism and Art: Writings in Aesthetics and Criticism.* New York: David McKay Co., Inc., 1972.

Leaska, Mitchell A. *The Novels of Virginia Woolf: From Beginning to End.* New York: John Jay, 1977.

Lee, Hermione. *The Novels of Virginia Woolf.* London: Methuen, 1977.

Lehman, John. *Virginia Woolf and her World.* London: Thames and Hudson, 1975.

Lewis, Thomas S. W., ed. *Virginia Woolf.* New York: McGraw-Hill, 1975.

Love, Jean O. *Virginia Woolf: Sources of Madness and Art.* Berkeley, Los Angeles, London: University of California Press, 1977.

Macherey, Pierre. *A Theory of Literary Production.* Trans. Geoffrey Wall. London: Routledge and Kegan Paul, 1978.

Marder, Herbert. *Feminism and Art: A Study of Virginia Woolf.* Chicago and London: University of Chicago Press, 1968.

McLaurin, Allen. *Virginia Woolf: The Echoes Enslaved.* Cambridge University Press, 1973.

Meisel, Perry. *The Absent Father: Virginia Woolf and Walter Pater.* New Haven and London: Yale University Press, 1980.

Moody, A. D. *Virginia Woolf.* Edinburgh and London: Oliver and Boyd, 1966.

Naremore, James. *The World Without a Self: Virginia Woolf and the Novel.* New Haven and London: Yale University Press, 1973.

Novak, Jane. *The Razor Edge of Balance: A Study of Virginia Woolf.* Coral Gables: University of Miami Press, 1978.
Poole, Roger. *The Unknown Virginia Woolf.* Cambridge University Press, 1978.
Poresky, Louise A. *The Elusive Self: Psyche and Spirit in Virginia Woolf's Novels.* Newark: University of Delaware Press, 1981.
Richter, Harvena. *Virginia Woolf: The Inward Voyage.* Princeton University Press, 1978.
Rigney, Barbara Hill. *Madness and Sexual Politics in the Feminist Novel: Studies in Bronte, Woolf, Lessing and Atwood.* Madison: University of Wisconsin Press, 1978.
Rose, Phyllis. *Woman of Letters: A Life of Virginia Woolf.* New York: Oxford University Press, 1978.
Rosenthal, Michael. *Virginia Woolf.* New York: Columbia University Press, 1979.
Schlack, Beverly Ann. *Continuing Presences: Virginia Woolf's Use of Literary Allusion.* University Park: Pennsylvania State University Press, 1979.
Spacks, Patricia Meyer. *The Female Imagination.* New York: Avon Books, 1976.
Spater, George, and Ian Parsons. *A Marriage of True Minds: An Intimate Portrait of Leonard and Virginia Woolf.* London: Hogarth Press, 1977.
Spilka, Mark. *Virginia Woolf's Quarrel with Grieving.* Lincoln and London: University of Nebraska Press, 1980.
Sprague, Claire, ed. *Virginia Woolf.* Twentieth Century Views. Englewood Cilffs, N.J.: Prentice-Hall, 1971.
Webber, Jeannette L., and Joan Grumman. *Woman as Writer.* Boston: Houghton and Mifflin, 1978.
Woolf, Leonard. *Beginning Again: An Autobiography of the Years 1911–1918.* London: Hogarth Press, 1968.
Woolf, Leonard. *Downhill All the Way: An Autobiography of the Years 1919–1939.* London: Hogarth Press, 1968.

ARTICLES

Ames, Kenneth J. "Elements of Mock-Heroic in Virginia Woolf's *Mrs. Dalloway*." *Modern Fiction Studies* 18, No. 3 (Autumn, 1972), 363–374.
Arakelian, Paul G. "Feature Analysis in Metaphor in *The Waves* and *Manhattan Transfer*." *Style* 12 (1978), 274–285.
Auerbach, Eric. "The Brown-Stocking." In *Virginia Woolf.* Twentieth Century Views. Ed. Claire Sprague. Englewood Cliffs, N.J.: Prentice-Hall, 1971. Also appears as a chapter in Auerbach's *Mimesis.*

Baldanza, Frank. "Orlando and the Sackvilles." *PMLA* 70 (March, 1955), 274–279. David Bonnell Green. "Orlando and the Sackvilles: Addendum." *PMLA* 71 (March, 1956), 268–269.

Bell, Millicent. *"Portrait of the Artist as a Young Woman." Virginia Quarterly Review* 52, No. 4 (Autumn, 1976), 670–686.

Bell, Quentin. "About Gerald Duckworth: Response to John Hulcoop's Review." *Virginia Woolf Miscellany* 6 (1977), p. 1.

Bell, Quentin. "Proposed Policy on Virginia Woolf's Unpublished Material." *Virginia Woolf Miscellany* 10 (1979), p. 3.

Blanchard, Margaret. "Socialization in *Mrs. Dalloway*." *College English* 34, No. 2 (Nov., 1972), 287–307.

Blotner, Joseph L. "Mythic Patterns in *To the Lighthouse*." In *Myth and Literature*. Ed. John B. Vickery. Lincoln: University of Nebraska Press, 1966, pp. 243–256.

Bovenschen, Sylvia. "Is There a Feminine Aesthetic?" *New German Critique* 10 (Winter, 1977), 111–137.

Brett, Sally Alexander. "No, Mrs. Ramsay: Feminist Dilemma in *To the Lighthouse*." *Ball State University Forum* 19, No. 1 (1978), 48–56.

Carroll, Berenice A. " 'To Crush Him in Our Own Country': The Political Thought of Virginia Woolf." *Feminist Studies* 4 (1978), 99–131.

Cohen, Steven. "Narrative Form and Death: *The Mill on the Floss* and *Mrs. Dalloway*." *Genre* 11 (1978), 109–129.

Cohen, Steven. "Why Mr. Ramsay Reads the Antiquary." *Women and Literature* 7, No. 2 (1979), 14–24.

Comstock, Margaret. " 'The Current Answers Don't Do': The Comic Form of *Night and Day*." *Women's Studies* 4 (1977), 153–171.

Comstock, Margaret. "The Loudspeaker and the Human Voice: Politics and the Form of *The Years*." *Bulletin of the New York Public Library* 80 (Winter, 1977), 252–275.

Cook, Blanche Wiesen. " 'Women Alone Stir My Imagination': Lesbianism and the Cultural Tradition." *Signs: Journal of Women in Culture and Society* 4 (1979), 718–739.

Cox, C. B. "Mental Images and the Style of Virginia Woolf." *The Critical Survey* 3, No. 4 (Summer, 1968), 205–208.

Cumings, Melinda F. *"Night and Day*: Virginia Woolf's Visionary Synthesis of Reality." *Modern Fiction Studies* 18, No. 3 (Autumn, 1972), 339–349.

Daiches, David. "Virginia Woolf." In *The Novel and the Modern World*. Rev. ed. Chicago and London: University of Chicago Press, 1960, pp. 187–217.

Delbaere-Garant, Jeanne. "The Divided Worlds of Emily Bronte, Virginia Woolf and Janet Frame." *English Studies* 60 (1979), 699–711.

DeSalvo, Louise A. "A Note on the Orlando Tapestries at Knole House." *Virginia Woolf Miscellany* 13 (1979), pp. 3–4.

DeSalvo, Louise A. "Katherine Mansfield and Virginia Woolf's Revisions of *The Voyage Out*." *Virginia Woolf Miscellany* 11 (1978), pp. 5–6.

DeSalvo, Louise A., and S. P. Rosenbaum. "*The Voyage Out*: Two More Notes on a Textual Variant." *Virginia Woolf Miscellany* 5 (1976), pp. 3–4.

Dick, Susan. "The Restless Searcher: A Discussion of the Evolution of 'Time Passes' in *To the Lighthouse*." *English Studies in Canada* 5 (1979), 311–329.

Dick, Susan. "Where Was James When His Mother Went to Town?" *Virginia Woolf Miscellany* 11 (1978), p. 7.

Dunbar, M. J. "Virginia Woolf to T. S. Eliot: Two Letters." *Virginia Woolf Miscellany* 12 (1979), pp. 1–3.

Eder, Doris L. "Portrait of the Artist as a Young Woman." Review. *Book Forum* 3, No. 2 (1977), 336–344.

Edwards, Lee R. "War and Roses: The Politics of *Mrs. Dalloway*." In *The Authority of Experience: Essays in Feminist Criticism*. Ed. Arlyn Diamond and Lee R. Edwards. Amherst: University of Massachusetts Press, 1977, pp. 160–177.

Farrell, Thomas J. "The Female and Male Modes of Rhetoric." *College English* 40 (1979), 909–921.

Farwell, Marilyn R. "Virginia Woolf and Androgyny." *Contemporary Literature* 16, No. 4 (Autumn, 1975), 433–451.

Ferguson, Suzanne. "The Face in the Mirror: Authorial Presence in the Multiple Vision of Third-Person Impressionist Narrative." *Criticism* 21 (1979), 230–250.

Fox, Stephen D. "The Fish Pond as Symbolic Center in *Between the Acts*." *Modern Fiction Studies* 18, No. 3 (Autumn, 1972), 467–473.

Frazer, Jane M. "*Mrs. Dalloway*: Virginia Woolf's Greek Novel." *Research Studies* 47 (1979), 221–228.

Fromm, Harold. "To the Lighthouse: Music and Sympathy." *Miscellany* 19 (1968), 181–195.

Fromm, Harold. "Virginia Woolf: Art and Sexuality." *Virginia Quarterly Review* 55 (1979), 441–459.

Ghiselin, Brewster. "Virginia Woolf's Party." *Sewanee Review* 80, No. 1 (Winter, 1972), 47–50.

Gillen, Francis. "'I am This, I am That': Shifting Distance and Movement in *Mrs. Dalloway*." *Studies in the Novel* 4, No. 3 (Fall, 1972), 484–493.

Gillespie, James. "Bolts of Iron." *Studies in the Novel* 8, No. 3 (Fall, 1976), 336–350.

Ginden, James. "Lots of Cotton Wool." *Studies in the Novel* 9 (1977), 312–325.

Gorsky, Susan. "'The Central Shadow': Characterization in *The Waves*." *Modern Fiction Studies* 18, No. 3 (Autumn, 1972), 449–466.

Graham, J. W. "Point of View in *The Waves*: Some Services of the Style." In *Virginia Woolf*. Ed. Thomas S. W. Lewis. New York: McGraw-Hill, 1975, pp. 94–112.

Gregor, Ian. "Spaces: To the Lighthouse." In *The Author in His Work: Essays on a Problem in Criticism*. Ed. Louis L. Martz and Aubrey Williams. New Haven: Yale University Press, 1978, pp. 375–389.

Gullette, Margaret Morganroth. "Virginia Woolf's Sanity." *North American Review* 264 (Sept., 1979), 56–61.

Hafley, James. "*The Years*." In *Virginia Woolf*. Ed. Thomas S. W. Lewis. New York: McGraw-Hill, 1975, pp. 113–124.

Hartman, Geoffrey H. "Virginia's Web." In *Beyond Formalism*. New Haven and London: Yale University Press, 1970, pp. 71–84.

Hawkes, Ellen. " 'Introduction' to 'Friendships Gallery.' " *Twentieth Century Literature* 25 (1979), 270–302.

Heine, Elizabeth. "The Earlier *Voyage Out*: Virginia Woolf's First Novel." *Bulletin of Research in the Humanities* 82 (1979), 294–316.

Heinemann, Jan. "The Revolt Against Language: A Critical Note on Twentieth Century Irrationalism with Special Reference to the Aesthetico-Philosophical Views of Virginia Woolf and Clive Bell." *Orbis Littererum* 32, No. 3 (1977), 212–228.

Henke, Suzette. "Virginia Woolf's *The Years*: Echoes of Joyce's *Ulysses*." *Modern British Literature* 4 (1979), 137–139.

Henke, Suzette. "Virginia Woolf's *To the Lighthouse*: In Defense of the Woman Artist." *Virginia Woolf Quarterly* 2, No. 1 (1975), 39–46.

Hessler, John G. "Moral Accountability in *Mrs. Dalloway*." *Renascence* 30, No. 3 (1978), 126–136.

Higden, David Leon. "Review Essay: Three Studies of Virginia Woolf." *Studies in the Novel* 3, No. 1 (Spring, 1971), 109–116.

Hoffman, A. C. "Subject and Object and the Nature of Reality: The Dialectic of *To the Lighthouse*." *Texas Studies in Literature and Language* 13, No. 4 (Winter, 1972), 691–703.

Hulcoop, John. " 'The Only Way I Keep Afloat': Work as Virginia Woolf's *Raison d'être*." *Women's Studies* 4 (1977), 223–245.

Humma, John B. " 'Time Passes' in *To the Lighthouse*; 'Governor Pyncheon' in *The House of the Seven Gables*." *Ball State University Forum* 20, No. 3 (1979), 54–59.

Hungerford, Edward A. " 'Introduction' to 'Byron and Mr. Briggs.' " (Text included.) *Yale Review* 63 (1979), 321–349.

Hunting, Constance. "Three More Hazards Towards Virginia Woolf." *Journal of Modern Literature* 4, No. 1 (Sept., 1974), 155–159.

Hunting, Robert. "Laurence Sterne and Virginia Woolf." *Études Anglaises* 32 (1979), 283–293.

Hyman, Virginia R. "The Metamorphosis of Leslie Stephen: 'Those Are Pearls That Were His Eyes.' " *Virginia Woolf Quarterly* 2, No. 1 (1975), 48–65.

Hynes, Samuel. "Stephen into Woolf." *Sewanee Review* 84, No. 3 (Summer, 1976), 510–517.

Kamiya, Miyeko. "Virginia Woolf: An Outline of a Study on her Personality, Illness and Work." *Confinia Psychiatrica* 8 (1965), 189–205.

Kaplan, Sydney Janet. "Virginia Woolf." In *Feminine Consciousness in the Modern British Novel*. Urbana, Chicago, London: University of Illinois Press, 1975, pp. 76–109.

Keats, John. "Letter to George and Tom Keats." (Dec. 21–27, 1817). In *English Romantic Writers*. Ed. David Perkins. New York: Harcourt, Brace, and World, 1967, p. 1209.

Kellerman, Frederick, "A New Key to Virginia Woolf's *Orlando*." *English Studies* 59 (1978), 138–150.

Kenney, Susan M. "Two Endings: Virginia Woolf's Suicide and *Between the Acts*." *University of Toronto Quarterly* 44, No. 4 (Summer, 1975), 265–289.

Kermode, Frank. "Yes Santa, There is a Virginia." *New York Review of Books* (Dec. 21, 1978), 31–32.

Kushen, Betty. " 'Dreams of Golden Domes': Manic Fusion in Virginia Woolf's *Orlando*." *Literature and Psychology* 29 (1979), 25–33.

Kushen, Betty. "The Psychogenic Imperative in the Works of Virginia Woolf." *Literature and Psychology* 27, No. 2 (1977), 52–66.

Leaska, Mitchell A. "The Death of Rachel Vinrace." *Bulletin of Research in the Humanities* 82 (1979), 328–337.

Leaska, Mitchell A. "Virginia Woolf, The Pargeter: A Reading of *The Years*." *Bulletin of the New York Public Library* 80 (Winter, 1977), 172–210.

Lilienfeld, Jane. "The Deceptiveness of Beauty: Mother Love and Mother Hate in *To the Lighthouse*." *Twentieth Century Literature* 23, No. 3 (Oct., 1977), 345–376.

Lipking, Joanna. "Looking at the Monuments: Woolf's Satiric Eye." *Bulletin of the New York Public Library* 80 (Winter, 1977), 141–145.

Little, Judy. "Festive Comedy in Woolf's *Between the Acts*." *Women and Literature* 5, No. 1 (Spring, 1977), 26–37.

Little, Judith. "Heroism in *To the Lighthouse*." In *Images of Women in Fiction*. Ed. Susan Koppelman Cornillon. Bowling Green, Ohio: Bowling Green Univ. Popular Press, 1972, pp. 237–242.

Lorsch, Susan E. "Structure and Rhythm in *The Waves*. The Ebb and Flow of Meaning." *Essays in Literature* 6 (1979), 195–206.

Lyons, Richard S. "The Intellectual Structure of Virginia Woolf's *Between the Acts*." *Modern Language Quarterly* 38, No. 2 (June, 1977), 149–166.

Maes-Jelinek, Hena. "Virginia Woolf." In *Criticism of Society in the English Novel Between the Wars*. Paris: Société d'Editions "Les Belles Lettres," 1970, pp. 101–158.

Marcus, Jane. "Art and Anger." *Feminist Studies* 4 (1978), 69–98.

Marcus, Jane. "Enchanted Organs, Magic Bells: *Night and Day* as Comic Opera." In *Virginia Woolf: Revaluation and Continuity*. Ed. Ralph Freedman. Berkeley, Los Angeles, London: University of California Press, 1980, pp. 97–122.

Marcus, Jane. "'No More Horses': Virginia Woolf on Art and Propaganda." *Women's Studies* 4 (1977), 265–290.

Marcus, Jane. "Pargeting 'The Pargiters': Notes of an Apprentice Plasterer." *Bulletin of the New York Public Library* 80 (1977), 416–435.

Marcus, Jane. "Some Sources for *Between the Acts*." *Virginia Woolf Miscellany* 6 (1977), pp. 1–3.

Marcus, Jane. "Tintinnabulations." *Marxist Perspectives* 2 No. 1 (1979), 144–167.

Marder, Herbert. "Beyond the Lighthouse: *The Years*." *Bucknell Review* 15, No. 1 (March, 1967), 61–70.

Marder, Herbert. "Virginia Woolf's 'System That Did Not Shut Out.'" *Papers on Language and Literature* 4, No. 1 (Winter, 1968), 106–111.

McConnell, Frank D. "'Death Among the Apple Trees': *The Waves* and the World of Things." In *Virginia Woolf*. Twentieth Century Views. Ed. Claire Sprague. Englewood Cliffs, N.J.: Prentice-Hall, 1971, pp. 117–129.

Mendez, Charlotte W. "I Need a Little Language." *Virginia Woolf Quarterly* 1, No. 1 (1972), 87–105.

Middleton, Victoria S. "The Years: 'A Deliberate Failure.'" *Bulletin of the New York Public Library* 80 (Winter, 1977), 158–171.

Miller, David Neal. "Authorial Point of View in Virginia Woolf's *Mrs. Dalloway*." *Journal of Narrative Technique* 2, No. 2 (May, 1972), 125–132.

Moore, Madeline. "Virginia Woolf's *The Years* and Years of Adverse Male Reviewers." *Women's Studies* 4 (1977), 247–263.

Morganstern, Barry S. "The Self-Conscious Narrator in *Jacob's Room*." *Modern Fiction Studies* 18, No. 3 (Autumn, 1972), 351–361.

Naremore, James. "Nature and History in *The Years*." In *Virginia Woolf: Revaluation and Continuity*. Ed. Ralph Freedman. Berkeley, Los Angeles, London: University of California Press, 1980, pp. 241–262.

Ohmann, Carol. "Culture and Anarchy in *Jacob's Room*." *Contemporary Literature* 18, No. 2 (Spring, 1977), 160–172.

Payne, Michael. "The Eclipse of Order: The Ironic Structure of *The Waves*." *Modern Fiction Studies* 15, No. 2 (Summer, 1969), 209–218.

Perrazzini, Randolph. "*Mrs. Dalloway*: Buds on the Tree of Life." *Midwest Quarterly* 18. No. 4 (Summer, 1977), 406–417.

Philipson, Morris. "'Mrs. Dalloway, What's the Sense of Your Parties?'" *Critical Inquiry* 1, No. 1 (Sept., 1974), 123–148.

Pitt, Rosemary. "The Exploration of Self in Conrad's *Heart of Darkness* and Woolf's *The Voyage Out*." *Conradiana* 10 (1978), 141–154.

Pomeroy, Elizabeth W. "Garden and Wilderness: Virginia Woolf Reads the Elizabethans." *Modern Fiction Studies* 24 (1979), 497–508.

Pratt, Annis. "Sexual Imagery in *To the Lighthouse*: A New Feminist Approach." *Modern Fiction Studies* 18, No. 3 (Autumn, 1972), 417–431.

Proudfit, Sharon Wood. "Lily Briscoe's Painting: A Key to Personal Relationships in *To the Lighthouse*." *Criticism* 13, No. 1 (Winter, 1971), 26–38.

Proudfit, Sharon L. "Virginia Woolf: Reluctant Feminist in *The Years*." *Criticism* 17 (Winter, 1975), 59–73.

Quick, Jonathan R. "The Shattered Moment: Form and Crisis in *Mrs. Dalloway* and *Between the Acts*." *Mosaic* 7, No. 3 (Spring, 1974), 127–136.

Rachman, Shalom. "Clarissa's Attic: Virginia Woolf's *Mrs. Dalloway* Reconsidered." *Twentieth Century Literature* 18, No. 1 (Jan., 1972), 3–18.

Radin, Grace. "'I Am Not a Hero': Virginia Woolf and the First Version of *The Years*." *Massachusetts Review* 16 (Winter, 1975), 195–208.

Richardson, Robert O. "Point of View in Virginia Woolf's *The Waves*." *Texas Studies in Literature and Language* 14, No. 4 (Winter, 1973), 691–709.

Rini, Roseanne. "Transcendent Perception in Virginia Woolf's *The Waves*." Unpublished essay. The Ohio State University.

[Rogat], Ellen Hawkes. "A Form of One's Own." *Mosaic* 8, No. 1 (Fall, 1974), 77–90. (Published under surname of Rogat; now Hawkes.)

[Rogat], Ellen Hawkes. "The Virgin in the Bell Biography." *Twentieth Century Literature* 20, No. 2 (April, 1974), 96–113.

Rosenberg, Stuart. "The Match in the Crocus: Obtrusive Art in Virginia Woolf's *Mrs. Dalloway*." *Modern Fiction Studies* 13, No. 2 (Summer, 1967), 211–220.

Rosenthal, Michael. "Virginia Woolf." *Partisan Review* 43, No. 4 (1976), 557–569.

Ruddick, Sara. "Learning to Live with the Angel in the House." *Women's Studies* 4 (1977), 181–200.

Rudikoff, Sonya. "How Many Lovers Had Virginia Woolf?" *The Hudson Review* 32 (1979), 540–566.

Ruotolo, Lucio P. "Clarissa Dalloway." In *Virginia Woolf*. Ed. Thomas S. W. Lewis. New York: McGraw-Hill, 1975), pp. 38–55.

Ruotolo, Lucio. "Mrs. Dalloway: The Journey Out of Subjectivity." *Women's Studies* 4 (1977), 173–178.

Samuels, Marilyn S. "The Symbolic Functions of the Sun in *Mrs. Dalloway*." *Modern Fiction Studies* 18, No. 3 (Autumn, 1972), 387–399.

Saunders, Judith P. "Mortal Stain: Literary Allusion and Female Sexuality in 'Mrs. Dalloway in Bond Street.'" *Studies in Short Fiction* 15 (1978), 139–144.

Schaefer, Josephine O'Brien. "The Vision Falters: *The Years*, 1937." In *Virginia Woolf*. Twentieth Century Views. Ed. Claire Sprague. Englewood Cliffs, N. J.: Prentice-Hall, 1971, pp. 130–144.

Schlack, Beverly Ann. "Virginia Woolf's Strategy of Scorn in *The Years* and *Three Guineas*." *Bulletin of the New York Public Library* 80 (Winter, 1977), 146–150.

Sears, Sallie. "Notes on Sexuality: *The Years* and *Three Guineas*." *Bulletin of the New York Public Library* 80 (Winter, 1977), 211–220.

Shanahan, Mary Steussy. "The Artist and the Resolution of *The Waves*." *Modern Language Quarterly* 36, No. 1 (March, 1975), 54–74.

Shanahan, Mary Steussy. "*Between the Acts*: Virginia Woolf's Final Endeavor in Art." *Texas Studies in Literature and Language* 14, No. 1 (Spring, 1972), 123–138.

Sharma, O. P. "Feminism as Aesthetic Vision: A Study of Virginia Woolf's *Mrs. Dalloway*." *Women's Studies* 3, No. 1 (1975), 61–73.

Shaw, Valerie. "The Secret Companion." *Critical Quarterly* 20, No. 1 (1978), 70–77.

Shore, Elizabeth M. "Virginia Woolf, Proust, and *Orlando*." *Comparative Literature* 31 (1979), 232–245.

Silver, Brenda R. "Virginia Woolf and the Concept of Community: The Elizabethan Playhouse." *Women's Studies* 4 (1977), 291–298.

Sitter, Deborah A. "The Debate of *The Waves*." *Durham University Journal* 37, No. 1 (Dec., 1975), 118–125.

Snider, Clifton. "'A Single Self': A Jungian Interpretation of Virginia Woolf's *Orlando*." *Modern Fiction Studies* 25 (1979), 263–268.

Snow, Lotus. "Charles Dalloway Revisited." *Research Studies* 46 (1978), 197–202.

Snow, Lotus. "Visions of Design: Virginia Woolf's 'Time Passes' and *Between the Acts*." *Research Studies* 44, No. 1 (March, 1976), 24–34.

Snow, Lotus. "The Wreckful Siege: Disorder in *The Waves*." *Research Studies* 42, No. 2 (June, 1974), 71–80.

Spilka, Mark. "On Mrs. Dalloway's Absent Grief: A Psycho-Literary Speculation." *Contemporary Literature* 20, (1979), 316–338.

Spilka, Mark. "The Robber in the Bedroom; or, The Thief of Love: A Woolfian Grieving in Six Novels and Two Memoirs." *Critical Inquiry* 5 (1979), 663–682.

Steele, Philip L. "Virginia Woolf's Spiritual Autobiography." *Topic* 18 (Fall, 1969), 64–74.

Stewart, Jack F. "Existence and Symbol in *The Waves*." *Modern Fiction Studies* 18, No. 3 (Autumn, 1972), 433–447.

Stewart, Jack. "Light in *To the Lighthouse*." *Twentieth Century Literature* 23, No. 3 (October, 1977), 377–389.

Temple, Ruth Z. "Never Say 'I': *To the Lighthouse* as Vision and Confession." In *Virginia Woolf*, Twentieth Century Views. Ed. Claire

Sprague. Englewood Cliffs, N.J.: Prentice-Hall, 1971, pp. 90–100.

Wasserman, Jerry. "Mimetic Form in *The Waves*." *Journal of Narrative Technique* 9 (1979), 41–52.

Watkins, Renee. "Survival in Discontinuity—Virginia Woolf's *Between the Acts*." *Massachusetts Review* 10, No. 2 (Spring, 1969), 356–376.

Wilkinson, Ann Y. "A Principle of Unity in *Between the Acts*." In *Virginia Woolf*. Twentieth Century Views. Ed. Claire Sprague. Englewood Cliffs, N. J.: Prentice-Hall, 1971, pp. 145–154.

Wilson, Angus. "The Always-Changing Impact of Virginia Woolf." *Studies in Literary Imagination* 11, No. 2 (1978), 1–9.

Wilson, J. J. "A Comparison of Parties, with Discussion of their Function in Woolf's Fiction." *Women's Studies* 4 (1977), 201–217.

Woolf, Leonard. "Transcript of BBC Interview with Malcolm Muggeridge." (Feb. 1, 1965.) Leonard Woolf Papers (II/7b). The University of Sussex Library.

Wyatt, Jean. "Art and Allusion in *Between the Acts*." *Mosaic* 11, No. 4 (1978), 91–100.

Zwerdling, Alex. "*Mrs. Dalloway* and the Social System." *PMLA* 92, No. 1 (Jan., 1977), 69–82.

Index

Academic persons: Woolf's view of, 17–18, 59, 61, 79, 146, 152–159
Aeschylus: 93
Aesthetic principles: as articulated by Woolf, 1–12, 15–16
Alardyce, Richard (in *Night and Day*): 38
Alexander, Jean: on *The Years*, 154
Amazon jungle: in *The Voyage Out*, 29
Ambrose, Helen (in *The Voyage Out*): 18, 19, 29
Androgyny: importance in writing: 2–9, 77; lighthouse as image of, 91; as theme—in *Between the Acts*, 178, 188, —in *Mrs. Dalloway*, 95–96, —in *Orlando*, 112–114, 115, 122–123, 185, —in *The Waves*, 133–134, 141–144, —in *The Years*, 162–163, —in *To the Lighthouse*, 86–87, 91, 95–96.
"Angel in the House, The": 65–68, 95–96, 150
Antigone: 153
Apple tree: as image, in *The Waves*, 139. *See also* Images
Ariosto: 112
Aristrocracy: Archduchess Harriett and Archduke Harry in *Orlando*, 114–115, 119–120; Dalloways in *The Voyage Out*, 20–21, 26–27; Lady Bradshaw in *Mrs. Dalloway*, 97–98; Lady Bruton in *Mrs. Dalloway*, 97; Orlando in *Orlando*, 116–125; Sir Hugh Whitbread in *Mrs. Dalloway*, 97, 102; Sir William Bradshaw in *Mrs. Dalloway*, 6, 96–98, 99
Art and ideology: relationship of, 2–9, 15–16
Artists: Bernard (in *The Waves*), 133–134, 141–144; Lily Briscoe, 76–78, 128;

Miss La Trobe, 173, 175–178, 179, 188; Woolf's view of, 5, 8, 77, 143
Ashton, Tony (friend of Edward Pargiter): 55. *See also* Jevons, Tony
Auerbach, Eric: on *To the Lighthouse*, 184
Austen, Jane: 3–4, 26, 47–48, 160, 185

Bankes, William (in *To the Lighthouse*): 78
Barfoot, Captain (in *Jacob's Room*): 54
Bartholomew (in *Between the Acts*): 168, 169
Bazin, Nancy: on *Between the Acts*, 177
Beggar woman (in *Mrs. Dalloway*): 93–94, 96
Bell, Quentin: on Thoby Stephen, 61
Bernard (in *The Waves*): as artist, 133–134, 141–144; character of, 127, 129, 131, 132, 135
Big Ben: as symbol, 94, 95. *See also* Images
Biography: Woolf's view of, 111–112, 123–124
"Blot fringed with flame": as symbol—in *Between the Acts*, 175, —in general, 15, 95, —in *Night and Day*, 45–46, 47, —in *The Years*, 162. *See also* Images
Bradshaw, Lady: 97–98
Bradshaw, Sir William: 6, 96–98, 99. *See also* Aristrocracy
Bramham, Nick (in *Jacob's Room*): 56
Brett, Sally: on *To the Lighthouse*, 82
Briscoe, Lily: as artist, 76–78, 128; and Charles Tansley, 79–80; and Mrs. Ramsay, 77–78, 82, 89–90, 91; and Mr. Ramsay, 89–90; view of sexuality, 106. *See also* Artists; Spinsters
Brontë, Charlotte: 3–4, 76, 185